ECONOMIC ISSUES, PROBLEMS AND PERSPECTIVES

STATE UNEMPLOYMENT LAWS

CHANGES AND COMPARISON

ECONOMIC ISSUES, PROBLEMS AND PERSPECTIVES

Additional books and e-books in this series can be found on Nova's website under the Series tab.

ECONOMIC ISSUES, PROBLEMS AND PERSPECTIVES

STATE UNEMPLOYMENT LAWS

CHANGES AND COMPARISON

JONAS LEMANN
EDITOR

snova
New York

Library of Congress Cataloging-in-Publication Data

ISBN: 978-1-53618-202-6

Published by Nova Science Publishers, Inc. † New York

CONTENTS

PREFACE

Chapter 1 analyzes recent changes to state Unemployment Compensation (UC) programs. Two categories of UC state law issues are considered: (1) changes in the duration of state UC unemployment benefits, and (2) changes in the UC weekly benefit amount.

Chapter 2 provides state-by-state information on workers covered, benefit eligibility, methods of financing, and other areas of interest in the Unemployment Insurance (UI) program. It also includes information on the temporary disability programs operated in six states.

Chapter 1 - This chapter analyzes recent changes to state Unemployment Compensation (UC) programs. Two categories of UC state law issues are considered: (1) changes in the duration of state UC unemployment benefits, and (2) changes in the UC weekly benefit amount. In recent years, some states have enacted legislation to decrease the maximum number of weeks of regular state UC benefits. Until 2011, all states paid at least up to 26 weeks of UC benefits to eligible, unemployed individuals. In 2011, however, six states passed legislation to decrease their maximum UC benefit durations: Arkansas, Florida, Illinois (only for calendar year 2012), Michigan, Missouri, and South Carolina. In 2012, Georgia also passed legislation to decrease the maximum UC benefit duration. In 2013, Kansas and North Carolina enacted similar legislation. Subsequently, in 2015, Arkansas and Missouri enacted additional state laws to further reduce their maximum UC durations. In the case of Missouri, however, the Missouri Supreme Court found the 2015 law unconstitutional; therefore, this further UC duration reduction is not in effect. In 2016, Idaho reduced its maximum UC duration. Arkansas passed a third reduction in its maximum UC duration in 2017. Finally, in 2019, Alabama reduced its maximum UC duration, effective January 1, 2020. As a result of these state law changes, depending on state unemployment, the shortest potential UC maximum duration is currently 12 weeks (in Florida and North Carolina), compared with 26 weeks prior to 2011. Changes in state UC benefit duration have consequences for the duration of federal unemployment benefits that may be available to unemployed workers, including Extended Benefits (EB) and benefits from the now-expired Emergency Unemployment Compensation (EUC08) program. Because state UC benefit duration is an underlying factor in the calculation of duration for additional federal unemployment benefits, reducing UC maximum duration also reduces the number of weeks available to unemployed workers in the federal extended unemployment programs (including EUC08, which is now expired, and EB). Prior to the EUC08 program's expiration on December 28, 2013 (December 29, 2013, in New York), states were temporarily subject to a *nonreduction rule* (under P.L. 111-205, as amended), which made the availability of federally financed EUC08 benefits contingent on not actively changing the state's method of calculating UC benefits, if it would have decreased weekly benefit amounts. Some states, however, make automatic adjustments to weekly benefit amounts under existing state law. Consequently, when these states experience certain conditions, such as a decrease in the average weekly wage used in the automatic adjustment calculation, their maximum weekly UC benefit amount may have been decreased without having violated the now-expired nonreduction rule. P.L. 112-96 provided a specific exception to the nonreduction rule in the case of state legislation enacted before March 1, 2012. In February 2013, North Carolina enacted legislation that actively reduced UC weekly benefit amount calculations beginning in July 2013. Due to this violation of the nonreduction rule, EUC08 benefits were no longer available in North Carolina, effective June 29, 2013. All EUC08 benefits expired as of the week ending on or before January 1, 2014 (i.e., December

28, 2013; or December 29, 2013, in New York State). Any reduction to the UC weekly benefit amount also translates into reduced EB weekly benefit amounts (and EUC08 benefit amounts when the program was authorized). Overall, the two types of changes to state UC laws and programs have consequences for the duration and amount of federal unemployment benefits. This report describes these changes and analyzes their consequences for UC, EUC08 (when it was authorized), and EB benefits. It will be updated, as needed, to reflect additional state UC changes.

Chapter 2 - The Comparison of State Unemployment Insurance Laws provides state-by-state information on workers covered, benefit eligibility, methods of financing, and other areas of interest in the Unemployment Insurance (UI) program. It also includes information on the temporary disability programs operated in six states. The Comparison is published annually. This edition reflects the provisions of state law as of January 1, 2019. The Comparison is issued solely for informational, reference, and research purposes. It is not an official interpretation of state UI laws. The state statutes should be consulted for the full text of state laws. Unless otherwise noted, the Comparison generally reflects state law, but not official interpretations of state laws, which are found in state rules and regulations, administrative and court decisions, and opinions of attorneys general.

In: State Unemployment Laws
Editor: Jonas Lemann

ISBN: 978-1-53618-202-6

Chapter 1

UNEMPLOYMENT INSURANCE: CONSEQUENCES OF CHANGES IN STATE UNEMPLOYMENT COMPENSATION LAWS (UPDATED)*

Katelin P. Isaacs

SUMMARY

This chapter analyzes recent changes to state Unemployment Compensation (UC) programs. Two categories of UC state law issues are considered: (1) changes in the duration of state UC unemployment benefits, and (2) changes in the UC weekly benefit amount.

In recent years, some states have enacted legislation to decrease the maximum number of weeks of regular state UC benefits. Until 2011, all states paid at least up to 26 weeks of UC benefits to eligible, unemployed individuals. In 2011, however, six states passed legislation to decrease their maximum UC benefit durations: Arkansas, Florida, Illinois (only for calendar year 2012), Michigan, Missouri, and South Carolina. In 2012,

---

* This is an edited, reformatted and augmented version of Congressional Research Service Publication No. R41859, Updated October 23, 2019.

Georgia also passed legislation to decrease the maximum UC benefit duration. In 2013, Kansas and North Carolina enacted similar legislation. Subsequently, in 2015, Arkansas and Missouri enacted additional state laws to further reduce their maximum UC durations. In the case of Missouri, however, the Missouri Supreme Court found the 2015 law unconstitutional; therefore, this further UC duration reduction is not in effect. In 2016, Idaho reduced its maximum UC duration. Arkansas passed a third reduction in its maximum UC duration in 2017. Finally, in 2019, Alabama reduced its maximum UC duration, effective January 1, 2020. As a result of these state law changes, depending on state unemployment, the shortest potential UC maximum duration is currently 12 weeks (in Florida and North Carolina), compared with 26 weeks prior to 2011.

Changes in state UC benefit duration have consequences for the duration of federal unemployment benefits that may be available to unemployed workers, including Extended Benefits (EB) and benefits from the now-expired Emergency Unemployment Compensation (EUC08) program. Because state UC benefit duration is an underlying factor in the calculation of duration for additional federal unemployment benefits, reducing UC maximum duration also reduces the number of weeks available to unemployed workers in the federal extended unemployment programs (including EUC08, which is now expired, and EB).

Prior to the EUC08 program's expiration on December 28, 2013 (December 29, 2013, in New York), states were temporarily subject to a *nonreduction rule* (under P.L. 111-205, as amended), which made the availability of federally financed EUC08 benefits contingent on not actively changing the state's method of calculating UC benefits, if it would have decreased weekly benefit amounts. Some states, however, make automatic adjustments to weekly benefit amounts under existing state law. Consequently, when these states experience certain conditions, such as a decrease in the average weekly wage used in the automatic adjustment calculation, their maximum weekly UC benefit amount may have been decreased without having violated the now- expired nonreduction rule. P.L. 112-96 provided a specific exception to the nonreduction rule in the case of state legislation enacted before March 1, 2012. In February 2013, North Carolina enacted legislation that actively reduced UC weekly benefit amount calculations beginning in July 2013. Due to this violation of the nonreduction rule, EUC08 benefits were no longer available in North Carolina, effective June 29, 2013. All EUC08 benefits expired as of the week ending on or before January 1, 2014 (i.e., December 28, 2013; or December 29, 2013, in New York State). Any reduction to the UC weekly benefit amount also translates into reduced EB weekly benefit amounts (and EUC08 benefit amounts when the program was authorized).

Overall, the two types of changes to state UC laws and programs have consequences for the duration and amount of federal unemployment benefits. This chapter describes these changes and analyzes their consequences for UC, EUC08 (when it was authorized), and EB benefits. It will be updated, as needed, to reflect additional state UC changes.

Introduction

Many states have enacted changes to their Unemployment Compensation (UC) programs in recent years. These changes may be a reaction to state UC financial stress, caused by the most recent recession (December 2007-June 2009), as well as a response to concerns about UC program integrity. In general, these states have been attempting to reduce the costs of UC benefits, which are financed through state taxes on employers. This reduction in state UC benefit spending may be achieved through two significant types of state UC changes: (1) a reduction in the duration of state UC employment benefits and (2) a reduction in the state UC weekly benefit amount.

This chapter first provides a brief overview of the unemployment compensation programs and benefits that may be available to eligible, unemployed individuals. It also analyzes the recent state UC financial stress and concerns about UC program integrity as context for state law changes.

Next, the two categories of UC state law issues are discussed:

1. changes in the duration of state UC unemployment benefits and
2. changes in the maximum UC weekly benefit amount.

Overview of Unemployment Benefits

Several unemployment insurance (UI) programs may provide benefits to unemployed workers. When eligible workers lose their jobs, the UC program may provide up to 26 weeks of income support through the payment of regular state UC benefits.[1] These UC benefits may be extended

[1] Or, in the case of the states described in the report section on "State Law Changes to UC Benefit Duration," UC currently pays fewer than up to 26 weeks. Additionally, the maximum UC

by the permanent-law Extended Benefits (EB) program, which may provide up to 13 or 20 weeks of additional unemployment benefits if certain economic situations exist within the state.[2] Until its expiration the week ending on or before January 1, 2014 (i.e., December 28, 2013; or December 29, 2013, in New York State), the temporary Emergency Unemployment Compensation (EUC08) program also provided up to four tiers of additional weeks of unemployment benefits to certain workers who had exhausted their rights to UC benefits in states with high unemployment.[3]

Provided below is a brief description of the benefits available through these three UI programs: UC, EUC08 (when it was authorized), and EB.

Unemployment Compensation Program

Authorized by the Social Security Act of 1935 (SSA; P.L. 74-271), UC is a joint federal-state program that provides unemployment benefits to eligible individuals. Although federal laws and regulations provide broad guidelines on UC benefit coverage, eligibility, and benefit determination, the specifics regarding UC benefits are determined by each state. This results in essentially 53 different programs.[4] Generally, UC eligibility is based on attaining qualified wages and employment in covered work over a 12-month period (called a base period) prior to unemployment. All states require a worker to have earned a certain amount of wages or to have worked for a

duration is 28 weeks in Montana and 30 weeks (if local economic conditions are met) in Massachusetts. When EB benefits are available in Montana, the total duration of UC and EB is capped at either 39 weeks (26 + 13) or 46 weeks (26 + 20). When EB benefits are available in Massachusetts, the maximum duration of UC benefits is capped at 26 weeks.

[2] See report section on "Calculation of Benefit Duration for EB Payable Periods" for the calculation of EB benefit durations in states that have reduced regular UC benefit duration.

[3] See report section on "Calculation of Benefit Duration for EUC08 Tiers" for the calculation of EUC08 benefit durations prior to EUC08 expiration in states with reduced regular UC benefit durations. In states without UC duration reductions, up to 47 weeks of total EUC08 benefits were generally available prior to EUC08 expiration in certain states with high unemployment. For more details on the structure and prior availability of EUC08 benefits, see CRS Report R42444, *Emergency Unemployment Compensation (EUC08): Status of Benefits Prior to Expiration*.

[4] The District of Columbia, Puerto Rico, and the Virgin Islands are considered to be states in UC law.

certain period of time (or both) within the base period to be monetarily eligible to receive any UC benefits. The methods states use to determine monetary eligibility vary greatly. Most state benefit formulas replace approximately half of a claimant's average weekly wage up to a weekly maximum. State taxes paid by employers on UC-covered wages finance UC benefits.

Maximum UC Benefit Duration

Until the recent state law changes described in this chapter, UC programs had been paying unemployment benefits for a maximum duration of 26 weeks. The only exceptions to the 26 week UC benefit maximum prior to these recent state law changes had been two states that provided more than 26 weeks of UC benefits (Montana: up to 28 weeks; Massachusetts: up to 30 weeks, depending on local economic conditions).[5] There is nothing in federal law, however, that requires states to set their UC benefit duration maximum at 26 weeks. Thus, states have the discretion to offer fewer than 26 weeks as the maximum as well as to set their own higher UC benefit durations via their state UC laws. In the early decades of the UC program, there was more variation in the maximum duration of UC benefits across states, which also tended to be lower than 26 weeks. Yet since the 1960s—and until the 2011 state law changes—all states had chosen to provide up to at least 26 weeks of UC benefits to eligible individuals.[6]

---

[5] When EB benefits are available in Montana, the total duration of UC and EB is capped at either 39 weeks (26 + 13) or 46 weeks (26 + 20). When EB benefits are available in Massachusetts, the maximum duration of UC benefits is capped at 26 weeks.

[6] Puerto Rico is an exception to this pattern of state convergence on 26 weeks as the maximum UC benefit duration in the 1960s. When it originally entered the federal-state UC system in 1961, Puerto Rico provided a lower maximum UC benefit duration (i.e., up to 16 weeks in 1961 and then up to 20 weeks for most of the 1970-1990 period). Puerto Rico did not provide up to 26 weeks of UC benefits until 1991. For more information on state UC benefit duration, including changes over time, see DOL's "Significant Provisions of State UI Laws," available at https://workforcesecurity.doleta.gov/unemploy/statelaws.asp#sigprou ilaws.

Emergency Unemployment Compensation Program (Now Expired)

On June 30, 2008, the Supplemental Appropriations Act of 2008 (P.L. 110-252) created a new temporary, federally financed unemployment insurance program, the EUC08 program. EUC08 was the eighth federal temporary program that Congress created to extend the number of potential weeks of UC available to eligible, unemployed individuals during an economic slowdown.[7] While it was authorized, state UC agencies administered the EUC08 benefit along with regular UC benefits. Prior to expiration, EUC08 benefits were financed with general revenue from the U.S. Treasury.

The authorization for this program expired the week ending on or before January 1, 2014 (December 28, 2013; December 29, 2013, for New York).[8] There was no grandfathering of any EUC08 benefit after that date. Therefore, no EUC08 benefits are currently available.[9]

Prior to program expiration, the EUC08 benefit amount was equal to the eligible individual's weekly regular UC benefits; the following four tiers of EUC08 benefits were available:

- *Tier I* was available in all states (except North Carolina),[10] up to 14 weeks.

---

[7] The other programs became effective in 1958, 1961, 1972, 1975, 1982, 1991, and 2002. See CRS Report RL34340, *Extending Unemployment Compensation Benefits During Recessions*, by Julie M. Whittaker and Katelin P. Isaacs.

[8] The EUC08 program was amended 11 times (P.L. 110-449, P.L. 111-5, P.L. 111-92, P.L. 111-118, P.L. 111-144, P.L.111-157, P.L. 111-205, P.L. 111-312, P.L. 112-78, P.L. 112-96, and P.L. 112-240). For more details on EUC08, including its legislative history, see CRS Report R42444, *Emergency Unemployment Compensation (EUC08): Status of Benefits Prior to Expiration*, by Katelin P. Isaacs and Julie M. Whittaker.

[9] Effective on or after July 1, 2013, EUC08 benefits were no longer available in North Carolina. North Carolina enacted legislation in February 2013 that included a provision to actively reduce UC weekly benefit amounts in the state. This state law provision violated the nonreduction rule and, therefore, terminated the EUC08 agreement between North Carolina and the Secretary of the U.S. Department of Labor.

[10] See previous footnote. North Carolina terminated its EUC08 agreement on July 1, 2013.

- *Tier II* was available in states with a Total Unemployment Rate (TUR) of at least 6% (not available in North Carolina), up to 14 weeks.[11]
- *Tier III* was available in states with a TUR of at least 7% (or an insured unemployment rate [IUR][12] of at least 4%; not available in North Carolina), up to 9 weeks.
- *Tier IV* was available in states with a TUR of at least 9% (or an IUR of at least 5%; not available in North Carolina), up to 10 weeks.

Extended Benefit Program

The Federal-State Extended Unemployment Compensation Act of 1970, P.L. 91-373, established the EB program. The EB program provides extended unemployment benefits in states that meet certain economic criteria. In all states, EB is available when a state's IUR or TUR reaches certain levels.[13]

The EB program imposes additional federal restrictions on individual eligibility for benefits beyond the state requirements for regular UC. In addition to all state requirements for regular UC eligibility, the EB program requires claimants to have at least 20 weeks of full-time insured employment or the equivalent in their base period and to conduct a systematic and sustained work search. Prior to the enactment of the Middle Class Tax Relief and Job Creation Act of 2012 (P.L. 112-96; enacted February 22, 2012), states were permitted to determine which benefit, EB or EUC08, was paid first, when EUC08 was authorized.[14] Effective with P.L. 112-96, states were required to pay EUC08 benefits before EB benefits until the EUC08 program expired December 28, 2013 (December 29, 2013, in New York State).

---

[11] The TUR (the total unemployment rate) is the seasonally-adjusted, three-month average of the ratio of unemployed workers to all workers (employed and unemployed) in the labor market.

[12] The IUR (the insured unemployment rate) is the ratio of UC claimants divided by individuals in UC-covered jobs.

[13] DOL's weekly trigger notices for the EB program are available online at https://workforcesecurity.doleta.gov/ unemploy/claims_arch.asp.

[14] Alaska was the only state to pay EB benefits first when this option was available under P.L. 110-252, as amended.

Under permanent law, EB benefits are funded half (50%) by the federal government and half (50%) by states. The American Recovery and Reinvestment Act of 2009 (P.L. 111-5), as amended, temporarily changed the financing of EB benefits to be 100% federal funding from February 2009 through December 2013.[15] (This temporary 100% federal funding for EB is now expired.) The EB benefit amount is equal to the eligible individual's weekly regular UC benefits.

There are two types of payable periods for EB benefits. First, if it meets certain state economic criteria and has certain state law trigger options in place, a state may pay EB benefits through an *EB Unemployment Period*. As discussed below, the duration of an EB Unemployment Period is based on the duration of regular UC benefits. For most states (i.e., those states with a UC maximum duration of up to 26 weeks), the EB Unemployment Period may provide up to 13 additional weeks of unemployment benefits to eligible individuals.[16]

Second, a state may pay benefits through an *EB High Unemployment Period* if that state meets certain state economic criteria and has certain state law trigger options in place. Because the duration of an EB High Unemployment Period is based on the duration of regular UC benefits in most states (i.e., those states with a UC maximum duration of up to 26 weeks), up to 20 additional weeks of EB benefits may be available to eligible individuals.[17]

---

[15] This temporary 100% federal financing of EB benefits did not include "non-sharable" benefits (generally, these are former state and local employees' EB benefits).

[16] All states must pay up to 13 weeks of EB if the insured unemployment rate (IUR; defined as the ratio of UC claimants divided by individuals in UC-covered jobs) for the previous 13 weeks is at least 5% and is 120% of the average of the rates for the same 13-week period in each of the two previous years. States may choose additional optional thresholds that may trigger an EB Unemployment Period: (1) an additional 13 weeks of benefits are payable if the state's IUR is at least 6%, regardless of previous years' averages; and/or (2) an additional 13 weeks of benefits are payable if the state's total unemployment rate (TUR; defined as the ratio of unemployed workers to all workers (employed and unemployed) in the labor market) is at least 6.5% and is at least 110% of the state's average TUR for the same 13 weeks in either of the previous two years. For additional information on these EB triggers, see CRS Report RL33362, *Unemployment Insurance: Programs and Benefits*, by Julie M. Whittaker and Katelin P. Isaacs.

[17] State may choose an optional EB trigger that provides an additional 20 weeks of benefits if the state's TUR is at least 8% and is at least 110% of the state's average TUR for the same 13 weeks in either of the previous two years. For additional information on these EB triggers,

Recent State UC Financial Stress

An original intent of the UC system, among other goals, was to help counter economic fluctuations, such as recessions.[18] This intent is reflected in the current UC program's funding and benefit structure. When the economy grows, UC program revenue rises through increased tax collection, and UC program expenditures fall as fewer workers are unemployed. The effect of collecting more taxes than are spent dampens demand in the economy. It also creates a surplus of funds, or a "cushion" of available funds, for the UC program to draw upon during a recession. In a recession, UC tax revenue falls and UC program spending rises as more workers lose their jobs and receive UC benefits. The increased amount of UC payments to unemployed workers dampens the economic effect of earnings losses by injecting additional funds into the economy.

As a result of the most recent recession, December 2007-June 2009, and its accompanying prolonged and high unemployment, states paid out large amounts of UC benefits: $75.3 billion in FY2009 and $63.0 billion in FY2010 versus $30.2 billion in FY2006 and $31.4 billion in FY2007.[19] This increase in state expenditures on UC benefits also led to large outstanding federal loans in many states.[20] According to the U.S. Department of Labor (DOL), 36 states depleted the balance of their state unemployment tax act (SUTA) revenues within their Unemployment Trust Fund accounts and took out federal loans to continue to pay UC benefits.[21] In 2010, for instance, outstanding federal loans to states totaled $40.2 billion at the end of the

---

see CRS Report RL33362, *Unemployment Insurance: Programs and Benefits*, by Julie M. Whittaker and Katelin P. Isaacs.

[18] See, for example, President Franklin Roosevelt's remarks at the signing of the Social Security Act at https://www.ssa.gov/history/fdrstmts.html#signing.

[19] U.S. Department of Labor (DOL), Office of Unemployment Insurance, *Unemployment Insurance Outlook*, various versions.

[20] For information on the authority and process under which states may request and take out federal loans to pay UC benefits, see CRS Report RS22954, *The Unemployment Trust Fund (UTF): State Insolvency and Federal Loans to States*, by Julie M. Whittaker.

[21] U.S. DOL, Office of Unemployment Insurance, *State Unemployment Insurance Trust Fund Solvency Report 2016*, February 2016, at http://www.workforcesecurity.doleta.gov/unemploy/docs/trustFundSolvReport2016.pdf.

calendar year.[22] As of October 23, 2019, all states except the Virgin Islands have paid back their federal loans from this most recent recessionary period.[23]

States may address this type of UC financial stress by (1) taking action to reduce UC expenditures (i.e., by decreasing UC benefits and/or limiting eligibility); (2) raising UC revenue (i.e., by increasing SUTA taxes); or (3) pursuing some combination of the first two options. The significant financial stress from the most recent recession contributed, in large part, to state legislative action during recent years. In response to similar state UC financial stress following prior recessions, states have typically reduced the amount of UC benefits paid to individuals through reductions in the maximum benefit amount or through changes in the underlying benefit calculations.[24]

UC PROGRAM INTEGRITY

Program integrity concerns constitute another factor to consider in understanding state UC reductions during recent years.[25] In addition to a significant increase in state expenditures on UC benefits during the 2011-2015 period, there were also significant federal expenditures on

---

[22] U.S. DOL, Office of Unemployment Insurance, *Unemployment Insurance Financial Data Handbook,* at https://workforcesecurity.doleta.gov/unemploy/hb394.asp.

[23] For the most recent DOL program data on outstanding federal loans, see https://oui.doleta.gov/unemploy/budget.asp.

[24] It should be noted, however, that reductions to UC duration or benefits were often coupled with other changes, including changes to UC financing. States enacted hundreds of laws over recent years. Although some of the laws that reduced UC benefits and eligibility were stand-alone laws, many of them included (1) multiple types of reductions, (2) other changes to UC benefits or financing generally, or (3) increased or altered employer tax rates. Additionally, states may and do have automatic triggers for changes to state UC programs, including reductions to UC benefits or increased employer taxes, that respond to changes in state UC finances. See U.S. DOL's *Reports on State Legislation*, various years, available at https://workforcesecurity.doleta.gov/unemploy/statelaws.asp#reports.

[25] *Program integrity activities* are defined by the Government Accountability Office (GAO) as "activities designed to prevent fraud, waste, and abuse of government resources." See, for example, GAO, *Program Integrity: Views on the Use of Commercial Data Services to Help Identify Fraud and Improper Payments*, GAO-16-624, June 30, 2016, p. 3, http://www.gao.gov/assets/680/678114.pdf.

unemployment benefits authorized through the EB and EUC08 programs during this period. For instance, in FY2011, $11.9 billion was paid out in EB benefits and $52.7 billion in EUC08 benefits, all federal expenditures.[26] Because states administer all unemployment benefits, including EB and EUC08 benefits (when authorized),[27] through their state UC programs, states were facing increased administrative pressure regarding program integrity. The Office of Management and Budget (OMB) has included UC in its list of "high-error" programs throughout this time period,[28] with the nominal amount of all improper UC payments peaking in FY2010 at $17.5 billion.[29] UC remains an OMB "high-error" program in the current year.[30]

In this climate, Congress has taken an active interest in trying to reduce UC improper payments, including UC, EB, and EUC08 overpayments made to individuals. For instance, Congress enacted three federal laws during the 2011-2015 period that either added or clarified state administrative

---

[26] U.S. DOL, Office of Unemployment Insurance, *Unemployment Insurance Outlook*, various versions.

[27] The Emergency Unemployment Compensation (EUC08) program was authorized between June 2010 and December 2013. For information on EUC08, see CRS Report R42444, *Emergency Unemployment Compensation (EUC08): Status of Benefits Prior to Expiration*, by Katelin P. Isaacs and Julie M. Whittaker.

[28] Programs are designated as "high-error" based on OMB guidance; they are "programs that reported roughly $750 million or more in improper payments in a given year, did not report an error amount in the current reporting year but previously reported an error amount over the threshold, or have not yet established a program error rate and have measured components that were above the threshold" (see overview available at https://payment accuracy.gov/high-priority-programs/).

[29] Improper payments include both overpayments and underpayments. For additional background information on UC improper payments, see https://oui.doleta.gov/unemploy/pdf/Overpayment_CauseDefinitions.pdf. According to DOL reporting, in 2010, there were $936 million in UC benefit underpayments and $16.5 billion in UC benefit overpayments. This total overpayment amount included $8.8 billion in overpayments that states were reasonably expected to detect and establish for recovery. See historical data on UC program integrity available at https://oui.doleta.gov/unemploy/improp_pay.asp.

[30] See https://paymentaccuracy.gov/high-priority-programs/. It should be noted that UC benefits are paid on a weekly basis (rather than monthly like other federal and state benefit programs). Therefore, there are additional opportunities for improper payments compared with other programs. At the same time, there are also additional opportunities for weekly improper payment detection and recovery. Historical data for UC benefit improper payment rate data for UC benefits are available at https://oui.doleta.gov/unemploy/ improp_payrate.asp#. For the 2004-2018 reporting years, the UC benefit overpayment rate ranged from 9% to 13%, whereas the rate of UC benefit overpayments that were reasonably expected to be detected and established for recovery ranged from 5% to 6%.

responsibilities to decrease benefit overpayments (P.L. 112-40;[31] P.L. 112-96;[32] and P.L. 113-67)[33] or imposed new restrictions on UC eligibility (P.L. 112-96).[34] Additionally, Congress held two hearings during this period to examine state UC program integrity: House Ways and Means Committee, Subcommittee on Human Resources, "Ending Cash for Convicts and Other Ways to Improve the Integrity of the UI Program" (September 11, 2013), and House Ways and Means Committee, Subcommittee on Human Resources, "Protecting the Safety Net from Waste, Fraud, and Abuse" (June 3, 2015).

DOL also prioritized program integrity efforts during this time period, for instance, by "making an immediate call to action to all state administrators to ensure that UI [unemployment insurance] integrity is a top priority and to develop state specific strategies to bring down the UI improper payment rate."[35] DOL also provided supplemental administrative funding opportunities to states during this period.[36] This heightened interest

---

[31] Among other provisions, P.L. 112-40, the Trade Adjustment Assistance Extension Act of 2011 (enacted 10/21/2011), added requirements that (1) states charge an employer's account (i.e., for the purposes of state unemployment taxes) when UC overpayments are the fault (through action or inaction) of the employer; (2) states assess a minimum 15% penalty on UC overpayments due to claimant fraud; and (3) employers to report any "rehired employee" to the National Directory of New Hires.

[32] Among other provisions, P.L. 112-96, the Middle-Class Tax Relief and Job Creation Act of 2012 (enacted 2/22/2012), added requirements that states (1) recover 100% of any erroneous UC benefit overpayment by reducing up to 100% of the UC benefit in each week until the overpayment is fully recovered (although allowed states to waive such deduction if it would be contrary to equity and good conscience); (2) recover certain federal benefits payments through reduced UC payments; and (3) provide reemployment and eligibility assessment activities to EUC08 claimants (the law provided $85 per person served through FY2013).

[33] Among other provisions, P.L. 113-67, the Bipartisan Budget Act of 2013 (enacted 12/26/2013), included a provision that required states (one year after the unemployment benefit overpayment debt was finally determined to be due) to recover any remaining state overpayments through reduced federal income tax refunds.

[34] P.L. 112-96 also (1) added a federal requirement that states require work search as a condition of eligibility for UC. (All states had such a requirement prior to the enactment of P.L. 112-96.); (2) required that individuals receiving EUC08 benefits be able to work, available to work, and actively seeking work; (3) clarified federal law to allow (but not require) states to engage in drug testing UC claimants under certain circumstances (and permitted states to deny benefits to an applicant who tests positive for drugs under those circumstances).

[35] U.S. DOL, Unemployment Insurance Program Letter (UIPL) 19-11, "National Effort to Reduce Improper Payments in the Unemployment Insurance (UI) Program," June 10, 2011, p. 1.

[36] For example, see U.S. DOL, UIPL 24-13, "Unemployment Insurance (UI) Supplemental Funding Opportunity for Program Integrity and Performance and System Improvements," July 25, 2013.

in UC program integrity may have encouraged states to reduce UC benefits via the state law changes, such as reductions to UC maximum duration or weekly benefit amount.

State Law Changes to UC Benefit Duration

In response to similar state UC financial stress following prior recessions, states have typically reduced the amount of UC benefits paid to individuals through reductions in the maximum benefit amount or through changes in the underlying benefit calculations. Prior to the expiration of EUC08, however, most states were temporarily prohibited from reducing UC benefit amounts through changes to benefit calculation[37] and, therefore, acted to reduce UC benefit duration as an alternative means to decrease total UC benefit payments. Therefore, these state UC benefit duration reductions are, in part, a response to UC financial crises facing states.

At the same time, however, the duration for current federal unemployment benefits—any EB periods (and each tier of the EUC08 program when it was authorized)—are calculated based on state UC benefit duration. Thus, states that have enacted laws to reduce the duration of regular UC benefits have also reduced the duration of EB benefits (and EUC08 benefits when that program was still authorized).

Currently, there are nine states with decreased maximum UC durations in effect:

- *Arkansas* decreased its state UC maximum duration from 26 weeks to 25 weeks, effective March 30, 2011. Effective October 1, 2015, Arkansas further reduced its UC maximum duration to up to 20 weeks. Effective January 1, 2018, Arkansas reduced its maximum duration to up to 16 weeks.

---

[37] For a fuller discussion of this issue, including details on states that have been able to reduce weekly UC benefit amounts, see the report section on "States with Reduced Weekly Benefit Amounts."

- *Florida* decreased the maximum UC duration from 26 weeks to a variable maximum duration, depending on the state unemployment rate and ranging from 12 weeks up to 23 weeks. Up to 12 weeks will be available if the state unemployment rate is 5% or less. Each 0.5% increase in the state unemployment rate above 5% will add an additional week of UC benefit duration. Finally, up to 23 weeks of regular UC benefits will be available if the state unemployment rate is at least 10.5%. This benefit reduction was effective January 1, 2012.
- *Georgia* decreased its UC maximum duration from 26 weeks to a variable maximum duration that ranges between 14 weeks and 20 weeks, depending on the unemployment rate in the state. A maximum UC duration of 14 weeks will be available if the state unemployment rate is 6.5% or less. Each 0.5% increase in the state unemployment rate above 6.5% will add additional weeks of UC benefit duration up to a maximum of 20 weeks of UC benefits if the state unemployment rate is at least 9%. This benefit reduction was effective May 2, 2012.
- *Idaho* decreased its UC maximum duration from 26 weeks to a variable maximum duration, ranging from 20 weeks up to 26 weeks and depending on the state unemployment rate. If the state unemployment rate is 2.9% or lower, then up to 20 weeks of UC benefits are available. Each subsequent 1.0% increase in the state unemployment rate raises the maximum UC duration by increments of one week, up to 26 weeks of UC benefits if the state unemployment rate is at least 8.0%.
- *Kansas* decreased its UC maximum duration from 26 weeks to a variable maximum duration, using a tiered system based on the state unemployment rate. Up to 16 weeks will be available if the state unemployment rate is less than 4.5%; up to 20 weeks if the state unemployment rate is at least 4.5% and less than 6.0%; and up to 26 weeks if the state unemployment rate is at least 6.0%. This benefit reduction was effective for individuals filing an initial claim for UC benefits beginning on or after January 1, 2014.

- *Michigan* decreased its UC maximum duration from 26 weeks to 20 weeks. This change was effective for individuals filing an initial claim for UC benefits on or after January 15, 2012.
- *Missouri* decreased its UC maximum duration from 26 weeks to 20 weeks, effective April 13, 2011. In 2015, Missouri enacted another law to further decrease its UC maximum duration from 20 weeks down to a variable duration based on state unemployment rate: (1) 13 weeks if state unemployment rate is less than 6.0%; (2) additional week added to 13 weeks for each 0.5% increase in state unemployment rate; (3) 20 weeks if state unemployment rate is at least 9.0%. In an opinion issued July 26, 2016, however, the Missouri Supreme Court found this 2015 law unconstitutional.[38] Therefore, UC maximum duration in Missouri remains up to 20 weeks.[39]
- *North Carolina* decreased the maximum UC duration from 26 weeks to a variable maximum duration, depending on the state unemployment rate and ranging from 12 weeks up to 20 weeks. Up to 12 weeks will be available if the state unemployment rate is 5.5% or less. Each 0.5% increase in the state unemployment rate above 5.5% will add an additional week of UC benefit duration. Finally, up to 20 weeks of regular UC benefits will be available if the state unemployment rate is greater than 9%. This benefit reduction is effective for individuals filing an initial claim for UC benefits on or after July 1, 2013.
- *South Carolina* also decreased its UC maximum duration from 26 weeks to 20 weeks, effective June 14, 2011.

---

[38] See http://www.courts.mo.gov/file.jsp?id=104054.

[39] See "Filing for Unemployment Insurance Benefits in Missouri: Basic Facts and Procedures," available at https://labor.mo.gov/sites/labor/files/pubs_forms/M-INF-288-5-AI.pdf.

One additional state has enacted a state law to decrease maximum UC duration that is not yet effective:

- *Alabama* is scheduled to decrease its maximum UC duration from 26 weeks to a variable duration, ranging from 14 to 20 weeks, depending on the average state unemployment rate. Up to 14 weeks of UC will be available in Alabama if the state unemployment rate is at or below 6.5%. Each 0.5% increase in the state unemployment rate above 6.5% will add an additional week of UC benefit duration. Finally, up to 20 weeks of regular UC benefits will be available if the state unemployment rate is at least 9.5%. This benefit duration change is scheduled to be effective January 1, 2020.[40]

Finally, one state enacted a law that decreased maximum UC duration only for a particular calendar year:

- *Illinois* enacted a law that decreased UC maximum duration in the state from 26 weeks to 25 weeks, effective only for calendar year 2012. Therefore, up to 26 weeks of UC benefits are currently available in Illinois.

Table 1 also provides details on these state changes to UC benefit duration.

[40] The same Alabama state law—Act 2019-204 (SB193, passed May 14, 2019)—will also provide an additional five weeks of UC benefits to individuals who have otherwise exhausted regular UC benefits and are "enrolled and making satisfactory progress in a job training or certification program approved by the Alabama Department of Labor. Each approved training program shall prepare individuals for entry into a high wage, high demand occupation." This provision is also scheduled to be effective January 1, 2020. Bill text available at http://arc-sos.state.al.us/PAC/ SOSACPDF.001/A0013121.PDF. Because these additional weeks of UC benefits are not available to all otherwise eligible UC claimants, they are not discussed in the remainder of this report.

Table 1. States with Unemployment Compensation (UC) Law Changes That Decrease Benefit Duration

State	State Bill or Act Number	Prior Maximum UC Duration	New Maximum UC Duration	Effective Date of New Maximum UC Duration
Alabama	Act 2019-204 (SB193)	26 weeks	Variable duration based on state unemployment rate: 14 weeks if state unemployment rate is 6.5% or below additional week added to 14 weeks for each 0.5% increase in state unemployment rate above 6.5% 20 weeks if state unemployment rate is at least 9.5%	Effective January 1, 2020 (Not yet effective)
Arkansas	Act 861, 88th General Assembly Act 412, 90th General Assembly Act 734, 91st General Assembly	26 weeks 25 weeks 20 weeks	25 weeks 20 weeks 16 weeks	Effective upon enactment (March 30, 2011) Effective October 1, 2015 Effective January 1, 2018
Florida	Chapter 2011-235, Laws of Florida	26 weeks	Variable duration based on state unemployment rate: 12 weeks if state unemployment rate is 5% or below additional	Effective January 1, 2012

Table 1. (Continued)

State	State Bill or Act Number	Prior Maximum UC Duration	New Maximum UC Duration	Effective Date of New Maximum UC Duration
			week added to 12 weeks for each 0.5% increase in state unemployment rate above 5% 23 weeks if state unemployment rate is at least 10.5%	
Georgia	Act 710 (House Bill 347), Georgia General Assembly, 2011-2012 Regular Session	26 weeks	Variable duration based on state unemployment rate: 14 weeks if state unemployment rate is 6.5% or below additional amount added to 14 weeks for each 0.5% increase in state unemployment rate above 6.5% 20 weeks if state unemployment rate is at least 9.0%	Effective May 2, 2012
Idaho	Session Law 280 (House Bill 485), Idaho Legislature, Second Regular Session, 2016	26 weeks	Variable duration based on state unemployment rate: 20 weeks if state unemployment rate is 2.9% or below additional week added to 20 weeks for each 1.0% increase in state unemployment rate above 2.9% 26 weeks if state unemployment rate is at least 8.0%	Effective July 1, 2016

State	State Bill or Act Number	Prior Maximum UC Duration	New Maximum UC Duration	Effective Date of New Maximum UC Duration
Illinois	Public Act 097-0001, 97th General Assembly	26 weeks	25 weeks	Effective January 1, 2012-December 31, 2012
Kansas	Substitute for HB 2105	26 weeks	Variable duration by tiers based on state unemployment rate: 16 weeks if state unemployment rate is less than 4.5% 20 weeks if state unemployment rate is at least 4.5% but less than 6.0% 26 weeks if state unemployment rate is at least 6.0%	Effective for individuals filing an initial claim for UC benefits on or after January 1, 2014
Michigan	Act No. 14, Public Acts of 2011	26 weeks	20 weeks	Effective for individuals filing an initial claim for UC benefits on or after January 15, 2012
Missouri	House Bill No. 163, 96th General Assembly	26 weeks	20 weeks	Effective upon enactment (April 13, 2011)
	House Bill No. 150, 95th General Assembly	20 weeks	Further reduced maximum UC duration from 20 weeks to variable duration based on state unemployment rate:	Not currently effective (due to a July 26, 2016, opinion by the Missouri Supreme Court)41

[41] See http://www.courts.mo.gov/file.jsp?id=104054.

Table 1. (Continued)

State	State Bill or Act Number	Prior Maximum UC Duration	New Maximum UC Duration	Effective Date of New Maximum UC Duration
			13 weeks if state unemployment rate is less than 6.0% additional week added to 13 weeks for each 0.5% increase in state unemployment rate 20 weeks if state unemployment rate is at least 9.0%	
North Carolina	Session Law 2013-2, General Assembly of North Carolina, Session 2013	26 weeks	Variable duration based on state unemployment rate: 12 weeks if state unemployment rate is 5.5% or below additional week added to 12 weeks for each 0.5% increase in state unemployment rate above 5.5% 20 weeks if state unemployment rate is greater than 9.0%	Effective July 1, 2013
South Carolina	Act No. 63, South Carolina General Assembly, 119th Session	26 weeks	20 weeks	Effective upon enactment (June 14, 2011)

Source: Compiled by the Congressional Research Service.

Consequences of Reduced UC Benefit Duration for Federal Unemployment Programs

Calculation of Benefit Duration for EUC08 Tiers (When EUC08 Was Authorized)

Prior to the expiration of EUC08, the duration of each tier of benefits was calculated through a formula based on state UC benefit duration.[43] Therefore, states that enacted laws to reduce the duration of regular UC benefits also experienced a reduction in the duration of EUC08 benefits when the program was authorized.

Specific formulas for the duration of each tier of EUC08 (when authorized) are presented below.[44] Examples of adjusted EUC08 benefit durations—based on a weekly benefit amount of $300 and a new maximum UC duration of 20 weeks—are also provided:[45]

- *Tier I of EUC08 (prior to expiration)*
  - Duration formula: 54% of the duration of an individual's total regular UC benefits in benefit year
  - Illustration of adjusted duration (formerly, the unreduced EUC08 tier I duration would have been up to 20 weeks—based on up to

---

[43] Prior to program expiration, the duration of benefits for each tier of EUC08 (as well as any EB payable period) was set through calculations based on the lesser of (1) the *state benefit criteria*, which is a set percentage of the duration of regular UC benefits (e.g., 54% of the individual's total regular UC duration in a benefit year for Tier I of EUC08 prior to expiration) or (2) the *maximum weekly amount criteria*, which is the multiple of an individual's average weekly benefit amount under the UC program (e.g., 13 times an individual's average weekly benefit amount in a benefit year for Tier I of EUC08 prior to expiration). In the event of state reduction in UC benefit durations, the former calculation—the state benefit criteria—would be lower and, thus, applicable. Therefore, this report's discussion of the benefit duration calculation for all tiers of EUC08 (when authorized) and all payable periods of EB focuses on this state benefit criteria formula in its explanations and illustrations of duration calculations.

[44] These EUC08 benefit duration formulas were effective for EUC08 tiers prior to expiration. The structure and availability of EUC08 tiers changed several times since the initial EUC08 program authorization. For more details on this legislative history, see CRS Report R42444, *Emergency Unemployment Compensation (EUC08): Status of Benefits Prior to Expiration*, by Katelin P. Isaacs and Julie M. Whittaker.

[45] The average weekly benefit amount was $315—or roughly $300—across all states as of July 2014 (DOL). Michigan, Missouri, and South Carolina have enacted state laws to reduce their maximum UC benefit duration to 20 weeks.

26 weeks of unreduced state UC benefits—at a weekly benefit amount of $300)
   - 54% of 20 weeks of UC = 10.8 weeks; up to 10 weeks at weekly benefit amount of $300 and the last week prorated at $240 ($300/0.8 = $240)
- *Tier II of EUC08 (prior to expiration)*
   - Duration formula: 54% of the duration of an individual's total regular UC benefits in benefit year
   - Illustration of adjusted duration (formerly, up to 14 weeks at $300)
   - 54% of 20 weeks of UC = 10.8 weeks; up to 10 weeks at weekly benefit amount of $300 and the last week prorated at $240 ($300/0.8 = $240)
- *Tier III of EUC08 (prior to expiration)*
   - Duration formula: 35% of the duration of an individual's total regular UC benefits in benefit year
   - Illustration of adjusted duration (formerly, up to 13 weeks at $300)
   - 35% of 20 weeks of UC = 7 weeks; up to 7 weeks at weekly benefit amount of $300
- *Tier IV of EUC08 (prior to expiration)*
   - Duration formula: 39% of the duration of an individual's total regular UC benefits in benefit year
   - Illustration of adjusted duration (formerly, up to 6 weeks at $300)
   - 39% of 20 weeks of UC = 7.8 weeks; up to 7 weeks at weekly benefit amount of $300 and the last week prorated at $240 ($300/0.8 = $240)

EUC08 tier duration calculations (prior to program expiration) for each state that enacted a reduction in regular UC benefit duration are provided in *Table 2.*

Calculation of Benefit Duration for EB Payable Periods

The duration of benefits for the two types of EB payable periods are set through calculations similar in structure to the calculations for EUC08 tier durations (when EUC08 was authorized).[46]

As was the case with the EUC08 program, state reductions in UC benefit durations lead to proportional reductions in the duration of the EB payable periods.

The EB payable period duration calculations and illustration of adjusted EB durations (using $300 as the weekly benefit amount and a new UC maximum duration of 20 weeks)[47] are below:

- *EB Unemployment Period*
  - Duration formula: 50% of the duration of individual's total regular UC benefits in benefit year
  - Illustration of adjusted duration (formerly up to 13 weeks at $300)
  - 50% of 20 weeks of UC = 10 weeks; up to 10 weeks at weekly benefit amount of $300
- *EB High Unemployment Period*
  - Duration formula: 80% of the duration of individual's total regular UC benefits in benefit year
  - Illustration of adjusted duration (formerly up to 20 weeks at $300)
  - 80% of 20 weeks of UC = 16 weeks; up to 16 weeks at weekly benefit amount of $300

Table 2 displays EB payable period duration calculations for each state that has enacted a reduction in regular UC benefit duration.

---

[46] See footnote 42 for more technical details.

[47] See footnote 44 for rationale behind these data points.

Table 2. Adjusted Maximum EUC08 (when authorized) and EB Benefit Duration Resulting from Changes to State Maximum UC Benefit Duration

State	Adjusted Maximum UC Duration	Adjusted Maximum EUC08 Tier I Duration (prior to expiration)	Adjusted Maximum EUC08 Tier II Duration (prior to expiration)	Adjusted Maximum EUC08 Tier III Duration (prior to expiration)	Adjusted Maximum EUC08 Tier IV Duration (prior to expiration)	Adjusted Maximum EB Unemployment Period Duration	Adjusted Maximum EB High Unemployment Period Duration	Effective Date for Adjusted UC Durations
Alabama	Variable duration based on state unemployment rate:							Effective 1/1/20 (Not yet effective)
	14 weeks if state unemployment rate is 6.5% or below additional week added to 14 weeks for each 0.5% increase in state	With 14-week UC duration: 7 weeks and 1 week at 0.56 × WBA	With 14-week UC duration: 7 weeks and 1 week at 0.56 × WBA	With 14-week UC duration: 4 weeks and 1 week at 0.9 × WBA	With 14-week UC duration: 5 weeks and 1 week at 0.46 × WBA	With 14-week UC duration: 7 weeks at WBA	With 14-week UC duration: 11 weeks at WBA and 1 week at 0.2 × WBA	

State	Adjusted Maximum UC Duration	Adjusted Maximum EUC08 Tier I Duration (prior to expiration)	Adjusted Maximum EUC08 Tier II Duration (prior to expiration)	Adjusted Maximum EUC08 Tier III Duration (prior to expiration)	Adjusted Maximum EUC08 Tier IV Duration (prior to expiration)	Adjusted Maximum EB Unemployment Period Duration	Adjusted Maximum EB High Unemployment Period Duration	Effective Date for Adjusted UC Durations
Alabama	unemployment rate above 6.5%							
	(3) 20 weeks if state unemployment rate is at least 9.5%	With 20-week UC duration: 10 weeks and 1 week at 0.8 × WBA	With 20-week UC duration: 10 weeks and 1 week at 0.8 × WBA	With 20-week UC duration: 7 weeks	With 20-week UC duration: 7 weeks and 1 week at 0.8 × WBA	With 20-week UC duration: 10 weeks	With 20-week UC duration: 16 weeks	
Arkansas	16 weeks	8 weeks and 1 week at 0.64 × WBA	8 weeks and 1 week at 0.64 × WBA	5 weeks and 1 week at 0.6 WBA	6 weeks and 1 week at 0.24 × WBA	8 weeks	12 weeks and 1 week at 0.8 × WBA	Effective 1/1/18
Florida	Variable duration based on state unemployment rate:							Effective 1/1/12
	12 weeks if state unemployment rate is 5% or below additional week added to 12 weeks for each	With 12-week UC duration: 6 weeks and 1 week at 0.48 × WBA	With 12-week UC duration: 6 weeks and 1 week at 0.48 × WBA	With 12-week UC duration: 4 weeks and 1 week at 0.2 × WBA	With 12-week UC duration: 4 weeks and 1 week at 0.68 × WBA	With 12-week UC duration: 6 weeks at WBA	With 12-week UC duration: 9 weeks at WBA and 1 week at 0.6 × WBA	

Table 2. (Continued)

State	Adjusted Maximum UC Duration	Adjusted Maximum EUC08 Tier I Duration (prior to expiration)	Adjusted Maximum EUC08 Tier II Duration (prior to expiration)	Adjusted Maximum EUC08 Tier III Duration (prior to expiration)	Adjusted Maximum EUC08 Tier IV Duration (prior to expiration)	Adjusted Maximum EB Unemployment Period Duration	Adjusted Maximum EB High Unemployment Period Duration	Effective Date for Adjusted UC Durations
Florida	0.5% increase in state unemployment rate above 5%							
	(3) 23 weeks if state unemployment rate is at least 10.5%	With 23-week UC duration: 12 weeks and 1 week at 0.42 × WBA	With 23-week UC duration: 12 weeks and 1 week at 0.42 × WBA	With 23-week UC duration: 8 weeks and 1 week at 0.05 × WBA	With 23-week UC duration: 8 weeks and 1 week at 0.97 × WBA	With 23-week UC duration: 11 weeks at WBA and 1 week at 0.5 × WBA	With 23-week UC duration: 18 weeks at WBA and 1 week at 0.4 × WBA	
Georgia	Variable duration based on state unemployment rate:							Effective 5/2/2012
	(1) 14 weeks if state unemployment rate is 6.5% or below	With 14-week UC duration: 7 weeks and 1 week at 0.56 × WBA	With 14-week UC duration: 7 weeks and 1 week at 0.56 × WBA	With 14-week UC duration: 4 weeks and 1 week at 0.9 × WBA	With 14-week UC duration: 5 weeks and 1 week at 0.46 × WBA	With 14-week UC duration: 7 weeks at WBA	With 14-week UC duration: 11 weeks at WBA and 1 week at 0.2 × WBA	

State	Adjusted Maximum UC Duration	Adjusted Maximum EUC08 Tier I Duration (prior to expiration)	Adjusted Maximum EUC08 Tier II Duration (prior to expiration)	Adjusted Maximum EUC08 Tier III Duration (prior to expiration)	Adjusted Maximum EUC08 Tier IV Duration (prior to expiration)	Adjusted Maximum EB Unemployment Period Duration	Adjusted Maximum EB High Unemployment Period Duration	Effective Date for Adjusted UC Durations
Georgia	(2) additional amount added to 14 weeks for each 0.5% increase in state unemployment rate above 6.5%							
	(3) 20 weeks if state unemployment rate is at least 9.0%	With 20-week UC duration: 10 weeks and 1 week at 0.8 × WBA	With 20-week UC duration: 10 weeks and 1 week at 0.8 × WBA	With 20-week UC duration: 7 weeks	With 20-week UC duration: 7 weeks and 1 week at 0.8 × WBA	With 20-week UC duration: 10 weeks	With 20-week UC duration: 16 weeks	
Idaho	Variable duration by tiers based on state unemployment rate:							Effective 7/1/2016
	(1) 20 weeks if state unemployment	With 20-week UC duration: 10 weeks and 1 week at	With 20-week UC duration: 10 weeks and 1 week at	With 20-week UC duration: 7 weeks	With 20-week UC duration: 7 weeks and 1 week at	With 20-week UC duration: 10 weeks	With 20-week UC duration: 16 weeks	

Table 2. (Continued)

State	Adjusted Maximum UC Duration	Adjusted Maximum EUC08 Tier I Duration (prior to expiration)	Adjusted Maximum EUC08 Tier II Duration (prior to expiration)	Adjusted Maximum EUC08 Tier III Duration (prior to expiration)	Adjusted Maximum EUC08 Tier IV Duration (prior to expiration)	Adjusted Maximum EB Unemployment Period Duration	Adjusted Maximum EB High Unemployment Period Duration	Effective Date for Adjusted UC Durations
Idaho	rate is 2.9% or below	0.8 × WBA	0.8 × WBA		0.8 × WBA			
	(2) additional week added to 20 weeks for each 1.0% increase in state unemployment rate above 2.9%							
	(3) 26 weeks if state unemployment rate is at least 8.0%	With 26-week UC duration: 14 weeks	With 26-week UC duration: 14 weeks	With 26-week UC duration: 9 weeks	With 26-week UC duration: 10 weeks	With 26-week UC duration: 13 weeks	With 26-week UC duration: 20 weeks	

State	Adjusted Maximum UC Duration	Adjusted Maximum EUC08 Tier I Duration (prior to expiration)	Adjusted Maximum EUC08 Tier II Duration (prior to expiration)	Adjusted Maximum EUC08 Tier III Duration (prior to expiration)	Adjusted Maximum EUC08 Tier IV Duration (prior to expiration)	Adjusted Maximum EB Unemployment Period Duration	Adjusted Maximum EB High Unemployment Period Duration	Effective Date for Adjusted UC Durations
Kansas	Variable duration by tiers based on state unemployment rate:							Effective for individuals filing initial claims for UC benefits on or after 1/1/14
	(1) 16 weeks if state unemployment rate is less than 4.5%	With 16-week UC duration: 8 weeks and 1 week at 0.64 × WBA	With 16-week UC duration: 8 weeks and 1 week at 0.64 × WBA	With 16-week UC duration: 5 weeks and 1 week at 0.6 × WBA	With 16-week UC duration: 6 weeks and 1 week at 0.24 × WBA	With 16-week UC duration: 8 weeks	With 16-week UC duration: 12 weeks and 1 week at 0.8 × WBA	
	(2) 20 weeks if State unemployment rate is at least 4.5% but less than 6.0%	With 20-week UC duration: 10 weeks and 1 week at 0.8 × WBA	With 20-week UC duration: 10 weeks and 1 week at 0.8 × WBA	With 20-week UC duration: 7 weeks	With 20-week UC duration: 7 weeks and 1 week at 0.8 × WBA	With 20-week UC duration: 10 weeks	With 20-week UC duration: 16 weeks	
	(3) 26 weeks if state unemployment rate is at least 6.0%	With 26-week UC duration: 14 weeks	With 26-week UC duration: 14 weeks	With 26-week UC duration: 9 weeks	With 26-week UC duration: 10 weeks	With 26-week UC duration: 13 weeks	With 26-week UC duration: 20 weeks	

Table 2. (Continued)

State	Adjusted Maximum UC Duration	Adjusted Maximum EUC08 Tier I Duration (prior to expiration)	Adjusted Maximum EUC08 Tier II Duration (prior to expiration)	Adjusted Maximum EUC08 Tier III Duration (prior to expiration)	Adjusted Maximum EUC08 Tier IV Duration (prior to expiration)	Adjusted Maximum EB Unemployment Period Duration	Adjusted Maximum EB High Unemployment Period Duration	Effective Date for Adjusted UC Durations
Michigan	20 weeks	10 weeks and 1 week at 0.8 × WBA	10 weeks and 1 week at 0.8 × WBA	With 20-week UC duration: 7 weeks	With 20-week UC duration: 7 weeks and 1 week at 0.8 × WBA	10 weeks	16 weeks	Effective for individuals filing initial claims for UC benefits on or after 1/15/12
Missouri	20 weeks	10 weeks and 1 week at 0.8 × WBA	10 weeks and 1 week at 0.8 × WBA	With 20-week UC duration: 7 weeks	With 20-week UC duration: 7 weeks and 1 week at 0.8 × WBA	10 weeks	16 weeks	Effective 4/13/11
North Carolina	Variable duration based on state unemployment rate:							Effective for individuals filing initial claims for UC benefits on or after 7/1/13
	(1) 12 weeks if state unemployment rate is 5.5% or below	NA	NA	NA	NA	With 12-week UC duration: 6 weeks at WBA	With 12-week UC duration: 9 weeks at WBA and 1 week at 0.6 × WBA	

State	Adjusted Maximum UC Duration	Adjusted Maximum EUC08 Tier I Duration (prior to expiration)	Adjusted Maximum EUC08 Tier II Duration (prior to expiration)	Adjusted Maximum EUC08 Tier III Duration (prior to expiration)	Adjusted Maximum EUC08 Tier IV Duration (prior to expiration)	Adjusted Maximum EB Unemployment Period Duration	Adjusted Maximum EB High Unemployment Period Duration	Effective Date for Adjusted UC Durations
North Carolina	(2) additional week added to 12 weeks for each 0.5% increase in state unemployment rate above 5.5%							
	(3) 20 weeks if state unemployment rate is greater than 9.0%	NA	NA	NA	NA	With 20-week UC duration: 10 weeks	With 20-week UC duration: 16 weeks	

Table 2. (Continued)

State	Adjusted Maximum UC Duration	Adjusted Maximum EUC08 Tier I Duration (prior to expiration)	Adjusted Maximum EUC08 Tier II Duration (prior to expiration)	Adjusted Maximum EUC08 Tier III Duration (prior to expiration)	Adjusted Maximum EUC08 Tier IV Duration (prior to expiration)	Adjusted Maximum EB Unemployment Period Duration	Adjusted Maximum EB High Unemployment Period Duration	Effective Date for Adjusted UC Durations
South Carolina	20 weeks	10 weeks and 1 week at 0.8 × WBA	10 weeks and 1 week at 0.8 × WBA	With 20-week UC duration: 7 weeks	With 20-week UC duration: 7 weeks and 1 week at 0.8 × WBA	10 weeks	16 weeks	Effective 6/14/11

Source: Compiled by Congressional Research Service.

Notes: The authorization for the EUC08 program expired the week ending on or before January 1, 2014. Consequently, EUC08 benefits were available through December 28, 2013 (December 29, 2013, for New York). Adjusted maximum EUC08 benefit durations and adjusted maximum durations from all programs reflect EUC08 benefits authorized prior to this expiration.

WBA: weekly benefit amount. All weeks of benefits are paid out in terms of full WBA unless a pro-rated WBA calculation is provided. States were authorized to augment pro-rated weeks of EUC08 tiers with amounts from subsequent EUC08 tiers to bring payments up to the full weekly benefit amount (Employment and Training Administration, U.S. Department of Labor, "Emergency Unemployment Compensation, 2008—Questions and Answers," Unemployment Insurance Program Letter 23-08, Change 3, December 24, 2008, http://wdr.doleta.gov/directives/attach/UIPL/UIPL23-08C3.pdf). The "Adjusted Benefit Duration Maximum from All Programs" column sums the total weeks from all four tiers of EUC08 and an EB High Unemployment Period, including full weeks of WBA and pro-rated weeks of WBA.

Illinois is not listed in this table because there is no UC maximum duration reduction effective in IL currently.

NA: not available. Due to a violation of the nonreduction rule (under P.L. 111-205, as amended), the EUC08 agreement between North Carolina and the Secretary of the U.S. Department of Labor was terminated. All tiers of EUC08 ended in North Carolina as of June 29, 2013.

The adjusted maximum benefit durations listed in the table for EUC08 and EB (and the maximum duration from all programs, which had previously been 93 weeks) apply to beneficiaries who file an initial claim for UC benefits after the effective date for adjusted UC durations. Individuals who received or are receiving UC benefits prior to the effective date for the state reduction in maximum UC benefits maintain the previous, unreduced UC, EUC08, and EB benefit durations. The EUC08 benefit duration formulas provided in this table were effective prior to EUC08 expiration. For more details, see CRS Chapter R42444, Emergency Unemployment Compensation (EUC08): Status of Benefits Prior to Expiration.

STATES WITH REDUCED WEEKLY BENEFIT AMOUNTS

P.L. 110-252, as amended, included a *nonreduction rule* that made the availability of federally financed EUC08 benefits (when authorized) contingent on not actively changing the state's method of calculating UC benefits, if the method would have decreased weekly benefit amounts. This nonreduction rule was a condition of the EUC08 federal-state agreement prior to EUC08 expiration. In general, states were not permitted to pay an average weekly UC benefit amount that is less than what would have been paid under state law prior to what was in effect as of June 2, 2010, and still be able to pay EUC08 benefits.[48] However, states could reduce weekly benefits if that reduction happens automatically in certain circumstances as required by a state law that was in place before the enactment of P.L. 111-5. Any reduction to the UC weekly benefit amount also translates into reduced EUC08 (when authorized) and EB weekly benefit amounts. The original goal of this nonreduction rule was to require states to maintain their previous efforts with regard to the level of UC benefit amounts during a period when there was a Federal Additional Compensation (FAC) payment of $25 a week added to all UI payments.[49]

Prior to P.L. 110-252, 36 states had enacted state laws that calculate the maximum weekly UC benefit via *automatic* adjustments based on the average weekly wage in a state.[50] Therefore, if the average weekly wage

---

[48] This nonreduction rule was put into place when P.L. 111-205 amended P.L. 110-252. There was a similar, but programmatically distinct nonreduction rule in P.L. 111-5, as amended, which prevented states from actively changing the method of calculation of the UC weekly benefit amount to pay UC benefit amounts less than what would have been paid under state law prior to December 31, 2008. No states acted to decrease UC benefit amounts between December 31, 2008, and June 2, 2010, when the federal authorization for this earlier nonreduction rule expired.

[49] This FAC was first authorized under the American Recovery and Reinvestment Act of 2009 (P.L. 111-5, enacted February 17, 2009), and it expired at the end of May 2010.

[50] The 36 states that calculate benefit amounts using automatic adjustments under prior state law are Arkansas, Colorado, Connecticut, District of Columbia, Hawaii, Idaho, Illinois, Iowa, Kansas, Kentucky, Louisiana, Maine, Massachusetts, Minnesota, Montana, Nevada, New Jersey, New Mexico, North Carolina, North Dakota, Ohio, Oklahoma, Oregon, Pennsylvania, Puerto Rico, Rhode Island, South Carolina, South Dakota, Texas, Utah, Vermont, Virgin Islands, Washington, West Virginia, Wisconsin, and Wyoming.

These 36 states could experience reductions in UC weekly benefit amounts under the nonreduction rule if (1) the average weekly wages in states declined and the corresponding

declines in these states, they may experience automatic reductions in UC average weekly benefit amount, which are permitted under the nonreduction rule. For instance, in 2011, New Jersey and Oklahoma appear to have met these conditions and to have experienced automatic reductions in their state UC weekly benefit amount. Similarly, in 2012, Hawaii also seems to have met the necessary conditions to automatically reduce the state UC weekly benefit amount.[51]

P.L. 112-96 provided a specific exception to this UC nonreduction rule in the case of state legislation that was enacted before March 1, 2012. States that made changes to the regular UC benefit amount prior to March 1, 2012, were not subject to the nonreduction rule.

In February 2013, North Carolina enacted legislation that included a provision to actively reduce UC weekly benefit amounts in the state. Effective on or after July 1, 2013, this state law provision violated the nonreduction rule and, therefore, terminated the EUC08 agreement between North Carolina and the Secretary of the U.S. Department of Labor. All tiers of EUC08 ended in North Carolina as of June 29, 2013.[52] With the expiration of the EUC08 program as of the week ending on or before January 1, 2014 (i.e., December 28, 2013; or December 29, 2013, in New York State), the nonreduction rule is no longer effective.

Any state UC benefit reductions also reduce weekly amounts for EB benefits (and EUC08 benefits when authorized), which are paid out in the same amount. Only individuals filing new state UC claims after the effective date for reduced UC durations, however, would experience reductions in UC, EUC08 (when authorized), or EB benefits.

---

methods of calculation formula resulted in a benefit decrease (for specific information regarding these state-specific methods of benefit calculation, see DOL's "Comparison of State Unemployment Laws, 2013," Chapter 3: Monetary Eligibility, Table 3.6, pp. 13-15, available at http://www.workforcesecurity.doleta.gov/unemploy/pdf/uilawcompar/2013/monetary.pdf) and (2) the state did not otherwise prevent this benefit amount reduction through enactment of new state legislation.

[51] See DOL's "Significant Provisions of State UI Laws," available at http://www.workforcesecurity.doleta.gov/ unemploy/statelaws.asp.

[52] See U.S. Department of Labor, EUC08 Trigger Notice No. 2013-24, effective June 30, 2013, http://www.workforcesecurity.doleta.gov/unemploy/euc_trigger/2013/euc_063013.html; and North Carolina Department of Commerce, Division of Employment Security, "Unemployment Insurance Law Changes—Claimants Questions and Answers," http://www.ncesc1.com/individual/2013LawChangeQA.asp.

In: State Unemployment Laws
Editor: Jonas Lemann

ISBN: 978-1-53618-202-6

Chapter 2

COMPARISON OF STATE UNEMPLOYMENT LAWS 2019*

U.S. Department of Labor

PREFACE

The Comparison of State Unemployment Insurance Laws provides state-by-state information on workers covered, benefit eligibility, methods of financing, and other areas of interest in the Unemployment Insurance (UI) program. It also includes information on the temporary disability programs operated in six states. The Comparison is published annually. This edition reflects the provisions of state law as of January 1, 2019.

The Comparison is issued solely for informational, reference, and research purposes. It is not an official interpretation of state UI laws. The state statutes should be consulted for the full text of state laws. Unless otherwise noted, the Comparison generally reflects state law, but not official

* This is an edited, reformatted and augmented version of U.S. Department of Labor Publication, dated January 1, 2019.

interpretations of state laws, which are found in state rules and regulations, administrative and court decisions, and opinions of attorneys general.

We recognize that the Comparison is useful only if it contains accurate data. States are encouraged to advise us of any needed corrections, either through their regional offices or through the contacts listed below. All users are invited to provide comments on the Comparison. We would like to thank those states that supplied updates and corrections.

State-specific information on filing a UI claim, employment assistance, or employer information is available online at https://www.careeronestop.org/localhelp/unemploymentbenefits/unemployment-benefits.aspx.

Click on the appropriate state on the blue map.

SECTION 1. COVERAGE

In General

This chapter provides information about the variations among states with respect to coverage – which employers are liable for Unemployment Insurance (UI) contributions and which workers accrue UI benefit rights.

When examining coverage, there is one overarching issue: are the services performed by a worker covered? To make that determination, the following questions must be answered.

- Were the services performed for an employer?
- Were the services performed in an employer-employee relationship?
- Were the services performed in employment?
- Were wages paid for the services?

If the answer is "yes" to all the questions listed then the services are covered by UI law. Note that not all payments may be considered "wages" for purposes of UI.

Other than service performed for the Federal government and railroads, Federal UI law does not technically "cover" services since no benefit rights accrue under Federal law. However, the taxing provisions of the Federal Unemployment Tax Act (FUTA) influence state coverage provisions since employers who pay taxes under an approved state UI law may credit their state contributions against a specified percentage of the FUTA tax owed.

Federal law requires, as a condition for approval of the state's UI law, that certain services not subject to the FUTA tax – services performed for state and local governments, certain nonprofit organizations, and federally recognized Indian tribes – must be covered by state law. Further, since states cannot tax the Federal government, coverage is extended to Federal service under the Unemployment Compensation for Federal Civilian Employees (UCFE) and Unemployment Compensation for Ex-Servicemembers (UCX) programs.

The Federal and state definitions of employment exclude from coverage certain types of service as well.

Since 1939, railroad workers have been excluded from the federal-state UI system. They are covered by a special Federal UI program administered by the Railroad Retirement Board. Since this program is not administered by the states, it is not discussed further in this publication.

State laws governing coverage generally incorporate the Federal exclusions, although nothing in Federal law requires them to do so. Most states permit voluntary election of coverage by employers for excluded workers. Also, most state laws provide that any service taxed by FUTA is covered under state law. Many state laws also automatically cover any service that Federal law requires to be covered as a condition of approval of the state's UI law.

Employers

As mentioned previously, one of the basic factors in determining coverage is whether services are performed for employers.

Table 1-1. Definition of employer (if different from FUTA 20 weeks/$1,500 rule)

State	Minimum Period of Time or Payroll	Alternative Conditions	State	Minimum Period of Time or Payroll	Alternative Conditions	State	Minimum Period of Time or Payroll	Alternative Conditions
AK	Any time		AR	1 employee for 10 or more days in a CY		CA	Over $100 in quarter	
DC	Any time		HI	Any time		IN	$1 or more in quarter	Employer liable for wages to 1 or more workers
IA	Any wages in current or preceding quarter		MD	Any time		MA	13 weeks	$1,500 in quarter
MI	20 weeks	$1,000 in CY	MN	Any time		MT	$1,000 in current or preceding year	
NV	$225 in quarter		NJ	$1,000 in year		NM	20 weeks	$450 in quarter
NY	$300 in quarter		OR	18 weeks	$1,000 in quarter	PA	Any time	
PR	Any time		RI	Any time		UT	Any time	
VI	Any time		WA	Any time		WY	Any time	

The coverage provisions of most state laws use the terms "employing unit" and "employer" to make the distinctions needed to address this issue. "Employing unit" is the more generic term. It applies to any one of several specified types of legal entities that has one or more individuals performing service for it within a state. An "employer" is an employing unit that meets the specific requirements of UI law. Hence, services provided for an employer are covered. As a result, an employer is subject to UI tax liability and its workers accrue rights for UI benefits.

For UI purposes, whether an employing unit is an employer depends on the number of days or weeks a worker is employed or the amount of the employing unit's quarterly or yearly payroll. Except for agricultural labor and domestic service, FUTA applies to employing units who, during any calendar quarter in the current or immediately preceding calendar year, paid wages of $1,500 or more, or to employing units with one or more workers on at least one day in each of 20 weeks during the current or immediately preceding calendar year.

About half of the states use this definition. The following table provides information on which employing units are considered employers in each state that uses a definition other than the one in FUTA.

Historical Note: The Federal law was originally applicable to employing units of eight or more workers on at least one day in each of 20 different weeks in a calendar year. This threshold was reduced to four workers in 1956 and to one in 1972.

Agricultural Labor

The FUTA agricultural labor provisions apply to employing units who paid wages in cash of $20,000 or more for agricultural labor in any calendar quarter in the current or preceding calendar year, or who employed 10 or more workers on at least one day in each of 20 different weeks in the current or immediately preceding calendar year. Most states have followed the FUTA provision and, therefore, have limited coverage to service performed on large farms. A few states cover services on smaller farms. The following table describes each state's agricultural labor provisions that differ from the FUTA provisions.

Most state laws follow the FUTA definition of agricultural labor. Under FUTA, agricultural labor is performed when workers:

- raise or harvest agricultural or horticultural products on a farm;
- work in connection with the operation, management, conservation, improvement, or maintenance of a farm and its tools and equipment;
- handle, process, or package any agricultural or horticultural commodity if a farm produced over half of the commodity (for a group of more than 20 operators, all of the commodity);
- do work related to cotton ginning, or processing crude gum from a living tree; or
- do housework in a private home if it is on a farm that is operated for profit.

Table 1-2. Agricultural labor provisions (if different from FUTA 20 weeks/$20,000 rule)

CA	1 at any time and wages in excess of $100 in a CQ
DC	1 at any time
FL	5 in 20 weeks or $10,000 in a CQ
MN	4 in 20 weeks or $20,000 in a CQ; agricultural labor performed by an individual 16 years of age or younger is excluded from agricultural coverage unless the employer is covered under Federal law
PR	1 or more at any time
RI	1 or more at any time
TX	3 in at least 20 different calendar weeks of the calendar year or wages in cash of $6,250 during a CQ
VI	1 or more at any time
WA	1 or more workers at any time, excluding workers attending or between terms in school; on corporate farms, does not include services performed by spouses or unmarried children under 18 years of age

The term "farm" includes stock, dairy, poultry, fruit, fur-bearing animals, and truck farms, as well as plantations, ranches, nurseries, ranges, greenhouses, or other similar structures used primarily for raising agricultural or horticultural commodities, and orchards. Agricultural labor does not include reselling activities that do not involve any substantial activity of raising agricultural or horticultural commodities, such as operation of a retail store or a greenhouse used primarily for display or storage.

> *Historical Note:* When the UI program began, all agricultural labor was excluded from the definition of employment regardless of the size of the agricultural employer. Administrative regulations of the Bureau of Internal Revenue first defined agricultural labor for Federal UI law purposes. All services on a farm in the raising and harvesting of any agricultural produce were excluded from coverage, as were services in some processing and marketing activities if performed for the farmer who raised the crop incidental to primary farming operations. A definition of agricultural labor, added to FUTA in 1939, also excluded from coverage some processing and marketing activities (services performed in the employ of someone other than the farmer) and services in the management and operation of a farm (if they were performed for the farm owner or operator). Amendments made to FUTA in 1970 changed the definition of agricultural labor, effectively extending coverage to some marginal agricultural activities. The 1976 amendments added the current dollar/employment thresholds that resulted in coverage of services performed on large farms.

States have the option of excluding from coverage service performed in agricultural labor on or after January 1, 1995, by aliens who are admitted to the United States pursuant to the Immigration and Nationality Act. However, these aliens are counted in determining whether an agricultural employer meets the wage or size-of-firm requirements for coverage.

The FUTA established a special rule for determining who will be treated as the employer and, therefore, liable for the FUTA tax, in the case of agricultural workers who are members of a crew furnished by a crew leader to perform services in agricultural labor for a farm operator. Workers who are members of a crew furnished by a crew leader to perform service in agricultural labor for a farm operator are treated as employees of the crew leader if the leader is registered under the Migrant and Seasonal Agricultural Protection Act, or if substantially all of the members of the crew operate or maintain mechanized equipment furnished by a crew leader. A member of a crew furnished by a crew leader to perform service in agricultural labor for a farm operator will not be treated as an employee of the crew leader if the individual is an employee of the farm operator within the meaning of the state law. Conversely, any worker who is furnished by a crew leader to perform service in agricultural labor for a farm operator but who is not treated as an employee of the crew leader is treated as an employee of the farm operator. This special rule is intended to resolve any question as to whether an individual's employer is the farm operator or crew leader. The same size-of-firm coverage provisions (10 in 20 weeks or $20,000 in a calendar quarter) apply to a crew leader as to a farm operator.

Domestic Service

FUTA applies to any employer who, during any calendar quarter in the current or preceding calendar year, paid wages in cash of $1,000 or more for domestic service in a private home, local college club, or local chapter of a college fraternity or sorority. As a result, all states cover such domestic service. The following table includes the provisions for states that do not utilize the FUTA provisions.

Table 1-3. Domestic service provisions (if different from FUTA $1,000 rule)

CA	Covers in-home supportive services provided under the Welfare and Institution Code
DC	At least $500 in quarterly wages
HI	Excludes domestic in-home and community-based services for a person with developmental and intellectual disabilities under the Medicaid home and community-based services program or when provided to individuals ineligible for Medicaid and performed by an individual in the employ of a recipient of social service payments unless the individual is an employee and not an independent contractor of the recipient of social service payments under FUTA
NY	At least $500 in quarterly wages
VA	Excludes: (1) medical services performed by an individual employed to perform those services in a private residence or medical institution if the employing unit is the person receiving the services; and (2) services performed under agreement with a Public Human Service Agency in the home of the recipient of the service or the provider of the service
VI	At least $500 in quarterly wages

Employer-Employee Relationship

Most state laws contain strict tests to determine whether there is sufficient absence of control by an employer that the worker is not an employee but an independent contractor. Many of the states provide criteria commonly called the "ABC" test under which service for remuneration is considered employment and the worker is an employee unless each of three factors are met.

- The worker is free from direction or control in the performance of the work under the contract of service and in fact.
- The service is performed either outside the usual course of the business for which it is performed or is performed outside of all places of business of the enterprise for which it is performed.
- The individual is customarily engaged in an independent trade, occupation, profession, or business.

Other states have variations of the "ABC" test. For example, in some states only the "A" and "C" tests apply.

The IRS uses the 20-factor test to determine whether direction and control exists in an employer/employee relationship, and to what degree. A few states use the 20-factor test instead of the "ABC" test. The 20-factor test is an analytical tool; there is no magic number of factors that must be met or not met. The 20-factor test looks for three basic types of evidence.

- Behavioral: Facts that illustrate whether there is a right to direct or control how the worker performed the specific task as opposed to what task the worker performed.
- Financial: Facts that illustrate whether there is a right to direct or control how the business aspects of a worker's activities are conducted.

Table 1-4. Workers considered employees unless

State	Workers Free From Control Over Performance (A)	Service Outside Regular Course or Place of Employer's Business (B)	Worker in an Independent Business (C)	Other Tests	State	Workers Free From Control Over Performance (A)	Service Outside Regular Course or Place of Employer's Business (B)	Worker in an Independent Business (C)	Other Tests
AK	X	X	X		AL				Master-servant[1]
AR				A and B or A and C	AZ				Service performed by an employee for the entity employing him
CA	X	X	X	Contract of hire, written or oral, express or implied[2]	CO	X		X	
CT	X	X	X		DC				Contract of hire, written or oral, expressed or implied
DE	X	X	X		FL	X	X	X	X[2]
GA	X		X	Determination from the IRS	HI	X	X	X	

State	Workers Free From Control Over Performance (A)	Service Outside Regular Course or Place of Employer's Business (B)	Worker in an Independent Business (C)	Other Tests	State	Workers Free From Control Over Performance (A)	Service Outside Regular Course or Place of Employer's Business (B)	Worker in an Independent Business (C)	Other Tests
IA	X			Contract of hire, written or oral, expressed or implied	ID	X		X	
IL	X	X	X		IN	X	X	X	20-factor test
KS	X				KY				Master-servant[1]; by judicial interpreta- tion
LA	X	X	X		MA	X	X	X	
MD	X	X	X		ME	X	X	X	
MI				20-factor test[3]	MN			X	Master-servant[1]
MO				Common law right to control[4]	MS	X			Master-servant[1]

Table 1-4. (Continued)

State	Workers Free From Control Over Performance (A)	Service Outside Regular Course or Place of Employer's Business (B)	Worker in an Independent Business (C)	Other Tests	State	Workers Free From Control Over Performance (A)	Service Outside Regular Course or Place of Employer's Business (B)	Worker in an Independent Business (C)	Other Tests
MT				Works under approved independent contractor exemption certificate	NC				Contract creating employee relationship
ND				20-factor test	NE	X	X	X	Contract creating employee relationship
NH	X	X	X		NJ	X	X	X	
NM	X	X	X		NV	X	X	X	
NY				Contract of hire, written or oral, expressed or implied	OH	X			Contract of hire, written or oral, expressed or implied
OK	X	X	X		OR	X		X	
PA	X		X		PR	X	X	X	
RI	X	X	X		SC				Contract of hire, written or oral, expressed or implied

State	Workers Free From Control Over Performance (A)	Service Outside Regular Course or Place of Employer's Business (B)	Worker in an Independent Business (C)	Other Tests	State	Workers Free From Control Over Performance (A)	Service Outside Regular Course or Place of Employer's Business (B)	Worker in an Independent Business (C)	Other Tests
SD	X		X		TN	X	X	X	
TX				Common law	UT	X		X	
VA				20-factor test	VI	X	X	X	
VT	X	X	X		WA	X	X	X	
WI				Statutory factors[5]	WV	X	X	X	
WY	X			X[6]					

[1] AL, KY, MN, and MS - master-servant refers generally to the employer's right of direction and control.

[2] CA and FL - in addition to the A, B, and C tests, the following tests are considered: 1) in locality, work is usually done by specialist without supervision; 2) specialized skill is required in the particular occupation; 3) length of time for which person is employed suggests an independent relationship; 4) method of payment is by the job rather than by time; 5) parties do not believe they are creating a master and servant relationship; 6) principal not in business; and 7) principal does not supply the instrumentalities, tools, and the place of work for the person doing the work.

[3] MI - an individual from whom an employer is required to withhold federal income tax will be prima facie considered to perform services in employment.

[4] MO - uses the 20-factor test for taxi-cab and rider referral service providers.

[5] WI - direction and control and independent business (i.e., A and C) tests used for governmental and nonprofit entities, loggers, and truckers.

[6] WY - individual must represent services to the public as being in self-employment or as an independent contractor, and individual must be able to substitute another individual to perform the services.

- Relationship: Facts that illustrate how the parties perceive their relationship to each other; whether the worker's activity is part of a regular business activity; employee benefits; and the intent of the parties.

Factors of lesser importance include whether the work is part-time or full-time, the place of the work, and hours of work. None of the 20 factors is singularly determinative, and some factors may not apply to certain occupations. The degree of importance of each factor may vary depending on the occupation.

The different tests used in states are listed in Table 1-4.

Employment

For UI purposes, employment is generally defined as the performance of any services, of whatever nature, by an employee for the person employing him or her. However, there are some exceptions. Also, since each state operates its own UI program, it is essential to determine which state covers a worker's employment. These topics are explored in the following section.

Location of Employment

Localization of Work

In general, workers are covered by the UI law of the state in which the work is performed. To avoid duplicate coverage or no coverage at all when a worker works for one employer in more than one state, states agreed in the early days of the UI program on how to determine which state would cover such workers. These provisions of states' UI laws are called "localization of work" provisions.

> *Historical Note:* Model state legislation to put this agreement into effect was developed by the U.S. Department of Labor and incorporated into all states' UI laws in the 1940s. The government of Canada agreed to the localization of work provisions in 1947. Additional guidance was provided in the September 1950 edition of the Manual of State Employment Security Legislation. Unemployment Insurance Program Letter (UIPL) 20-04 was issued to address new concerns, such as telecommuting.

There are four tests to determine the state in which service should be reported (hence, the state in which a worker is covered). The tests are applied in the following sequence until a determination is made.

- Are the workers' services localized in any state?
    - Are the services performed entirely in one state; or
    - Are the services performed out of that state incidental (e.g., temporary or transitory) to the services performed in that state?
- If the workers' services are not localized in any state, do the workers perform some service in the state in which their base of operations is located?
- If the workers do not perform any service in the state in which their base of operations is located, do they perform any service in the state from which the services are directed and controlled?
- If the workers do not perform any service in the state from which their services are directed and controlled, do they perform any service in the state in which they live?

Thus, even if a worker's services are not localized in any state, the last three tests listed will help in determining the state in which a worker is covered.

Election of Coverage of Services Performed Outside of the State

The laws of most states permit employers to elect coverage of workers who perform their services entirely outside the state if they are not covered by any other state or Federal UI law. Of the states permitting such elections, most states require residence in the state of election.

Coverage of Services Performed Outside the United States

Prior to the 1970 amendments to the FUTA, employment included only services performed within the United States, with the exception of certain services performed in connection with an American vessel or aircraft. With respect to services performed after 1971, Federal law also requires coverage of services performed outside the United States by an American citizen for an American employer. Coverage of such services is not applicable to services performed in a contiguous country with which the United States has an agreement relating to UI (Canada).

In determining the state of coverage, the following four tests are applicable to the state in which the:

- employer has the principal place of business;
- employer is located;
- employer elects coverage; or
- individual files a claim.

Election of Coverage through Reciprocal Coverage Arrangement

If none of the localization of work tests determine the state in which a worker is covered, most state laws allow the employer, all of its employees, and all states involved to sign an agreement for the services to be covered by a state. An employer may cover all the services of such a worker in any state in which any part of the service is performed, the state of residence, or the state in which the employer maintains a place of business. A few states do not participate in these arrangements.

All states have provisions for the election of coverage of services outside the state not covered elsewhere or of services allocated to the state under a reciprocal agreement.

Table 1-5. Significant exclusions from coverage

State	Insurance Agents on Commission	Real Estate Agents on Commission	Casual Labor Not in Course of Employer's Business	Part-Time Service for Nonprofit Organizations Exempt from Federal Income Tax[1]	State	Insurance Agents on Commission	Real Estate Agents on Commission	Casual Labor Not in Course of Employer's Business	Part-Time Service for Nonprofit Organizations Exempt from Federal Income Tax[1]
AL	X	X	X	X	AK	X	X	X	X[2]
AZ	X	X	X	X	AR	X	X	X	X
CA		X	X	X	CO	X	X	X	X
CT	X	X	X	X	DE	X	X		
DC	X		X	X	FL	X	X	X	X
GA	X	X	X		HI	X	X	X	X[2]
ID	X	X			IL	X	X		X
IN	X		X	X	IA		X		
KS	X	X	X	X	KY	X	X	X	X
LA	X	X	X	X	ME	X	X		X[1]
MD	X	X	X	X	MA	X	X	X	X
MI	X	X		X	MN	X[3]	X[3]	X	
MS	X	X	X	X	MO	X	X		
MT	X	X	X		NE	X	X	X	X
NV		X			NH	X	X	X	X
NJ	X	X			NM	X	X		
NY	X	X			NC	X	X	X	X
ND	X	X	X	X	OH	X		X	X
OK	X	X			OR	X	X	X	

Table 1-5. (Continued)

State	Insurance Agents on Commission	Real Estate Agents on Commission	Casual Labor Not in Course of Employer's Business	Part-Time Service for Nonprofit Organizations Exempt from Federal Income Tax[1]	State	Insurance Agents on Commission	Real Estate Agents on Commission	Casual Labor Not in Course of Employer's Business	Part-Time Service for Nonprofit Organizations Exempt from Federal Income Tax[1]
PA	X	X	X		PR		X	X	
RI	X[3]	X	X	X	SC	X	X	X	X
SD	X			X	TN	X	X		
TX	X	X			UT	X	X	X	X
VT	X	X	X	X	VA	X	X	X	X
VI			X		WA	X	X	X	
WV	X				WI	X	X		X
WY		X	X						

[1] All states - this exclusion is limited to remuneration of less than $50 in any CQ, except in AK (less than $250), and ME (less than $150).

[2] AK and HI - exclusion not limited to part-time service.

[3] MN - does not exclude such service if performed by a corporate officer; RI - does not exclude such service if performed for a corporation or by industrial and debit insurance agents.

Employment Specifically Excluded

State exclusions from employment generally follow the FUTA exclusions. However, the states often exclude other types of employment as well. This section presents a brief discussion of each of the exclusions that occur in all or nearly all of the state laws. Exclusions that occur in only a few states, and affect relatively small groups, are not included. The following table provides an overview of some of the significant exclusions from the definition of employment used by states.

Service for Relatives

All states exclude service performed for an employer by a spouse or minor child and, with few exceptions, service of an individual in the employ of a son or daughter.

Service by Students and Spouses of Students

FUTA excludes service performed in the employ of a school, college, or university by a student enrolled and regularly attending classes at such school. FUTA excludes service performed by a student's spouse for the school, college, or university at which the student is enrolled and regularly attending classes, provided the spouse's employment is under a program designed to give financial assistance to the student, and the spouse is advised that the employment is under such student-assistance program and is not covered by any UI program. Also excluded is service by a full-time student in a work-study program provided that the service is an integral part of the program. The following table provides additional information about states' provisions with respect to student employment.

Service by Patients for Hospitals

These services may be excluded from coverage under the state law whether they are performed for a hospital operated for profit, not-for-profit, or by a state.

Table 1-6. Student employment excluded from coverage

State	Student Nurses and Interns in Employ of a Hospital	Students Working for Schools[1]	State	Student Nurses and Interns in Employ of a Hospital	Students Working for Schools[1]	State	Student Nurses and Interns in Employ of a Hospital	Students Working for Schools[1],	State	Student Nurses and Interns in Employ of a Hospital	Students Working for Schools[1]
AL	X	X	AK	X	X[2]	AZ	X	X	AR	X	X[2]
CA	X	X	CO		X	CT	X	X	DE		X[2]
DC	X	X[2]	FL	X	X[2]	GA	X	X	HI	X	X2
ID	X	X[2]	IL	X	X	IN	X	X	IA		X
KS		X[2]	KY	X	X	LA	X	X[2]	ME	X	X[2]
MD	X	X	MA	X	X	MI		X	MN	X	X[2]
MS	X	X	MO		X	MT		X	NE	X	X
NV		X	NH	X	X	NJ	X[3]	X	NM		X[2]
NY		X	NC		X	ND	X	X	OH	X	X[2]
OK	X	X	OR	X	X	PA	X	X	PR		X[2]
RI		X[2]	SC	X	X	SD	X	X	TN		X
TX	X	X[2]	UT	X	X	VT		X	VA	X	X[2]
VI		X[2]	WA		X	WV		X[2]	WI	X	X
WY		X									

[1]All states exclude students in work-study programs; however, DC and HI - exclude only elementary or secondary school students. DC - excludes services performed by a student in the employ of an organization exempt from Federal income tax if the remuneration does not exceed $50 in a CQ.

[2]AK, AR, DE, DC, FL, HI, ID, KS, LA, ME, MN, NM, OH, PR, RI, TX, VA, VI, and WV - do not exclude service by the spouse of a student in the employ of the school; all other states exclude such service.

[3] NJ - Exclusion does not apply to service by an intern who has completed a four-year course in medical school.

Service for Federal Instrumentalities

An amendment to FUTA, effective with respect to services performed after 1961, permits states to cover Federal instrumentalities that are neither wholly nor partially owned by the United States, nor exempt from the FUTA tax by virtue of any other provision of law that specifically refers to such section of the Internal Revenue Code in granting such exemptions. All states, except New Jersey, have provisions in their laws that permit the coverage of service performed for non-wholly or partially owned Federal instrumentalities.

Maritime Workers

FUTA permits a state to cover maritime services if the operation of an American vessel operating on navigable waters within, or within and without, the United States is ordinarily regularly supervised, managed, directed, and controlled by such state. Most state laws currently cover such services.

> *Historical Note:* The FUTA and most state laws initially excluded maritime workers, principally because it was thought that the Constitution prevented the states from covering such workers. Supreme Court decisions in *Standard Dredging Corporation v. Murphy* and *International Elevating Company v. Murphy*, 319 U.S. 306 (1943), were interpreted to mean that there is no such bar. In 1946, the current FUTA provision was added.

Voluntary Coverage of Excluded Employment

Most states allow employers to elect to cover most types of employment that are exempt under their state laws.

Self-Employment

Employment, for purposes of UI coverage, is employment of workers who work for others for wages; it does not include self-employment. Although the protection of the Federal old-age, survivors, and disability insurance program has been extended to most of the self-employed, protection under the UI program is not feasible, largely because of the difficulty of determining whether in a given week a self-employed worker is unemployed.

Coverage of Officers of Corporations

Under FUTA, an officer of a corporation is defined as an employee of the corporation, and wages paid to the employee are subject to the FUTA tax. However, some states have enacted exclusions from coverage and restrictions on benefits for corporate officers (with the exception of any corporate officers for whom coverage is required). Since FUTA contains no exclusion, when states exclude these services, the employers of corporate officers are liable for the full FUTA tax on wages paid to these individuals. The following table outlines the exclusions and restrictions for which states have opted.

Table 1-7. Corporate Officers

State	Provisions
AK	Services are exempt only if the corporation is not a nonprofit or governmental entity and the employee is an executive officer of the corporation.
CA	Exempts services performed by an individual in the employ of a corporation of which he/she is the majority or controlling shareholder and an officer, if not subject to FUTA. Also exempts an officer or shareholder of an agricultural corporation unless the corporation is an employer defined under FUTA.
DE	Exempts services performed by an officer of a corporation organized and operated exclusively for social or civic purposes, provided the services performed by the officer are part-time and when the remuneration received does not exceed $75 in any CQ.
HI	An individual will not be eligible for benefits if an owner-employee of a corporation brings about his/her unemployment by divesting ownership, leasing the business interest, terminating the business, or by other similar actions. Also, excludes from coverage services for a family-owned private corporation, organized for profit, that employs family members who own at least 50% of the corporate shares, provided certain criteria are met.
IA	Exempts services performed by an individual in the employ of a corporation of which he/she is the majority or controlling shareholder and an officer, if not subject to FUTA.

State	Provisions
ID	Permits exemption of corporate officers from coverage and permits reinstatement of corporate officers previously exempted. A corporate officer whose benefit claim is based on wages with a corporation in which he or she or a family member has an ownership interest is not "unemployed" and is ineligible for benefits in any week during his/her term of office with the corporation. However, the corporate officer is unemployed in any week not employed by the corporation for an indefinite period of time due to circumstances beyond his/her control or the control of a family member who has an ownership interest in the corporation; if at any time during the BY the corporate officer resumes, or returns to, work for the corporation, there is a rebuttable presumption that his/her unemployment was within his/her control, and all benefits paid are considered an overpayment. A corporation that is a public company may elect to exempt from coverage any corporate officer who is voluntarily elected or voluntarily appointed, is a shareholder of the corporation, exercises substantial control in the daily management of the corporation, and whose primary responsibilities do not include the performance of manual labor; a corporation that is not a public company may elect to exempt from coverage any corporate officer, without regard to his/her performance of manual labor, if he/she is a shareholder of the corporation, voluntarily agrees to be exempted from coverage, and exercises substantial control in the daily management of the corporation that has a class of shares registered with the Federal Securities and Exchange Commission.
MI	Limits to no more than 7 weeks benefits payable based on services performed in a family corporation in which the individual or his/her son, daughter, spouse, or parent owns more than 50% of the proprietary interest in the corporation.
MN	An individual who has been paid 4 times his/her WBA may not use wages paid by an employing unit if the individual (a) individually or jointly with a spouse, parent, or child owns or controls 25% or more interest in the employing unit; or (b) is the spouse, parent, or minor child of any individual who owns or controls 25% or more interest in the employing unit; and (c) is not permanently separated from employment. Also exempts officers or shareholders in a family agricultural corporation. Contracts to obtain a taxpaying employer's workforce must include coverage of corporate officers for the duration of the contract.
NJ	Excludes corporate officers and individuals with at least 5% ownership of employing business.
ND	Exempts corporate officers when ¼ or more of the ownership interest was owned or controlled by the individual's spouse, child, or parent or by any combination of them if the corporation requests exemption from coverage.
OK	Exempts services, not considered nonprofit, if he/she owns 100% of the stock.
OR	Exempts services performed by corporate officers who are directors of the corporation, who have a substantial corporate ownership interest, and who are related by family if the corporation elects not to provide coverage for the related family members.
TX	An individual will not be eligible for benefits from the date of the sale of a business and until he/she is re-employed and eligible for benefits based on the wages received through the new employment if the business was a corporation and the individual was an officer or a majority or controlling shareholder in the corporation, and was involved in the sale of

Table 1-7. (Continued)

State	Provisions
	the corporation; or if the business was a limited or general partnership and the individual was a limited or general partner who was involved in the sale of the partnership; or the business was a sole proprietorship and the individual was the proprietor who sold the business.
SC	Exempts service performed by an officer of a corporation. A corporation may elect, in writing, to cover its officers and must notify its officers they are ineligible for UI benefits if the corporation does not elect to provide coverage. Coverage must be provided for at least 2 calendar years and shall terminate January 1 subsequent to the 2-year period if the employer files a written application before January 15 of that year.
WA	Exempts services performed by corporate officers unless corporation elects coverage for all officers; wages for corporate officer must be less than 25 percent of total base year wages to be eligible for benefits. However, this exemption does not apply to corporate officers employed by nonprofit or governmental employers.
WI	The amount of BPW used to compute total benefits payable to an individual may not exceed 10 times the individual's WBA based on the individual's employment with a corporation or a limited liability company that is treated as a corporation if ½ or more of the ownership interest in the corporation or limited liability company during the employment was owned or controlled by the individual's spouse or by the individual's parent if the individual is under age 18, or by a combination of 2 or more of them; or in the case of a corporation, if ¼ or more of the ownership interest in the corporation during the employment was owned or controlled by the individual. Also, a corporate employer having taxable payrolls less than the amount used to establish separate solvency contribution rates may elect not to have the principal officers covered if the officers have a direct or indirect substantial ownership interest in the corporation.

Coverage Required under Federal Law

As a result of amendments to FUTA made in 1970, 1976, and 2000, certain services performed for nonprofit organizations, state and local governments, and Indian tribes must be covered as a condition for approval of the state's law. These special "required coverage" provisions exist because the services are not taxable under FUTA. Normally, if a state law fails to cover services that are taxed under the FUTA, the employer must pay the full FUTA tax. Since this scheme does not encourage coverage for services not subject to the FUTA tax, Federal law requires services performed for the previously mentioned entities to be covered as a condition of approval and, as a result, a necessary condition for all employers in the state to receive credits against the FUTA tax.

States are required to pay UI benefits based on services performed for governmental entities, nonprofit organizations, and federally recognized Indian tribes in the same amounts and under the same terms and conditions as for services covered under state law. There are, however, special provisions applicable to school personnel. They are commonly called "between-and-within-terms denial provisions." (For more information, see Nonmonetary Chapter.)

Federal law permits states to exclude from this required coverage all of the exclusions from employment available for private employers. Moreover, additional exclusions are available for nonprofit organizations, state and local governments, and federally recognized Indian tribes. These include services performed:

- by an individual receiving rehabilitation help in a facility that carries out programs for individuals whose earning capacity is impaired by age, physical or mental deficiency, or injury;
- as part of an unemployment work-relief or work-training program financed partially or completely by a governmental entity; or
- by an inmate of a custodial or penal institution.

Other exclusions are listed in the following sections relating to nonprofit organizations and governmental entities.

State law is also required to give governmental entities, nonprofit organizations, and federally recognized Indian tribes a choice concerning benefit financing. They can pay taxes as employers do or they can reimburse UI benefits paid that are attributable to services performed for them.

Nonprofit Organizations

State coverage is required for services performed for religious, charitable, or educational nonprofit organizations. These organizations are described in section 501(c)(3) of the Federal Internal Revenue Code of 1986, and are exempt from Federal income tax under section 501(a) of the Code.

Although coverage is required only for those organizations employing four or more workers in 20 weeks, a number of states have provisions that cover smaller nonprofit organizations as well. The following table lists the states that have expanded their coverage provisions beyond Federal requirements.

Table 1-8. States covering organizations with one or more employees

Arkansas	California	Connecticut	District of Columbia	Hawaii	Idaho
Iowa	Maryland	Massachusetts	Michigan	Minnesota	Montana
New Hampshire	New Jersey	New Mexico	Oregon	Pennsylvania	Puerto Rico
Rhode Island	Virgin Islands	Washington			

Federal law permits states to exclude from required coverage services performed by a minister in the exercise of ministerial duties or services performed in the employ of:

- a church, convention, or association of churches;
- an organization operated primarily for religious purposes, which is operated, supervised, controlled, or principally supported by a church, convention, or association of churches; or
- an elementary or secondary school operated primarily for religious purposes, regardless of affiliation with a church, convention, or association of churches.

Governmental Entities

Federal law requires states to cover most services for the state and its political subdivisions. When service is performed for an instrumentality owned by more than one state or political subdivision, coverage is determined based on the location of the work.

Since Federal law includes no size-of-firm restrictions for governmental entities as it does for nonprofit organizations, all governmental entities, regardless of size, must be covered. There are, however, certain types of services Federal law permits states to exclude from governmental coverage. These include service performed:

- as an elected official;
- as a member of a legislative body or a member of the judiciary;
- as a member of the state National Guard or Air National Guard;
- as an employee serving on a temporary basis in case of fire, storm, snow, earthquake, flood, or similar declared emergency; or
- in a position which, under the state law, is designated as a major, non-tenured, policymaking or advisory position, or a part-time policymaking position which ordinarily requires eight or fewer hours a week.

Most states have opted to exclude all types of services mentioned previously. For states that do not exclude all of the aforementioned types of services, the following table shows which services are excluded under state law.

Table 1-9. State and local governments - service excluded from coverage

State	Elected Officials	Legislators and Members of Judiciary	Members of State National Guard and Air National Guard	Temporary Emergency Employees	Policymaking and Advisory Positions
AK	X	X	X	X	
AR	X	X	X		X
FL	X	X		X	X
GA	X	X	X		X
MT	X				
NE	X	X	X	X	
NV			X		
WA	X		X		X

Indian Tribes

Amendments to FUTA made in 2000 added federally recognized Indian tribes to the set of entities for whom coverage is required although they are not liable for FUTA taxes. As a result, workers performing services for tribes are now potentially eligible to receive UI benefits. Coverage is required when service is performed for any tribal or native entity recognized and eligible for Federal assistance by the United States Bureau of Indian Affairs. The same permissible exclusions from coverage applicable to other governmental entities also apply to services performed for Indian tribes. If an Indian tribe fails to make payments to states as required, it loses its FUTA tax exemption and may lose coverage.

Unemployment Compensation for Federal Civilian Employees and for Ex-Servicemembers

Two Federal UI programs – one for Federal civilian employees and the other for ex-servicemembers are provided by Federal law (5 U.S.C. 8501 et seq.). Under agreements entered into between the Secretary of Labor and the state UI agencies, the Federal programs of unemployment compensation for Federal civilian employees and for ex-servicemembers are administered by the state agencies as agents of the United States government.

Federal civilian and military wages are assigned to the appropriate state agency in accordance with Federal law. The claims of Federal civilian employees and ex-servicemembers are subject to the same eligibility and disqualification provisions as those filed by any other individual claiming benefits under that state's UI law.

Unemployment Compensation for Federal Employees (UCFE)

An unemployed Federal civilian worker's eligibility is determined under the UI law of the state where:

- the worker's official duty station was located for the most recent Federal civilian employment;
- there was subsequent private covered employment in the state in which the covered employment was performed; or
- the worker resides when filing the claim, if employed outside the United States.

States determine UCFE eligibility under the same terms and conditions as those applied to services covered under state law.

Unemployment Compensation for Ex-Servicemembers (UCX)

States administer the UCX program on behalf of the Federal government under agreements with the U.S. Department of Labor (Department). States must follow the Department's guidance in operating the program, including the use of the Federal Schedule of Remuneration, to determine UCX benefit eligibility. The Department issues an updated schedule yearly.

In general, ex-servicemembers must be honorably discharged and have completed their first full term of service to qualify for UCX. However, ex-servicemembers who did not complete their first full term of service, were separated under honorable conditions, and were separated for certain "acceptable narrative reasons" may qualify for UCX. Some "acceptable narrative reasons" for separation require 365 days of service to be applicable. Narrative reasons are found in Block 28 of the DD Form 214, Certificate of Release or Discharge from Active Duty. A consolidated list of acceptable narrative reasons for separation from the military for UCX claim purposes is attached to UIPL No. 9-10.

Members of the National Guard and Reserves must have 180 days of continuous active service and be separated under honorable conditions to qualify for UCX benefits.

SECTION 2. FINANCING

The Federal Tax and the Federal Unemployment Trust Fund (UTF)

Amount of Tax

Under the provisions of the Federal Unemployment Tax Act (FUTA), a Federal tax is levied on covered employers at a rate of 6.0 percent on wages up to $7,000 per calendar year paid to a worker in covered employment. The law, however, provides a credit against Federal tax liability of up to 5.4 percent to employers who pay state taxes timely under an approved state UI program. This credit is allowed regardless of the amount of the tax paid to the state by the employer. Accordingly, in states meeting the specified requirements, employers pay an effective Federal tax of 0.6 percent or a maximum of $42 per covered worker, per year. The Federal tax is not levied on workers.

Historical Note: Initially, the Federal tax was 1.0 percent (0.1 percent effective tax) of the total wages of a worker. By 1940 it had increased to 3.0 percent (0.3 percent effective tax) on wages up to $3,000. Since then, the rate has increased a number of times, occasionally on a temporary basis. In 1985, the Federal tax reached 6.2 percent (0.8 percent effective tax) on taxable wages. On July 1, 2011, the Federal tax was reduced to 6.0 percent. The taxable wage base increased to $4,200 in 1972, $6,000 in 1978, and $7,000 in 1983.

The credit against the Federal tax may be reduced if the state has an outstanding advance (commonly called a "loan"). When states lack the funds to pay UI benefits, they may obtain advances from the Federal government. To assure that these advances are repaid Federal law provides that, when a state has an outstanding advance balance on January 1 of two consecutive years, the full amount of the advance must be repaid before November 10 of the second year or the credit available to employers will be reduced. The amount of the reduction increases annually until the advance is repaid unless certain conditions are met. Federal law provides for certain limits and exceptions on this credit reduction. Except for cash flow loans (advances obtained from January through September and repaid by September 30 of the same calendar year), interest is charged on all advances made on or after April 1, 1982. The rate is the lesser of 10 percent or the rate of interest paid on the state reserve balance in the Federal UTF for the last quarter of the preceding calendar year. Interest payments may not be made from the state's unemployment fund.

Use of Federal Revenues

The Federal tax funds the following costs:

- Federal and state administrative costs for the UI program;
- Federal share of benefits paid under the Federal-State Extended Unemployment Compensation Act of 1970 (this program "triggers on" during periods of high and rising unemployment);
- the fund from which an individual state may obtain advances (or "loans") whenever the state's trust fund lacks funds to pay UC; and
- labor exchange services under the Wagner-Peyser Act, employment and training services for veterans and disabled veterans, and some labor market information program activities.

The Unemployment Trust Fund (UTF)

The UTF in the U.S. Treasury consists of 59 accounts.

- Each state (defined as the 50 states, District of Columbia, Puerto Rico, and the Virgin Islands) has an account which consists of the contributions and reimbursements collected by the state; interest earned on these amounts is credited to the state's account. Money is withdrawn from state accounts for payment of benefits and refunds of contributions erroneously paid.
- The Employment Security Administration Account (ESAA). Each year, Congress appropriates from this account the funds necessary for administering the federal-state UI program, labor exchange services under the Wagner-Peyser Act, employment and training services for veterans and disabled veterans, and some labor market information program activities.
- The Extended Unemployment Compensation Account (EUCA). Funds from this account reimburse states for the Federal share of extended benefits. This fund is also used at times to cover the cost of temporary extensions.
- The Federal Unemployment Account (FUA). This fund provides states with repayable advances for paying UC.

- The Federal Employees Compensation Account (FECA). This fund finances benefit payments to former Federal and military employees.
- Two accounts related to the Railroad Retirement Board.

All Federal payroll taxes are deposited into the ESAA. Amounts equal to one-tenth of net monthly collections are automatically transferred to the EUCA.

On September 30 of each year, the net balance in the ESAA is determined. If the amount in this account exceeds 40 percent of the prior year's appropriation by Congress, then an "excess" exists. This excess is transferred to the EUCA and/or the FUA as provided by the Social Security Act (SSA) unless the balance of each of these accounts exceeds its statutory ceiling. The net balances of the EUCA and the FUA are also determined on September 30 of each year. The statutory ceiling in the EUCA equals 0.5 percent of total wages in covered employment for the preceding calendar year. For the FUA, the statutory ceiling equals 0.5 percent of total wages in covered employment for the calendar year. Excess balances are transferred between these accounts or to the ESAA as required by the SSA. If all three accounts are at their statutory limits, the excess amounts are distributed to the state accounts in the UTF in amounts equal to each state's covered payrolls bear to the aggregate covered payrolls of all states. These are commonly called "Reed Act" distributions and are governed by section 903, SSA.

Technical Note: The SSA provides that the maximum balance in the extended unemployment compensation account is the *greater* of $750 million or 0.5 percent of total wages in covered employment. Due to the growth in covered employment, the $750 million figure is effectively obsolete. A similar provision relating to the Federal unemployment account ($550 million) is also effectively obsolete.

With certain exceptions authorized by Federal law, Reed Act moneys may only be used for benefit payments. A state may, through an appropriation of its legislature, use Reed Act moneys under certain conditions to supplement Federal administration grants in financing its UI program and system of public employment offices.

Most states' UI laws contain permanent provisions regarding the use of moneys transferred under Section 903 of the SSA. These provisions usually mirror the requirements of Federal law pertaining to "traditional" Reed Act distributions, including a provision that the moneys be used for the payment of UC unless appropriated by the legislative body of the state for the administration of the state's UI law or the state's system of public employment offices.

State Unemployment Fund

As mentioned above each state has its own account in the Unemployment Trust Fund (UTF). Each state's unemployment fund is comprised of this account, and two other accounts that are outside of the UTF. These two accounts are the state's clearing account and benefit payment account. When an employer pays its state tax the funds are initially deposited into the clearing account, then the funds are transferred to the state's account in the UTF where the funds remain until needed to pay benefits. Benefits are paid from the state's benefit payment account using funds that are drawn down from the state's account in the UTF. See Appendix III.

State Taxes and Other State Revenues

To enable employers to obtain credit against the Federal tax, all states finance the costs of UI benefits by imposing payroll taxes, commonly called "contributions," on employers. In addition, three states require employee contributions under certain conditions. Federal law requires that nonprofit organizations, state and local governmental entities, and federally recognized Indian tribes be given the option of making "payments in lieu of contributions" (commonly called "reimbursements").

Employer Taxes

The amount of tax an employer pays depends on the number of its employees, the state's taxable wage base, and the contribution rate assigned the employer.

> *Technical Note:* Federal and state laws provide for a "standard rate" of contributions. At one time, the standard rate for Federal and state law purposes was identical; now this is not always the case. For Federal purposes, a state must have a standard rate of at least 5.4 percent if its employers are to obtain the full credit against the Federal tax. As a result, the Department of Labor accepts a 5.4 percent rate (or in its absence, the highest rate assigned based on experience) as being the standard rate for Federal law purposes. Many state laws use the term standard rate in this sense. Other state laws use the term differently; it may, for example, be the new employer rate.

State laws provide for assignment of a contribution rate of 5.4 percent or higher to enable employers to receive the maximum credit of 5.4 percent against the Federal tax. In all states, an employer pays a contribution rate based on its "experience." In all states, new and newly covered employers pay a "new employer rate" until they meet the requirements for experience rating. In some states, additional contributions are required when fund levels drop to specified points or to restore amounts expended for noncharged or ineffectively charged benefits. Noncharged benefits are those charged to a general account rather than to an individual employer account. Ineffectively charged benefits include those charged to inactive and terminated accounts, and those charged to an employer's experience rating account after the previously charged benefits to the account were sufficient to qualify the employer for the maximum contribution rate. In some states, the state UI agency collects additional taxes imposed on the employer's payroll. Although the revenues from these additional taxes are not deposited in the state's unemployment fund, they sometimes serve UI or employment and training purposes.

In every state, an employer who has overpaid contributions, based on the law in effect at the time of the overpayment, is entitled to a refund. These refunds may be made within time limits ranging from one to six years; in a few states no limit is specified.

Employee Taxes

Only Alaska, New Jersey, and Pennsylvania levy UI taxes on workers. The tax base is that applicable to employers except in Pennsylvania, where employee contributions are calculated on total gross covered wages paid for employment. Worker taxes are deducted by the employer from the worker's pay and forwarded with the employer's taxes to the state agency. In Alaska, the tax rate is equal to 27 percent of the average benefit cost rate, but not less than 0.5 percent or more than 1.0 percent. In New Jersey, the tax rate is 0.3825 percent. Depending on the adequacy of the fund balance in a given year, Pennsylvania employees pay contributions ranging from 0.0 percent to 0.08 percent of total gross covered wages earned in employment.

Interest and Penalty Funds

In every state an employer is subject to certain interest or penalty payments for delay or default in payment of contributions, and may incur penalties for failure to file or delinquency in filing required reports. Many states have set up special administrative funds, made up of such interest and penalties, to meet special needs. The most usual statement of purpose includes covering one or more of these three items:

- expenditures for which Federal funds have been requested but not yet received, subject to repayment to the fund;
- costs of administration found not to be properly chargeable against funds obtained from Federal sources; or

Table 2-1. Taxable wage bases

State	Taxable Wage Base	Wages Include Remuneration Over $7,000 if Subject to FUTA	State	Taxable Wage Base	Wages Include Remuneration Over $7,000 if Subject to FUTA	State	Taxable Wage Base	Wages Include Remuneration Over $7,000 if Subject to FUTA
AL	$8,000	X	AK*	$39,900		AZ	$7,000	X
AR	$10,000	X	CO	$13,100	X	CT	$15,000	X
DE	$16,500	X	DC	$9,000	X	FL	$7,0001	X
GA	$9,500	X	HI*	$46,800	X	ID*	$40,000	
IL*	$12,960	X	IN	$9,500	X	IA*	$30,600	X
KS	$14,000	X	KY	$10,500	X	LA*	$7,700	X
ME	$12,000	X	MD	$8,500	X	MA	$15,000	X
MI	$9,000	X	MN*	$34,000		MS	$14,000	X
MO*	$12,000	X	MT*	$33,000	X	NE	$9,000	X
NV*	$31,200	X	NH	$14,000		NJ*	$34,400	X
NM*	$24,800	X	NY	$11,400	X	NC*	$24,300	X
ND*	$36,400	X	OH	$9,500		OK*	$18,100	
OR*	$40,600	X	PA	$10,000	X	PR	$7,0002	
RI*	$23,600[3] $25,100	X	SC	$14,000	X	SD	$15,000	X
TN*	$7,000	X	TX	$9,000		UT*	$35,300	X

State	Taxable Wage Base	Wages Include Remuneration Over $7,000 if Subject to FUTA	State	Taxable Wage Base	Wages Include Remuneration Over $7,000 if Subject to FUTA	State	Taxable Wage Base	Wages Include Remuneration Over $7,000 if Subject to FUTA
VT*	$15,600	X	VA	$8,000		VI*	$26,500	
WA*	$49,800		WV*	$12,000	X	WI	$14,000	X
WY*	$25,400	X						

NOTE: California is not included in this table since they have neither a taxable wage base above $7,000 nor a provision in their law that automatically adjusts the taxable wage base if FUTA is amended to apply to a higher amount than that specified under state law.

[1] Taxable wage base is $7,000 but increases to $8,000 any year principal is due on Title XII advances.

[2] Increase up to $10,500 at Secretary's discretion.

[3] Two-tier UI taxable wage base. Tier I sets the state's UI taxable wage base at 46.5% of the statewide average annual wage for most employers. Tier II impacts only employers in the highest tax group, and sets the taxable wage base $1,500 higher than the wage base for employers in lower tax groups.

* Flexible taxable wage base, see following table for additional information.

Table 2-2. Computation of flexible taxable wage bases

State	Indexed Taxable Wage Base					Variable Taxable Wage Base Based on Trust Fund Balance (5 States)
	Computed As		Period of Time Used			
	% of State Average Annual Wage (14 States)	Other (5 States)	Preceding CY (7 States)	12 Months Ending June 30 (6 States)	Second Preceding CY (4 States)	
AK	75 rounded to nearest $100			X		N/A
HI	100 rounded to nearest $100			X		N/A
ID	100 rounded to nearest $100				X	N/A
IL	N/A					X
IA		66⅔% of the state AWW, multiplied by 52, or the Federal taxable wage base; rounded to higher $100	X			N/A

Table 2-2. (Continued)

State	**Indexed Taxable Wage Base**					**Variable Taxable Wage Base Based on Trust Fund Balance (5 States)**
	Computed As		Period of Time Used			
	% of State Average Annual Wage (14 States)	Other (5 States)	Preceding CY (7 States)	12 Months Ending June 30 (6 States)	Second Preceding CY (4 States)	
LA	N/A					X
MN	60 rounded to nearest $1,000		X			N/A
MO	N/A					X
MT	80 rounded to nearest $100		X			N/A
NV	66⅔ rounded to nearest $100		X			N/A
NJ		28 x state AWW rounded to higher $100			X	N/A
NM	60 rounded to higher $100			X		N/A
NC	50 rounded to nearest $100		X			N/A
State	Indexed Taxable Wage Base					Variable Taxable Wage Base Based on Trust Fund Balance (5 States)
	Computed As		Period of Time Used			
	% of State Average Annual Wage (14 States)	Other (5 States)	Preceding CY (7 States)	12 Months Ending June 30 (6 States)	Second Preceding CY (4 States)	
ND	70 rounded to nearest $100			X		N/A
OK	40-50 (dependent upon the condition factor in place) rounded to nearest $100				X	N/A
OR	80 rounded to nearest $100				X	N/A

State	Indexed Taxable Wage Base					Variable Taxable Wage Base Based on Trust Fund Balance (5 States)
	Computed As		Period of Time Used			
	% of State Average Annual Wage (14 States)	Other (5 States)	Preceding CY (7 States)	12 Months Ending June 30 (6 States)	Second Preceding CY (4 States)	
RI	46½ rounded to higher even multiple of $200		X			N/A
TN	N/A					X
UT		75% of the prior average fiscal year wage rounded to the higher $100				N/A
VT	N/A	When trust fund has positive balance, TWB increases by same percentage as the increase in the state's AAW	N/A			N/A
VI	60 rounded to higher $100					N/A
WA		115% of previous year's taxable wage base rounded to the lower $100, but not to exceed 80% of AAW for the 2nd preceding CY rounded to the lower $100				N/A
WV	N/A					X
WY	55 rounded to lower $100					N/A

- reimbursement for funds lost or improperly expended for purposes other than, or in amounts in excess of, those found necessary for proper administration of the UI program.

A few states provide for the use of such funds for purchasing land and buildings for agency use, or for the payment of interest on Federal advances. In some states, the fund is capped; when it exceeds a specified sum, the excess is transferred to the unemployment fund or, in one state, to the general fund.

Taxable Wages

Almost all states have adopted a higher tax base than that applicable under FUTA. In these states, an employer pays a tax on wages paid to (or earned by) each worker within a calendar year up to the specified amount. In addition, most of the states provide an automatic adjustment of the wage base if the FUTA is amended to apply to a higher taxable wage base than that specified under state law.

Some states have established flexible tax bases, i.e., bases that are automatically adjusted, generally on an annual basis. Most of these states key the adjustment to some measure of previous wages.

Experience Rating

All state laws use a system of experience rating by which individual employers' contribution rates are varied on the basis of their experience with the risk of unemployment.

Experience rating systems are designed to: encourage employers to stabilize employment; equitably allocate the costs of unemployment; and encourage employers to participate in the system by providing eligibility information.

Federal Requirements for Experience Rating

State experience rating provisions have developed on the basis of the additional credit provisions of section 3303(a), FUTA. Federal law allows employers additional credit for a lowered rate of contribution if the rates are based on not less than three years of "experience with respect to unemployment or other factors bearing a direct relation to unemployment risk." FUTA allows the states to extend experience rating tax reductions to new and newly covered employers after they have had at least one year of such experience. Further, states allow new and newly covered employers a reduced rate (but not less than 1.0 percent) on a reasonable basis.

State Requirements for Experience Rating

In most states, 3 years of experience with unemployment means more than 3 years of coverage and contribution experience. Factors affecting the time required to become a "qualified" employer include:

- coverage provisions of the state law ("at any time" vs. "20 weeks");
- in states using benefits or benefit derivatives in the experience-rating formula, the type of base period and benefit year, and the lag between these two periods, which determine how soon a new employer may be charged for benefits;

> *Historical Note:* The first state UI system in this country (Wisconsin) set up a separate reserve for each employer. Employer contributions were credited to this reserve and benefits paid to former employees were charged to it as long as the account had a credit balance. Most of the states enacted "pooled-fund" laws on the theory that the risk of unemployment should be spread among all employers and that workers should receive benefits regardless of the balance of the contributions paid by the individual employer and the benefits paid to such workers. All states now have pooled unemployment funds.

- type of formula used for rate determination; and
- length of the period between the date as of which rate computations are made and the effective date for rates.

Experience Rating Formulas

Within the broad Federal requirements, the experience rating provisions of state laws vary greatly. The most significant variations grow out of differences in the formulas used for rate determinations. The factor used to measure experience with unemployment is the basic variable that makes it possible to establish the relative incidence of unemployment among the workers of different employers. At present there are four distinct systems, usually identified as reserve-ratio, benefit-ratio, benefit- wage-ratio, and payroll variation formulas. A few states have combinations of the systems.

All systems have certain common characteristics. All formulas are devised to establish the relative experience of individual employers with unemployment or with benefit costs. To this end, all have factors for measuring each employer's experience with unemployment or benefit expenditures, and all compare this experience with a measure of exposure (usually payrolls) to establish the relative experience of large and small employers. However, the four systems differ greatly in the construction of the formulas, in the factors used to measure experience and the methods of measurement, in the number of years over which the experience is recorded, in the presence or absence of other factors, and in the relative weight given the various factors in the final assignment of rates.

Reserve-Ratio Formula

The reserve-ratio [(contributions minus benefits charged) divided by payroll] was the earliest of the experience rating formulas and continues to be the most popular. The system is essentially cost accounting. On each employer's record are entered the amount of payroll, contributions, and the benefits paid to workers. The benefits are subtracted from the contributions, and the resulting balance is divided by the payroll to determine the size of the balance in terms of the potential liability for benefits. The balance carried forward each year under the reserve-ratio plan is ordinarily the difference between the employer's total contributions and the total benefits received by workers since the employer became subject to the UI law.

Table 2-3. Reserve-ratio formula states

State	Years of Benefits and Contributions Used	Years of Payrolls Used[1]	State	Years of Benefits and Contributions Used	Years of Payrolls Used[1]
AZ	All past years	Average of 3 years, ending 6 months before computation date	AR	All past years	Average last 3 or 5 years, whichever is lower[2]
CA	All past years	Average of 3 years, ending 6 months before computation date	CO	All past years	Average 3 years
DC	All since July 1, 1939	Average of 3 years, ending 3 months before computation date	GA	All past years	Average 3 years
HI	All past years	Average 3 years	ID	All since Jan.1, 1940	Average 4 years
IN	All past years	Aggregate 3 years	KS	All past years	Average 3 years
KY	All past years	Aggregate 3 years	LA	All since Oct.1, 1941	Average 3 years
ME	All past years	Average 3 years	MA	All past years	Average 3 years
MO	All past years	Average 3 years	MT	All years since Oct. 1, 1981	Average 3 years
NE	All past years	Average 4 years	NV	All past years	Average 3 years
NH	All past years; last 5 years under specified conditions	Average 3 years	NJ	All past years	Average last 3 or 5 years, whichever is higher
NY	All past years	Average of 5 years, ending 3 months before computation date	NC	All past years	Aggregate 3 years
ND	Last 6 years	Average 3 years	OH	All past years	Average 3 years
PR	Last 3 years	Last 3 years	RI	All since October 1, 1958	Average 3 years
SD	All past years	Aggregate 3 years	TN	All past years	Average 3 years
VI	Last 3 years	Last 3 years	WV	All past years	Average 3 years
WI	All past years	Last year			

[1] Years immediately preceding or ending on computation date, unless noted.

[2] Experience rated employers may elect to be rated on the basis of total taxable wages paid during the preceding CY.

Rates are assigned according to a schedule for specified ranges of reserve ratios; the higher the ratio, the lower the rate. Also, fluctuations in the state fund balance can affect the rate an employer will pay; an increase in the fund may trigger a tax rate schedule in which a lower rate is assigned and, conversely, a decrease in the fund balance may trigger a tax schedule requiring a higher rate.

Benefit-Ratio Formula

Table 2-4. Benefit-ratio formula states

State	**Years of Benefits Used**	**Years of Payrolls Used (Years Immediately Preceding or Ending on Computation Date, Unless Noted)**	**State**	**Years of Benefits Used**	**Years of Payrolls Used (Years Immediately Preceding or Ending on Computation Date, Unless Noted)**
AL	Last 3 fiscal years	Last 3 fiscal years	CT	Last 3 years	Last 3 years, ending 6 months before computation date
FL	Last 3 years	Last 3 years, ending June 30th	IL	Last 3 years	Last 3 years
IA	Last 5 years	Last 5 years	MD	Last 3 years	Last 3 years
MI[1]	Last 3 years	Last 3 years	MN	Last 4 years	Last 4 years
MS	Last 3 years	Last 3 years	NM	Last 3 years	Last 3 years
State	Years of Benefits Used	Years of Payrolls Used (Years Immediately Preceding or Ending on Computation Date, Unless Noted)	State	Years of Benefits Used	Years of Payrolls Used (Years Immediately Preceding or Ending on Computation Date, Unless Noted)
OR	Last 3 years	Last 3 years	PA[1]	All past years	Average 3 years
SC	Last 3 years	Last 3 years	TX	Last 3 years	Last 3 years
UT	Last 4 years; if 4 years not available, will use up to 1 year minimum	Last 4 years; if 4 years not available, will use up to 1 year minimum	VT	Last 3 years	Last 3 years
VA	Last 4 years	Last 4 years	WA	Last 4 years	Last 4 years
WY	Last 3 years	Last 3 years			

[1] Benefit-ratio predominates. State also has a reserve ratio component.

The benefit-ratio formula (benefits charged divided by employer's payroll) also uses benefits as the measure of experience, but eliminates contributions from the formula and relates benefits directly to payrolls. The theory is that, if each employer pays a rate that approximates his benefit ratio, the program will be adequately financed. Rates are further varied by the inclusion in the formulas of schedules (effective at specified levels of the state fund in terms of dollar amounts), proportion of payrolls, or fund adequacy percentage.

Unlike the reserve-ratio, the benefit-ratio system is geared to short-term experience. The following table shows the number of years used for each state in determining benefit ratios.

Benefit-Wage-Ratio Formula

The benefit-wage-ratio formula is radically different. This formula is designed to assess variable rates, which will raise the equivalent of the total amount paid out as benefits. The percentage relationship between total benefit payments and total benefit wages in the state during three years is determined. This ratio, known as the state experience factor, means that, on average, the workers who drew benefits received a certain amount of benefits for each dollar of benefit wages paid and the same amount of taxes per dollar of benefit wages is needed to replenish the fund. The total amount to be raised is distributed among employers in accordance with their benefit-wage-ratios; the higher the ratio, the higher the rate.

Individual employers' rates are determined by multiplying the employer's experience factor by the state experience factor. The multiplication is facilitated by a table, which assigns rates that are the same as, or slightly more than, the product of the employer's benefit-wage-ratio and the state factor. The range of the rates is, however, limited by a minimum and maximum. The minimum and the rounding upward of some rates tend to increase the amount that would be raised if the plan were effected without the table; the maximum, however, decreases the income from employers who would otherwise have paid higher rates.

Table 2-5. Benefit-wage-ratio formula states

State	Years of Benefits Used	Years of Payrolls Used (Years Immediately Preceding or Ending on Computation Date)
DE	Last 3 years	Last 3 years
OK	Last 3 years	Last 3 years

Payroll Variation Plan

The payroll variation plan is independent of benefit payments to individual workers. Neither benefits nor any benefit derivatives are used to measure unemployment under this formula.

Experience with unemployment is measured by the decline in an employer's payroll from quarter to quarter. The declines are expressed as a percentage of payrolls in the preceding period, so that experience of employers with large and small payrolls may be compared. If the payroll shows no decrease or only a small percentage decrease over a given period, the employer will be eligible for the largest proportional reductions.

Alaska measures the stability of payrolls from quarter to quarter over a 3-year period; the changes reflect changes in general business activity and also seasonal or irregular declines in employment. Also, Alaska arrays employers according to their average quarterly decline quotients and groups them on the basis of cumulative payrolls in 20 rate classes plus a 21st class (the penalty rate).

Charging Methods

Since various methods are used to identify the employer(s) who will be charged with benefits when a worker becomes unemployed and receives benefits, the laws address this issue in some detail. In the reserve- ratio and benefit-ratio states, it is the worker's benefit payments that are charged; in the benefit-wage-ratio states, the benefit wages. There is no charging of benefits in the payroll-decline systems.

In most states, the maximum amount of benefits to be charged is the maximum amount for which any worker is eligible under the state law.

In states with benefit-wage-ratio formulas, the maximum amount of benefit wages charged is usually the amount of wages required for maximum annual benefits.

Charging Most Recent or Principal Employer

Some states charge the most recent employer on the theory that this employer has primary responsibility for the unemployment. All of the states that charge benefits to the last employer relieve the employer of these charges if only casual or short-time employment is involved. Charging the most recent base-period employer assumes that liability for benefits is inherent in wage payments.

Table 2-6. States that charge most recent or principal employer

State	Employer Specified	State	Employer Specified
GA	Most recent	ID	Employer who paid largest amount of BPW; charges omitted if worker continues to perform services for the employer
IL	Most recent; charges omitted for employers who employed individual less than 30 days, except if the earnings from the employer allow the individual to requalify following a disqualification	KY	Most recent; charges omitted for employers who employed individual less than 10 weeks
ME	Most recent; charges omitted for employers who employed individual less than 6 weeks	MI	Most recent employer charged for first 2 weeks of benefits; Thereafter, BP employers charged proportionately (with respect to wages)
NV	Employer who paid 75% of an individual's BPW, except if a reimbursing employer is liable	NH	Most recent; charges omitted for employers who paid individual less than 12 consecutive weeks; benefits paid following disqualifications for voluntary leaving, discharge for misconduct, and refusal of suitable work will be charged to the employer's account who furnished the employment

Table 2-6. (Continued)

State	Employer Specified	State	Employer Specified
NY	Most recent employer charged 7 x individual's WBA; thereafter, BP employers charged proportionately (with respect to wages)	PR	Most recent employer charged 50% of benefits paid and the remaining 50% charged proportionately to all BP employers
RI	Most recent BP employer	SC	Most recent; charges omitted for employers who employed individual less than 8 x WBA
VA	Most recent; charges omitted for employers who employed individual less than 30 days or 240 hours		

Charging Base-Period Employers in Inverse Chronological Order

Some states limit charges to base-period employers but charge them in inverse order of employment. This method combines the theory that liability for benefits results from wage payments with the theory of employer responsibility for unemployment; responsibility for the unemployment is assumed to lessen with time, and the more remote the employment from the period of compensable unemployment, the less the probability of an employer being charged. A maximum limit is placed on the amount that may be charged any one employer; when the limit is reached, the next previous employer is charged. The limit is usually fixed as a fraction of the wages paid by the employer or as a specified amount in the base period or in the quarter, or as a combination of the two. Usually the limit is the same as the limit on the duration of benefits in terms of quarterly or base-period wages.

If a worker's unemployment is short, or if the last employer in the base period employed the individual for a considerable part of the base period, charging employers in inverse chronological order gives the same results as charging the last employer in the base period. If a worker's unemployment is long, such charging gives much the same results as charging all base-period employers proportionately.

All the states that provide for charging in inverse order of employment have determined, by regulation, the order of charging in case of simultaneous employment by two or more employers.

Table 2-7. States that charge base-period employers in inverse chronological order

State	Inverse Order of Employment up to Amount Specified	Stat e	Inverse Order of Employment up to Amount Specified
CO	⅓ wages up to ⅓ of 26 x current WBA	IA	In proportion to BPW
MA	36% of BPW	NE	⅓ BPW
SD	In proportion to BPW; charges omitted for employers who paid worker less than $100		

Charging in Proportion to Base-Period Wages

On the theory that unemployment results from general conditions of the labor market more than from a given employer's separations, the largest number of states charge benefits against all base-period employers in proportion to the wages earned by the worker with each employer.

Table 2-8. States that charge in proportion to base-period wages

State	Special Provisions	State	Special Provisions
AL	X	AZ	X
AR	X	CA	X
CT	Charges omitted for employers who paid individual less than $500	DE	X
DC	X	FL	Charges omitted for employers who paid worker less than $100
HI	X	IN	Law also provides for charges to BP employers in inverse order
KS	X	LA	X
MD	Principal employer will be charged for shut-downs for convenience; employers participating in shared work will bear all charges	MN	X
MS	X	MO	Charges omitted for employers who employed individual less than 28 days or paid individual less than $400
MT	X	NJ	X

Table 2-8. (Continued)

State	Special Provisions	State	Special Provisions
NM	X	NC	Amount charged to a BP employer's account is the benefit allocated to such employer multiplied by 120%
ND	X	OH	X
OK	If employer recalls a laid-off or separated employee and the employee continues to be employed, or voluntarily terminates employment or is discharged for misconduct within the BY, benefit charges may be reduced by the ratio of remaining weeks of eligibility to the total weeks of entitlement	OR	X
PA	X	TN	X
TX	X	UT	X
VT	X	VI	X
WA	Charged to separating employer for certain quits with good cause	WV	X
WI	Benefits are not charged to an employer constituting less than 5% of an individual's BPW	WY	X

Their charging methods assume that liability for benefits is inherent in the wage payments creating the worker's eligibility. (Note that states combining this method with charging the most recent employer are listed on the "Charging Most Recent or Principal Employer" table.)

Noncharging of Benefits

Many states do not charge individual employers for benefit costs under certain limited circumstances.

These "noncharging" provisions are found in practically all state experience rating laws. In the states that charge benefits, certain benefits are omitted from charging as indicated in the following information; in the states that charge benefit wages, certain wages are not counted as benefit-wages.

Table 2-9. Benefits excluded from charging

State	Federal-State Extended Benefits	Benefit Award Finally Reversed	Reimbursements on Combined Wage Claims[1]	Voluntary Leaving	Discharge for Misconduct	Refusal of Suitable Work	Continues to Work for Employer on Same Part-Time Basis
AL		X		X, including quit to relocate with military-connected spouse	X		X
AZ		X	X	Limited to compelling personal reasons not attributable to employer and not warranting disqualification, and to leaving work due to mutually-agreed-upon mandatory retirement age[2]	X		X
AR	X			X	X		X
CA		X		Limited to quit to take other job, quit to accompany spouse, and irresistible impulse to use intoxicants[2]	X		X
CO		X	X	X[2, 3]	X		
CT				X, including quit to accompany spouse due to change in location of spouse's employment	X	X	

Table 2-9. (Continued)

State	Federal-State Extended Benefits	Benefit Award Finally Reversed	Reimbursements on Combined Wage Claims[1]	Voluntary Leaving	Discharge for Misconduct	Refusal of Suitable Work	Continues to Work for Employer on Same Part-Time Basis
DE		X	X	X, including quit to accompany spouse or to care for ill or disabled family member	X		X
DC				X	X		X
FL		X		X	X	Limited to refusal of reemployment	
GA		X	X	X, includes quit to follow military spouse or to accept a better job	X	Limited to refusal of reemployment in suitable work	
HI	X		X	X	X		X
ID	X	X	X	X	X		
IL		X	X	X, including quit to accept another job, or to accompany a spouse who has been reassigned by the military[2]	X	X	X
IN			X	X	X		X
IA	X	X	X	X	X	X	
KS	X			X	X		X
KY			X	X	X		

State	Federal-State Extended Benefits	Benefit Award Finally Reversed	Reimbursements on Combined Wage Claims[1]	Voluntary Leaving	Discharge for Misconduct	Refusal of Suitable Work	Continues to Work for Employer on Same Part-Time Basis
LA		X		X, including quit from part-time or interim job to protect full-time or regular job, or to accompany a spouse who has been reassigned by the military	X	X	X
ME	X	X	X	X	X	Limited to refusal of reemployment in suitable work	X
MD		X		X, including quit without good cause attributable to work, to accept a better job, or to enter approved training[2]	Only for gross and aggravated misconduct		X
MA		X		X[2]	For individual convicted of felony or misdemeanor		
MI				X, including quit to accompany military spouse to new duty location	X		X
MN			X	X	X		
MS				X, including quit to accompany military spouse to new duty location	X	X	X

Table 2-9. (Continued)

State	Federal-State Extended Benefits	Benefit Award Finally Reversed	Reimbursements on Combined Wage Claims[1]	Voluntary Leaving	Discharge for Misconduct	Refusal of Suitable Work	Continues to Work for Employer on Same Part-Time Basis
MO		X	X	X[4]	X	X	
MT	X	X		X[2]	X2		X
NE		X	X	X, including quit to accompany spouse to spouse's new employment in a different city or new military duty station, or to accept insured work in construction industry	X		X
NV	X		X	X, including quit to accompany military spouse or to take other employment	X		
NH			X	X, including quit resulting from physician-certified inability to perform job duties due to pregnancy, illness, or non work-related injury, including quit to accompany spouse, or quit to accept better employment			X

State	Federal-State Extended Benefits	Benefit Award Finally Reversed	Reimbursements on Combined Wage Claims[1]	Voluntary Leaving	Discharge for Misconduct	Refusal of Suitable Work	Continues to Work for Employer on Same Part-Time Basis
NJ		X		X, including BY employer if worker left that job by a disqualifying separation[2]	X, including BY employer if worker left that job by a disqualifying separation[2]	X, including BY employer if separation due to failure to accept suitable work without good cause	
NM	X	X		X, including quit to accompany military spouse or to take other employment[2]	X[2]		
NY	X			X	X		X
NC		X		X, including quit to accompany military spouse or to take other employment	X		X
ND		X		X, including quit directly attributable to sexual assault[2]	X		
OH		X	X	X, including quit from interim or part- time job to protect full-time job	X	X, only if due to participation in approved training	X
OK		X		X, including quit due to compelling family circumstances[2]	X		X
OR	X	X	X	X	X		X
PA		X		X	X		X

Table 2-9. (Continued)

State	Federal-State Extended Benefits	Benefit Award Finally Reversed	Reimbursements on Combined Wage Claims[1]	Voluntary Leaving	Discharge for Misconduct	Refusal of Suitable Work	Continues to Work for Employer on Same Part-Time Basis
PR	X						
RI		X		X	X		
SC	X	X		X[2]	X[2]	X, limited to refusal of reemployment in suitable work	
SD	X	X		X, including quit to accompany military spouse	X		
TN		X		X, including quit to accompany military spouse	X		X
TX		X		X[2]	X[2]		
UT	X	X	X	X, including quit to accompany military spouse	X		X
VT			X	X	X	X	X
VA			X	X[5]	Separation due to violation of law leading to jail time	Refusal of rehire due to participation in approved training	
VI							
WA	X	X		X[2]	X		X
WV		X		X, including quit to relocate with military spouse	X		

State	Federal-State Extended Benefits	Benefit Award Finally Reversed	Reimbursements on Combined Wage Claims[1]	Voluntary Leaving	Discharge for Misconduct	Refusal of Suitable Work	Continues to Work for Employer on Same Part-Time Basis
WI		X		X, including quit due to illness, disability, or to accompany spouse[2, 6]			
WY	X	X		X, including quit to follow military spouse[2]	X		X

[1] Most states limit noncharging to specific situations such as benefits paid in excess of amount payable under state law or if individual would have been ineligible using only the in-state wages.

[2] Includes separations due to domestic violence.

[3] If quit one construction job to take a better construction job when conditions of law are met. Also, does not charge employer if individual separates due to compelling family reasons, or to relocate to a new residence from which it is impractical to commute due to death of military spouse who was an active duty member of the US. Armed Forces, stationed in Colorado, and who was killed in combat.

[4] For individual leaving to accept more remunerative job or who quit unsuitable work within 28 days.

[5] For quit to accept other employment, to enter approved training, because of a non job-related injury or medical condition, or required in work release programs as a condition of release/parole. Also for quit to accompany active duty military spouse to new assignment if relocation is due to permanent change of station order, new location is not readily accessible from individual's place of employment, and spouse's new duty assignment is located in a state that does not consider a person accompanying a military spouse to be leaving work voluntarily without good cause.

[6] Benefits are charged when a claimant voluntarily terminates employment because of the illness or disability of a family member when the period of time needing to be off is longer than the employer is willing to grant leave.

The postponement of charges until a certain amount of benefits has been paid results in noncharging of benefits for workers whose unemployment is very short in duration. In many states, charges are omitted when benefits are paid on the basis of an early determination in an appealed case and the determination is eventually reversed. In many states, charges are omitted in the case of benefits paid under a combined wage claim. In some states with dependents' allowances, those payments are not charged to employers' accounts.

Additionally some states noncharge benefits paid following a period of disqualification for a voluntary quit, misconduct, or a refusal of suitable work. The intent is to relieve the employer of charges for unemployment caused by circumstances beyond the employer's control. The provisions differ with variations in the employer to be charged and with the disqualification provisions, particularly with respect to the cancellation and reduction of benefit rights. In this summary, no attempt is made to distinguish between noncharging following a period of disqualification and noncharging where no disqualification is imposed. Most states provide for noncharging where voluntary leaving or discharge for misconduct is involved and, in some states, refusal of suitable work. A few of these states limit noncharging to cases where a worker refuses reemployment in suitable work.

The following table provides information on some of the reasons benefits are excluded from charging. Alaska, a payroll variation state, is excluded because benefit charges are not a factor in determining experience rates.

A few state have special provisions or regulations for identifying the employer to be charged in the case of benefits paid to seasonal workers. In general, seasonal employers are charged only with benefits paid for unemployment occurring during the season, and nonseasonal employers with benefits paid for unemployment at other times. In one state the individual must also have seasonal base-period wages for the seasonal employer to be charged benefits during the season.

Several states noncharge benefits for reasons other than those listed in Table 2-9, or in addition to those reasons listed in Table 2-9. For example, some states noncharge benefits paid to individuals who:

- were unable to work due to a disaster;
- quit for personal reasons such as lack of adequate child care, to relocate with a military spouse, or to care for a sick or disabled family member;
- were in training with the approval of the UI agency;
- were laid off when a permanent employee who was called to military duty returned and claimed his/her job; or
- were laid off when the employer was called to active military duty.

Federal law prohibits states from relieving an employer of benefit charges if the employer's (or its agent's) failure to respond timely and adequately has resulted in an inappropriate payment and if the employer (or agent) has established a pattern of failing to respond for information. However, states are permitted to charge an employer for fault after the first instance of failure to respond timely or adequately to requests for information related to a UC claim.

Taxes Payable to Unemployment Fund

The requirements for rate assignments vary greatly among the states. Each state law incorporates at least the Federal requirements for assigning reduced rates. Many states require that all necessary contribution reports must have been filed and all contributions due must have been paid.

Taxes not paid into the state's unemployment fund are listed later in this chapter under the heading "Additional Taxes."

Rates and Rate Schedules

Schedules are used to convert the results of the formula used (that is, the reserve-ratio, benefit-ratio, benefit-wage-ratio, or payroll variation) into a tax rate. In a few benefit-ratio states, the benefit ratio is itself the employer's rate. Several states use an "array" system where employers are annually ranked against each other, rather than through a schedule using predetermined experience levels. Rate classes in array systems are determined by segregating wages paid by all employers. For example, the highest rate class will consist of employers with the highest costs. A new rate class will be triggered when employers in the highest class represent a certain percentage of the wages paid under state law.

Minimum and Maximum Rates

Tax rates depend on the state's fund balance and other factors in state law. In most states, low balances trigger schedules with higher rates and higher balances trigger schedules with lower rates.

> *Note:* The following table indicates the range of base contribution rates provided for in state law. It does not indicate what rates are in effect for the current year. For that information, the appropriate state UI agency should be contacted.

In some states, state law establishes an overall contribution rate that is the sum of various components (e.g., basic contribution rate, a solvency rate, social cost add-on, and adjustments for other purposes). Components that are treated by state law as distinctly separate are listed in Table 2-11.

Limitation on Rate Increases

Wisconsin prevents sudden increases of rates for individual employers by limiting an employer's rate increase in any year to no more than 1.0 percent higher than the previous rate for positive rated employers, or 2.0 percent higher than the previous rate for negative rated employers. In Oklahoma, for employers with rates of 3.4 percent or more, the limitation on the rate increase is percent in any year. For employers with rates below 3.4 percent, their rate may not be increased to more than 5.4 percent in any year.

Table 2-10. Fund requirements and range of rates

State	Most Favorable Schedule			Least Favorable Schedule		
	When Fund Balance	Range of Rates		When Fund Balance	Range of Rates	
		Minimum	Maximum		Minimum	Maximum
AL	≥125% of desired level	0.14%	5.4%	<70% of desired level	0.65%	6.8%
AK	Law authorizes agency to set rates	≥1.0%	≤6.5%	Law authorizes agency to set rates	≥1.0%	≤6.5%
AZ	≥12% of taxable payrolls	0.02%	5.4%	<3.0% of taxable payrolls	0.02%	≥5.4%
AR[1]	Based on reserve ratio	0.1%	6.0%	Based on reserve ratio	0.1%	6.0%
CA	>1.8% of taxable payrolls	0.1%	5.4%	<0.6% of taxable payrolls	1.5%	6.2%
CO	Fund reserve ≥1.4	0.51%	6.28%	Fund reserve <0.0	0.75%	10.39%
CT	Based on benefit ratio	0.5%	5.4%	Based on benefit ratio	0.5%	5.4%
DE	Dependent upon the state experience factor	0.1%	8.0%	Dependent upon the state experience factor	0.1%	8.0%
DC	>3.0% of payrolls	0.1%	5.4%	≤0.8% of payrolls	1.9%	7.4%
FL	Current adjusted benefit ratio	0.1%	5.4%	Current adjusted benefit ratio	0.1%	5.4%
GA	State-wide reserve ratio of ≥2.7%	0.0125%	5.4%	State-wide reserve ratio of <1.25%	0.0375%	8.1%
HI	Ratio of the current reserve fund to the adequate reserve fund is >1.69	0.0%	5.4%	Ratio of the current reserve fund to the adequate reserve fund is <0.2	2.4%	6.6%
ID	State calculated average high cost multiple	0.18%	5.4%	State calculated average high cost multiple	0.96%	6.8%
IL[2]	Dependent upon the adjusted state experience factor	0.0%	The greater of 6.4% or the product of 6.4% and the adjusted state experience factor	Dependent upon the adjusted state experience factor	0.0%	The greater of 6.4% or the product of 6.4% and the adjusted state experience factor

Table 2-10. (Continued)

State	Most Favorable Schedule			Least Favorable Schedule		
	When Fund Balance	Range of Rates		When Fund Balance	Range of Rates	
		Minimum	Maximum		Minimum	Maximum
IN	≥1.6% of payrolls	0.0%	5.4%	<0.2% of payrolls	0.75%	10.2%
IA	Current reserve fund ratio/highest benefit cost ratio ≥1.3	0.0%	7.0%	Current reserve fund ratio/ highest benefit cost ratio <0.3	0.0%	9.0%
KS	Based on reserve ratio	0.2%	7.6%	Based on reserve ratio	0.2%	7.6%
KY	≥1.18% of payrolls	0.0%	9.0%	<$150 million	1.0%	10.0%
LA	Based on reserve ratio	0.09%	6.0%	Based on reserve ratio	0.09%	6.0%
ME	Reserve multiple of >1.58	Varies	≥5.4%	Reserve multiple of <0.25	Varies	≥5.4%
MD	>5.0% of taxable payrolls	0.3%	7.5%	<3.0% of taxable payrolls	2.2%	13.5%
MA	≥1.65% of taxable payrolls	0.56%	8.62%	<0.3% of taxable payrolls	1.21%	18.55%
MI	Based on benefit ratio	0.0%	6.3%	Based on benefit ratio	0.0%	6.3%
MN	≥0.75% of payrolls	0.1%	9.0%	<0.55% of payrolls	0.4%	9.3%
MS	Depends on statutory variables that comprise the general experience rate	0.0%	5.4%	Depends on statutory variables that comprise the general experience rate	0.0%	5.4%
MO[3]	>$750 million	0.0%	5.4%	<$350 million	0.0%	7.8%
MT	≥2.6% of payrolls	0.0%	6.12%	<0.25% of payrolls	1.62%	6.12%
NE	No requirements for fund balance in law	0.0%	≥5.4%	No requirements for fund balance in law	Not specified	≥5.4%
NV	Rates set by agency in accordance with authorization in law	0.25%	5.4%	Rates set by agency in accordance with authorization in law	0.25%	5.4%
NH	≥$300 million	0.1%	7.0%	<$250 million	0.1%	8.5%
NJ	≥3.5% of taxable wages	0.3%	5.4%	≤0.99% of taxable wages	1.3%	7.7%
NM	Based on benefit ratio	0.33%	5.4%	Based on benefit ratio	0.33%	5.4%

State	Most Favorable Schedule			Least Favorable Schedule		
	When Fund Balance	Range of Rates		When Fund Balance	Range of Rates	
		Minimum	Maximum		Minimum	Maximum
NY	≥5.0% of payrolls	0.0%	5.9%	<0% of payrolls	1.5%	8.9%
NC	>1.25% of payrolls	0.06%	5.76%	<1.0% of payrolls	0.06%	5.76%
ND	Rates set by agency in accordance with authorization in law	0.01%	≥5.4%	Rates set by agency in accordance with authorization in law	0.01%	≥5.4%
OH	≥30% above minimum safe level	0.0%	6.3%	≤60% below minimum safe level	≥0.3%	≥6.7%
OK	≥3.5 x 5-year average of benefits	0.1%	5.5%	<2 x 5-year average of benefits	0.3%	9.2%
OR	≥200% of cumulative taxable payroll limit	0.5%	5.4%	<100% of cumulative taxable payroll limit	2.2%	5.4%
PA	Law authorizes agency to set rates	0.0%	8.95%	Law authorizes agency to set rates	0.0%	8.95%
PR	>$589 million	1.0%	5.4%	<$370 million	2.5%	5.4%
RI	≥6.4% of payrolls	0.21%	7.4%	<1.0% of payrolls	1.2%	10.0%
SC	Based on benefit ratio	0.0%	>5.4%	Based on benefit ratio	0.0%	>5.4%
SD	Average High Cost Multiplier ≥1.6%	0.0%	9.35%	Average High Cost Multiplier <1.6%	0.0%	9.45%
TN	≥$850 million	0.01%	10.0%	<$450 million	0.5%	10.0%
TX	Based on benefit ratio	0.0%	6.0%	Based on benefit ratio	0.0%	6.0%
UT	Based on reserve factor calculation	0.0%	7.0%	Based on reserve factor calculation	0.0%	7.0%
VT	≥2.5 x highest benefit cost rate	0.4%	5.4%	<1.0 x highest benefit cost rate	1.3%	8.4%
VA	Fund balance factor is ≥120%	0.0%	5.4%	Fund balance factor is ≤50%	0.1%	6.2%
VI	Based on reserve ratio	0.0%	6.0%	Based on reserve ratio	0.0%	6.0%
WA	Based on benefit ratio	0.0%	5.4%	Based on benefit ratio	0.0%	5.4%

Table 2-10. (Continued)

State	Most Favorable Schedule			Least Favorable Schedule		
	When Fund Balance	Range of Rates		When Fund Balance	Range of Rates	
		Minimum	Maximum		Minimum	Maximum
WV	≥3.0% of gross covered wages	0.0%	7.5%	<1.75% of gross covered wages	1.5%	7.5%
WI	≥$1.2 billion	0.0%	10.7%	<$300 million	0.07%	10.7%
WY	Based on benefit ratio	0.0%	8.5%	Based on benefit ratio	0.0%	8.5%

GENERAL NOTE: Table 2-10 incorporates the various methods of determining the minimum and maximum rates under the least and most favorable circumstances. The rates above reflect only those tax rate ranges for contributions deposited into the Unemployment Trust Fund. In some states, under certain circumstances, the rates shown above are reduced.

[1] The rates shown above do not include the additional contribution assessments (applicable to certain maximum rated deficit employers) of up to an additional 8.0%.

[2] The maximum rate is capped at 5.4% for "small" employers.

[3] The maximum rates do not include the surcharge (applicable to certain maximum rated deficit employers) of up to 1.5%.

Adjustments

The previous table does not include taxes that are treated by state law as distinctly separate from the employer's contribution rate.

These adjustments may be in the form of a direct modification of the employer's tax rate (for example, by adding 0.1 percent to, or subtracting 0.1 percent from, the employer's tax rate) or by taking these costs into account when calculating the employer's experience rate (for example, charging a prorated portion of socialized costs to the employer's account in a reserve-ratio state). Reimbursing employers are exempted from solvency adjustments since they already reimburse the state's unemployment fund for 100 percent of their benefit costs. The following table provides an overview of states that treat the adjustments separately. Note that, depending upon the solvency of a state's fund and other factors in state law, not all of the following adjustments are levied in a given year.

Table 2-11. Surcharges, surtaxes, and adjustments

State	Name	Amount	Purpose
AL	Shared Cost Assessment[1]	Varies	Social Cost
AK	Trust Fund Solvency Adjustment[1]	-0.4% - 1.1%	Solvency
AR	Extended Benefit Tax	When in effect, 0.1%	Extended Benefits
	Stabilization Tax[2]	-0.1% - 0.8%	Solvency
CO	Solvency Surcharge	When in effect, the rate varies	Solvency
CT	Fund Balance Tax Rate	Up to 1.4%	Solvency
DE	Supplemental Assessment Rate	0.2%	Solvency
IL	Fund Building Factor	0.4% - 0.55%	Solvency
	Solvency Surcharge	0.3%	Solvency
IN	Unemployment Insurance Surcharge[3]	Varies	Solvency
KS	Solvency Adjustment	-0.5% - 1.6%	Solvency
LA	Social Charge Tax	Varies[4]	Social Cost
	Solvency Adjustment[5]	-0.1% - 0.3% of contributions due	Solvency
MA	Secondary Adjustment	When in effect, from 0.3% - 0.9%	Solvency
MI	Account Building Component	0.0% - 3.0%	Solvency
	Nonchargeable Benefit Component	0.0% - 1.0%	Social Cost
MN	Additional Assessment Rate	0.0% - 14.0%	Solvency
	Falling Trust Fund Adjustment	When in effect, 0.1%	Solvency

Table 2-11. (Continued)

State	Name	Amount	Purpose
NH	Emergency Surcharge	When in effect, 0.5%	Solvency
	Emergency Power Surcharge	When in effect, 0.5%	Solvency
NJ	Solvency Adjustment	When in effect, 25% reduction or 50% reduction[6]	Solvency
NY	Subsidiary Contribution	When in effect, 0.0% - 0.925%	Solvency
OH	Mutualized Contributions	When in effect, up to 0.5%	Social Cost
OK	Temporary Surcharge	When in effect, up to 33⅓%	Solvency
PA	Solvency Measures[1]	Surcharge adjustment of 5.4% and additional contributions of 0.5%	Solvency
SD	Adjustment Percentage	When in effect, 0.1% - 1.5%[7]	Solvency
TX	Replenishment Tax Rate	Varies	Social Cost
	Deficit Tax Rate	When in effect, up to 2.0%	Solvency
	Surplus Credit Rate	When in effect, the rate varies	Solvency
UT	Social Tax Rate	Varies	Social Cost
VA	Fund Balance Factor	Varies	Solvency
	Pool Cost Charge Rate	Varies	Social Cost
WA	Social Cost Factor	Varies	Social Cost
	Solvency Surcharge	When in effect, up to 0.2%	Solvency
WI	Solvency Rate	0.0% - 1.3%8	Solvency
WY	Adjustment Factor	Up to 1.5%	Social Cost & Solvency

GENERAL NOTE: Social cost recoupments are generally payable each year. Solvency adjustments are triggered by fund balances.

[1] Excludes new employers.

[2] Portion of stabilization tax proceeds are deposited in the Training Trust Fund and Unemployment Insurance Administrative Fund.

[3] If funds from this surcharge are used to pay interest on advances those payments may not be credited to an employer's experience rating account.

[4] The social charge rate is calculated to the nearest 0.01% and may not raise an employer's total rate above 6.2%.

[5] If the balance in the trust fund exceeds $1.4 billion an additional 10% reduction applies.

[6] Not applicable to maximum rated employers.

[7] Contribution rate may not exceed 12% with the adjustment percentage.

[8] Seasonal employers pay an additional 2.0% solvency rate (total rate capped at 10.7% + solvency rate applicable that year).

Computation, Fund Trigger, Effective Dates, and New Employers

The computation date is the end of the period used to determine the employer's experience. For example, a benefit- ratio state may compute an employer's experience rate using the benefits paid in the three years immediately preceding the computation date. If a new or newly-covered employer has accrued sufficient experience as required under state law as of the computation date, the employer will henceforth be assigned a rate based on experience. Under FUTA, experience rates must be effective within 27 weeks of the computation date.

Table 2-12. Computation, fund trigger, effective dates, and new employers

State	Computation Date	Fund Trigger Date	Effective Date for New Rates	Years Needed to Qualify for Experience Rating[1]	Reduced Rate for New Employers[2]
AL	June 30	Sept. 30	Jan. 1	1	2.7%
AK	June 30	Sept. 30	Jan. 1	1[1]	Average industry rate
AZ	July 1	July 31	Jan. 1	1	2.0%
AR	June 30	June 30	Jan. 1	3	2.9%[3]
CA	June 30	Sept. 30	Jan. 1	1	3.4%
CO	July 1	July 1	Jan. 1	1	Greater of 1.7%, actual rate, or, for construction industry, average industry rate
CT	June 30	June 30	Jan. 1	1[1]	Higher of 1% or state's 5-year benefit cost rate
DE	Oct. 1	Sept. 30	Jan. 1	2	Average industry rate
DC	June 30	Sept. 30	Jan. 1	3	2.7% or average rate for all employers if higher
FL	June 30	June 30	Jan. 1	2½	2.7%
GA	June 30	June 30	Jan. 1	3	2.64%
HI	Dec. 31	Nov. 30	Jan. 1	1	1.7% - 5.2% based upon the rate schedule in effect
ID	June 30	Sept. 30	Jan. 1	1	1.0% - 3.36% based upon fund balance calculation
IL	June 30	June 30	Jan. 1	3[1]	2.9% multiplied by the state experience factor
IN	June 30	Sept. 30	Jan. 1	3[1]	2.5%; 1.6% for government employers
IA	July 1	July 1	Jan. 1	3	1.0% - 3.0% based upon the rate schedule in effect; 7.0% - 9.0% for construction

Table 2-12. (Continued)

State	Computation Date	Fund Trigger Date	Effective Date for New Rates	Years Needed to Qualify for Experience Rating[1]	Reduced Rate for New Employers[2]
KS	June 30	June 30	Jan. 1	2	2.7%; construction employers receive 6.0%
KY	July 31	Sept. 30	Jan. 1	3	2.7%; foreign and domestic construction firms receive maximum rate
LA	June 30	Sept. 1	Jan. 1	3	Up to 6.2% based on average industry rate
ME	June 30	Sept. 30	Jan. 1	2	Greater of predetermined yield or 1%
MD	July 1	Sept. 30	Jan. 1	2	2.6%; foreign contractors assigned average industry rate
MA	Sept. 30	Sept. 30	Jan. 1	1	2.42%; construction employers receive 6.91%
MI	June 30	June 30	Jan. 1	2[4]	2.7%; construction employers receive average industry rate
MN	June 30	March 31	Jan. 1	1	Higher of 1.0% or the state's 4-year benefit cost rate; higher of regular new employer rate or 4-year benefit cost rate for high experience rated employers up to 8.9%
MS	June 30	Nov. 1	Jan. 1	1	1.0% - 1.2% depending on years of liability
MO	June 30	Oct. 15	Jan. 1	1	Greater of 2.376% or rate assigned to employer's industrial classification; 1.0% for nonprofit
MT	Sept. 30	Oct. 31	Jan. 1	3	Ranges from 1.7% - 4.10% based on average industry rate
NE	Dec. 31	May 315	Jan. 1	1[1]	Lessor of category 12 rate or 2.5%, but not less than 1.25%; construction employers 5.4%
NV	June 30	June 30	Jan. 1	2½	2.95%

State	Computation Date	Fund Trigger Date	Effective Date for New Rates	Years Needed to Qualify for Experience Rating[1]	Reduced Rate for New Employers[2]
NH	Jan. 31	Jan. 315	July 1	1	1.7%
NJ	Dec. 31	March 31	July 1	3	2.6825% - 3.5825% based on the tax schedule in effect
NM	June 30	June 30	Jan. 1	3	Greater of 1% or average industry rate
NY	Dec. 31	Dec. 31	Jan. 1	1	Highest rate assigned to employers with positive account balances or 3.4%, whichever is less
NC	Aug. 1	June 30	Jan. 1	1	1.0%
ND	Sept. 30	Sept. 30	Jan. 1	3	1.21% for positive balance non- construction employers, 6.15% for negative balance non-construction; and 9.75% for construction employers
OH	July 1	July 1	Jan. 1	1	2.7%, except construction employers pay industry average rate
OK	July 31	Dec. 316	Jan. 1	1	1.5%
OR	June 30	Aug. 31	Jan. 1	1	2.0% - 3.3% based on the tax schedule in effect
PA	June 30	June 30	Jan. 1	1½[1]	3.689%; construction employers pay 10.2238%
PR	June 30	Dec. 31	Jan. 1	1	2.7% - 3.4% depending upon the tax schedule in effect
RI	Sept. 30	Sept. 30	Jan. 1	3	Higher of 1.0% or the 5-year benefit cost rate for non-ratable employers up to a maximum of 4.2%
SC	July 1	June 30	Jan. 1	1[1]	Rate applicable to rate class 12
SD	June 30	June 30	Jan. 1	2	1.2% for first year and 1.0% for second and third years if employer has positive balance;

Table 2-12. (Continued)

State	Computation Date	Fund Trigger Date	Effective Date for New Rates	Years Needed to Qualify for Experience Rating[1]	Reduced Rate for New Employers[2]
					construction pays 6.0% for first year and 3.0% for second and third years if they have a positive balance
TN	Dec. 31	Dec. 315	July 1	3	2.7%, except average industry rate when industry reserve ratio is 0.0% or less
TX	Oct. 17	Oct. 1	Jan. 17	1	Greater of 2.7% or industry rate
UT	July 1	June 30	Jan. 1	1	Average industry rate up to 9.5%
VT	Dec. 31	Dec. 31	July 1	1	Lower of average industry rate or rate class eleven, but not less than 1%8
VA	June 30	June 30	Jan. 1	1	2.5%, plus any applicable add-ons
VI	Dec. 31	Sept. 30	Jan. 1	3	2.0%
WA	July 1	Sept. 30	Jan. 1	2[1]	90, 100, or 115% of industry average rate depending upon benefits charged and taxes collected from new employers during the previous three years
WV	June 30	Jan. 1	Jan. 1	3	2.7%; construction and foreign entities pay 7.5%

State	Computation Date	Fund Trigger Date	Effective Date for New Rates	Years Needed to Qualify for Experience Rating[1]	Reduced Rate for New Employers[2]
WI	June 30	June 30	Jan. 1	3	2.5%; except construction employers pay average industry rate
WY	June 30	Oct. 31	Jan. 1	3	Average industry rate

[1] Period shown is period throughout which employer's account was chargeable or during which payroll declines were measurable. AK, CT, IN, and WA - in states noted, requirements for experience rating are stated in the law in terms of subjectivity; IL and PA - in which contributions are payable; NE - in addition to the specified period of chargeability, contributions payable in the 2 preceding CYs; SC - coverage.

[2] When rate varies, it must be no less than 1%.

[3] New employers who have been experience rated in another state are given the option of using their previous experience or the new employer rate. The new employer rate must be at least 1.0% plus the stabilization tax rate in effect.

[4] An employer's rate will not include a nonchargeable benefits component for the first 4 years of subjectivity.

[5] MO - uses a calculation based on the average balance of the 4 CQs; NE - May 30 is the last day the administrator decides the next year's tax rate based on quarterly trust fund balances of preceding year; NH - can also use quarterly trust fund levels to activate quarterly changes in tax rates; TN - can also use June 30 trust fund balance to activate a 6-month tax schedule.

[6] In some circumstances, the trust fund trigger date can be July 1.

[7] For newly qualified employers, computation date is end of quarter in which employer meets experience requirements and effective date is immediately following quarter.

[8] Exception: Foreign corporations classified in 236, 237, or 238 North American Industry Classification System code shall pay the average rate as of most recent computation date paid by all employers so classified.

The fund trigger date is the date the fund's balance is determined for purposes of determining which rate schedule is used for the following tax year.

All state laws contain provisions describing the treatment of employers who are not eligible for experience rates. To conform to Federal law, all states assign employers with three years of experience a rate based on experience. Federal law allows states to reduce the experience period to no less than one year before assigning rates based on experience, and allows states to assign new employer rates on a "reasonable basis," but not less than 1 percent. Typically, states assign either a flat rate to all new employers or a rate based on the new employer's industry type. In some states, these two methods are combined. Most new employers receive a flat rate, while some high-cost industries, such as construction, receive the higher industry rate. In some cases, the flat rate varies from year to year, depending on such factors as the fund balance.

Rate Reduction through Voluntary Contributions

In about half of the states employers may obtain lower rates by making voluntary contributions by an established deadline. In reserve ratio states, a voluntary contribution increases the balance in the employer's reserve so that a lower rate is assigned that will save more than the amount of the voluntary contribution. In benefit-ratio states, an employer pays voluntary contributions to cancel benefit charges to its account, thereby reducing its benefit ratio.

Table 2-13. States permitting rate reduction through voluntary contributions

State	Due Date[1]	Additional Information[2]
AZ	On or before February 28	No additional information
AR	On or before March 31	Not permitted if rate increased because of knowingly violating/attempting to violate state law regarding transfers of experience and assignment of rates
CA	By last working day in March in CY to which reduced rate would apply	Cannot reduce by more than 3 rates; employer must not have negative account balance or not have any unpaid amounts owed; not allowed for any year in which schedule E or F or emergency solvency surcharge in effect
CO	Before March 15	No additional information
GA	Within 30 days following the date upon which a notice is mailed	No additional information
IN	Within 30 days of receipt of rate notice	No additional information
KS	Within 30 days of mailing of rate notice	No rate may be reduced more than five rate groups for positive balance employers; negative balance employers may have their rates reduced to the highest five rates for positive balance employers
KY	Within 20 days following mailing of rate notice	No additional information

State	Due Date[1]	Additional Information[2]
LA	Within 30 days of mailing of notice of benefits charged to employer's experience rating account	May not be permitted if solvency tax, advance interest tax, or special assessment to finance bonds used to prepay Federal loan is assessed
ME	Within 30 days of mailing of rate notice; can be extended for 10 days for good cause	No additional information
MA	No later than 30 days after date of issuance of notice of employer's contribution rate	Employer must be assigned contribution rate, file all required reports, and pay all contributions, interest, and penalties due
MI	Within 30 days of mailing of notice of adjusted contribution rate	No additional information
MN	Within 120 days of January 1	Contribute up to amount of benefits charged to account during period ending June 30 of preceding year plus 25% surcharge; not refundable unless request made in writing within 30 days of mailing of notice of new tax rate; must not be delinquent in any amount
MO	On or before following January 15	Employer must be eligible for experience rate and must include signed written statement identifying it as voluntary payment
NE	Before January 10	Limited to amount likely to reduce one rate category
NJ	Within 30 days of mailing of employer's rate notice; may be extended 60 days for good cause; if contribution not made within extended period, employer becomes subject to a penalty of 5% or $5.00, whichever is greater, up to $50.00	If employer transfers all/part of business to a successor in interest and both parties at time of transfer are under common ownership or control, neither may make voluntary contributions in year of transfer and the following year
NM	On or before March 1	No additional information
NY	On or before April 1	No additional information
NC	Within 30 days of mailing of rate notice	No additional information
ND	Within 4 months of beginning of year	No additional information
OH	By December 31 following computation date	No additional information
PA	Within 30 days of mailing of rate notice; can extend for good cause	No additional information
RI	Within 30 days of mailing rate notice or prior to 120 days after the start of the calendar year, whichever is earlier	No additional information

Table 2-13. (Continued)

State	Due Date[1]	Additional Information[2]
SD	Before February 1	No additional information
TX	No later than 60 days after mailing date of rate notice; may extend an additional 15 days; if payment insufficient to cause decrease in employer's rate, Commission will notify employer and grant an extension, not to exceed total of 75 days	No additional information
WA	By February 15	May contribute part or all of benefit charges from most recent 2 years ending June 30; only eligible if tax rate increased at least 12 rate classes from prior tax rate year
WV	Within 30 days of mailing of rate notice	No additional information
WI	By November 30	Can only lower one rate unless catastrophic event; not available for 5 years for certain employer's whose benefit charges exceed their contributions

[1] Federal law requires that voluntary contributions be made "prior to the expiration of 120 days after the beginning of the rate year" (Section 3303(d), FUTA). This column contains additional state limitations for the voluntary contribution to affect the applicable rate year.

[2] Since Federal law limits refunds to erroneous payments, if a voluntary contribution does not lead to a reduced rate or if an employer changes its mind, no refund can be made.

Transfer of Employers' Experience

Because of Federal experience rating requirements states must maintain a record of the employer's experience with the factors used to measure unemployment. Without such a record, there would be no basis for a rate determination. For this reason, all state laws specify the conditions under which the experience record of a predecessor employer may be transferred to an employer who, through purchase or otherwise, acquires the predecessor's business. In some states, the authorization for transfer of the record is limited to total transfers; i.e., the record may be transferred only if a single successor employer acquires the predecessor's organization, trade, or business, and substantially all of its assets. In other states, the provisions authorize partial as well as total transfers; in these states, if only a portion of a business is acquired by any one successor, that part of the predecessor's record pertaining to the acquired portion of the business may be transferred to the successor.

To address concerns regarding employers who avoid liability for UI benefits charged to their accounts through the manipulation of payrolls, Congress enacted the SUTA Dumping Prevention Act of 2004. This Act required state UI laws to provide for:

- mandatory transfers of experience when there is substantial commonality of ownership, management, or control at the time of acquisition of trade or business; and
- no transfers of experience when the acquiring party is not otherwise an employer at the time of acquisition and when the state agency finds that acquiring the business was solely or primarily for the purposes of obtaining a lower rate of contributions.

Most states establish by statute or regulation the rate to be assigned to the successor employer from the date of the transfer to the end of the rate year in which the transfer occurs. The rate assignments vary with the status of the successor employer prior to the acquisition of the predecessor's business. Most states provide that an employer who has a rate based on experience with unemployment shall continue to pay that rate for the remainder of the rate year; the others provide that a new rate be assigned based on the employer's own record combined with the acquired record. In all other situations, it is left to the states to determine the circumstances under which experience may be transferred.

Additional Taxes

This section discusses various payroll taxes that are not deposited into the state's unemployment fund.

Loan and Interest Repayment Taxes

Some states have the authority to sell bonds to pay benefit costs, thereby avoiding the need to obtain Federal advances. In these states, special taxes may be assessed to pay off the bond as well as any costs associated with the bond. Since Federal advances are subject to interest and interest may not be paid from the state's unemployment fund, several states have established special taxes to pay the costs of this interest.

Table 2-14. States with loan and interest repayment taxes

State	Tax	Amount[1]	When Payable	Specific Purposes
AL	Additional rate	Rate determined based on amount due[2]	By May 15th following year interest becomes due	Pay interest on Federal advances
AZ	Special assessment	0.5%	Quarterly	Pay principal and interest
AR	Advance interest tax	0.2%	When interest is due on Federal advances	Pay interest on Federal advances
CO	Advance interest	Rate determined based on amount due[2]	When interest is due on Federal advances	Pay interest on Federal advances
	Bond assessment	Rate determined based on amount due	When bonds are outstanding	Pay bonds issued to pay UC, Federal advances, and bond costs
CT	Bond assessment	Not specified; assessment is a percent of employer's charged tax rate	When bonds are outstanding	Pay bonds issued to pay UC, Federal advances, and bond costs
	Special assessment	Rate determined based on amount due[2]	When interest is due on Federal advances	Pay interest on Federal advances
DE	Temporary emergency assessment	Rate determined based on amount due[2]	When interest is due on Federal advances	Pay interest on Federal advances
DC	Interest surcharge	1%	When interest is due on Federal advances	Pay interest on Federal advances
FL	Additional rate	Rate determined based on amount due	When interest is due on Federal advances	Pay interest on Federal advances

State	Tax	Amount[1]	When Payable	Specific Purposes
HI	Special assessment	Rate determined based on amount due	When interest is due on Federal advances	Pay principal and interest
ID	Advance interest repayment tax	Rate determined based on amount due[2]	When interest is due on Federal advances	Pay interest on Federal advances
IA	Temporary emergency surcharge	Rate determined based on amount due[2]	When interest is due on Federal advances	Pay interest on Federal advances
LA	Bond repayment assessment	1.4% on $15,000 wage base[2]	When bonds are outstanding	Pay bonds issued to pay Federal advances and bond costs
ME	Special assessment	Rate determined based on amount due[2]	When interest is due on Federal advances	Pay interest on Federal advances
MI	Obligation assessment	Rate determined based on amount due[2]	When bonds are outstanding	Pay bonds issued to pay Federal advances and bond costs
	Solvency Tax	Lesser of ¼ of the Account Building Component or 2%	When there is an unrepaid interest balance on a Federal advance on Dec 31	Pay interest on Federal advances
MN	Special assessment	Up to 8% of quarterly taxes	When interest is due on Federal advances	Pay interest on Federal advances
MO	Advance interest	Rate determined based on amount due[2]	When interest is due on Federal advances	Pay interest on Federal advances
	Bond and loan assessment	Rate determined based on amount due	When bonds or loans are outstanding	Pay principle, interest, and administrative expenses related to bonds and loans
NV	Special assessment	Rate determined based on amount due[2]	When interest is due on Federal advances	Pay interest on Federal advances
	Special bond contributions	Rate determined based on amount due[2]	When bonds are outstanding	Pay bonds issued to pay Federal advances and bond costs
NJ	Federal loan interest assessment	Rate determined based on amount due[2]	When interest is due on Federal advances	Pay interest on Federal advances
NY	Interest assessment surcharge	Rate determined based on amount due	When interest is due on Federal advances	Pay interest on Federal advances
OR	Advance interest repayment tax	Rate determined based on amount due[2]	When interest is due on Federal advances	Pay bond obligations and interest on Federal advances
PA	Advance interest tax	Capped at 1.1%[2]	When interest is due on Federal advances	Pay interest on Federal advances
PR	Advance interest tax	Rate determined based on amount due	When interest is due on Federal advances	Pay interest on Federal advances

Table 2-14. (Continued)

State	Tax	Amount[1]	When Payable	Specific Purposes
SC	Additional surcharge	Rate determined based on amount due	When interest is due on Federal advances	Pay interest on Federal advances
TN	Interest tax	Rate determined based on amount due[2]	When interest is due on Federal advances	Pay interest on Federal advances
TX	Obligation assessment	Based on amount due[2]	When bonds or loans are outstanding	Pay interest and cost of bonds
WA	Interest payment tax	Not to exceed 0.15%[2]	Based on balance of interest payment fund and projected interest due	Pay interest on Federal advances
WV	Assessment	0.35% on employees, % on employers on $21,000 tax wage base = to employee assessment	When bonds are outstanding	Retire bonds used to pay Federal advances and cost of bonds
WI	Assessment	Rate determined based on amount due	When interest is due on Federal advances	Pay interest on Federal advances

[1] Percentage figures include percent of taxable payroll, unless otherwise indicated.

[2] AL, CT, ID, LA, ME, MI, MO, NV, OR, PA, TX, and WA - exclude reimbursing employers; CO - excludes governmental entities, reimbursing nonprofit organizations, political subdivisions electing the special rate, negative balance employers, and employers with positive balances of 7.0% or more; DE - excludes reimbursing governmental entities or instrumentalities and nonprofit organizations; ID – excludes deficit employers from rate class 6; IA - excludes governmental employers and employers assigned a zero rate; NJ - excludes reimbursing employers, nonprofit organizations, and governmental entities or instrumentalities; OR - excludes zero rated employers; PA - excludes new employers. In some states, it is not clear whether the tax applies only to contributory employers; and TN - excludes employers with no benefit charges for 2 years and no negative balance for the same 2 years.

Reserve Taxes

These taxes are deposited in a reserve fund established under state law. The principal in the reserve fund is used for UI purposes (such as paying benefits or interest on Federal advances). Any interest earned on the reserve fund is deposited in another fund where it is used for other purposes, such as job training and paying the collection costs of the reserve tax. Unlike employer contributions, which are held in the Federal Unemployment Trust Fund until needed to pay benefits, these reserve fund moneys are not protected by the Federal withdrawal standard, which restricts the use of contributions to the payment of benefits and other specified purposes. This means that state legislatures may, if the state constitution allows, redirect the reserve fund's principal to other uses. Even if the taxing authority has expired, reserve taxes are listed in the following table when the reserve fund continues in existence.

Table 2-15. Reserve taxes - principal used for ui purposes, interest used for UI or non-UI purposes

State	Surtax	Amount[1]	When Payable	Purpose
ID	Reserve	Taxable wage rate less the assigned contribution rate and training tax rate	If as of September 30th of the preceding year the Reserve Fund balance is <1% of state taxable wages or ≤49% of the Employment Security Fund	Loans to the employment security fund, and interest on loans; interest accrued is deposited in the Dept. of Commerce and Labor Special Administration Fund
IA	Reserve	0-50% of contributions due, not to exceed $50,000,000 in total contributions annually	If as of July 1st of the preceding year the Reserve Fund balance is <$150,000,000	Pay UI; interest accrued is used for UI and Employment Service administrative costs
NE	State UI	0-20% of contributions due	When unemployment fund meets specified solvency requirements[2]	Pay UI; interest accrued is deposited into the Jobs Training and Support Fund
NC	Reserve Fund	20% of contributions due	Except if as of September 1st of the preceding year the balance of the state's account in the Unemployment Trust fund exceeds $1,000,000,000	Pay UI; principle or interest on Federal advances; administrative cost related to the surtax

[1] Percentage figures include percent of taxable payroll, unless otherwise indicated.

[2] The reserve tax is in effect unless any of the following occur: the average balance in the state unemployment fund at the end of any 3 months in the preceding CY is greater than 1% of state taxable wages for the same preceding year; the balance in the state unemployment fund equals or exceeds 30% of the average month-end balance of the state's account in the Unemployment Trust Fund for the three lowest calendar months in the preceding year; or the state advisory council determines that a 0% state UI tax rate is in the best interests of preserving the integrity of the state's account in the Unemployment Trust Fund.

Taxes for UI Administration or Non-Ui Purposes

States also collect a variety of taxes established for administrative purposes. These purposes may be UI administration, job training, employment service administration, or special improvements in technology. These taxes are not deposited in the state's unemployment fund, but in another fund designated by state law. Since Federal grants for the administration of the UI program may not be used to collect non-UI taxes, almost all legislation establishing non-UI taxes provides that a portion of the revenues generated will be used for payment of costs of collecting the tax. Expired taxes are not listed. In some states, certain contributions to the state's unemployment fund are reduced when other taxes or assessments are in effect.

Table 2-16. States with taxes for UI administration or non-UI purposes

State	Tax Name	Amount[1]	When Payable	Purpose
AL	Employment Security Administrative Enhancement Assessment	0.06%[2]	Quarterly	Job search/placement
AK	State Training and Employment Program	0.1%[3]	Each year	Development of skilled workforce
	Technical and Vocational Education Program	0.15% [2,3]	Each year	Vocational and technical training
AR	Stabilization Tax[2, 4]	0.025% of taxable wages collected	Through June 30, 2019	Training
		0.025% of taxable wages collected	Through June 30, 2019	Administration
CA	Employment and Training Tax	0.1% (excluding negative balance employers)	Each year	Training and administration costs
DE	Special Assessment	0.085%	Quarterly	Counseling, training, placement of dislocated workers

State	Tax Name	Amount[1]	When Payable	Purpose
DC	Unemployment and Workforce Development Administrative Assessment	0.2%	Quarterly	Improve benefit claim eligibility determinations, reemployment services, fraud prevention, cost of collecting/administering assessment
GA	Administrative Assessment	0.06%[2]	Quarterly	Employment services and administration
HI	Employment and Training Fund Assessment	0.01%[2]	Quarterly	Employment services and training
ID	Training Tax	3.0% of taxable wage rate	Excludes deficit employers from rate class 6	Training
KY	Service Capacity Upgrade Fund	0.075%[5, 10]	Quarterly	Technology acquisition & upgrade
	Additional Contribution	0.3%	When Federal funds are not available	Administration
LA	Social Charge Tax	Varies6	When trust fund balance is >$750 million	Training and specified UI and employment functions
ME	Competitive Skills Scholarship Fund Contributions	Varies[7, 10]	Quarterly	Training and related administrative costs
MA	Unemployment Health Insurance Contribution	0.36%	Quarterly, applies to employers with 6 or more employees and 2 years as a subject employer	Medical Security Trust Fund
	Workforce Training Fund Contribution	0.056%[8]	Quarterly	Training
MN	Workforce Development Assessment	0.10%[2]	Quarterly	Dislocated worker training

Table 2-16. (Continued)

State	Tax Name	Amount[1]	When Payable	Purpose
MS	Workforce Enhancement Contributions	0.15% of taxable wages[2, 5]	Quarterly, suspended if IUR >5.5% until IUR <4.5%	Training to enhance productivity
		0.04% of taxable wages[2, 5]	Quarterly, suspended if IUR >5.5% until IUR <4.5%	Mississippi Works
		0.01% of taxable wages[2, 5]	Quarterly, suspended if IUR >5.5% until IUR <4.5%	Workforce investment
MT	Administrative Fund Tax	0.13% or 0.18% (depending upon rate class)[9]	Quarterly	Administration
NV	Employment and Training	0.05%[2]	Quarterly	Employment and training of the unemployed
NH	Administrative Contribution	0.2%	Quarterly	Administration and training
NJ	Supplemental Workforce Fund for Basic Skills	0.0175%[10]	Quarterly	Remedial education
	Workforce Development Partnership Tax	0.1% - Employer rate10 0.025% - Employee rate	Quarterly	Customized training grants to employers and unions for incumbent workers, individual training grants for displaced workers, OSHA training grants, youth transition-to- work grants
NY	Re-Employment Service Fund	0.075%	Quarterly	Automation, re-employment services, administration

State	Tax Name	Amount[1]	When Payable	Purpose
OK	Technology Reinvestment Apportionment	5.0% of unemployment taxes owed[10]	Quarterly	Technology modernization
OR	Administration Tax	0.09%[2, 10]	Quarterly	Employment Department administration
	Wage Security	0.03%[2, 10]	1st quarter of every odd-numbered year	Pays last payroll checks of bankrupt employers
PR	Special Tax	1.0%[2]	Quarterly	Employment, training, and administration
RI	Job Development Assessment	Varies[2, 10]	Quarterly	Rhode Island Human Resource Investment Council (HRIC) and Employment Services and Unemployment Insurance activities
SC	Administrative Contingency Assessment	0.06%[2]	Quarterly	Job placement for individuals
SD	Investment Fee	0 - 0.53% rated employers; 0.55% new employers[2]	Quarterly	Research and economic development
	Administrative Fee	0.02%[11]	Quarterly	Administration
TX	Employment Training Investment Assessment	0.1%[12]	Quarterly	Job training
WA	Employment Assistance Tax	0.02%[2]	Quarterly, terminates if Federal funding increases	Employment Assistance Program
WI	Administrative Account Contribution	0.2%, but agency may reduce	Quarterly	UI and ES administration

Table 2-16. (Continued)

State	Tax Name	Amount[1]	When Payable	Purpose
WY	Adjustment Factor	40% of annual noncharged/ineffectively charged adjustment factor[2]	Quarterly	Workforce development program, administration

[1] Percentage figures include percent of taxable payroll unless otherwise indicated.

[2] AL - excludes new employers, excludes reimbursing employers, and excludes employers paying at least 5.4%; AK, AR, MN, RI, SD, WA, and WY - exclude reimbursing employers; GA - excludes reimbursing employers, employers who are assigned the minimum positive reserve rate, or maximum deficit reserve rate; HI - excludes reimbursing employers, employers assigned either the minimum, or maximum tax rate; MS - excludes state boards, instrumentalities, political subdivisions, and nonprofit organizations; NV - excludes reimbursing employers, and employers who pay 5.4%; OR - excludes employers paying 5.4%; PR - excludes governmental entities and political subdivisions; those employers with a rate of higher than 4.4% shall have the special tax rate capped so as to not increase the employer's rate above 5.4%; SC - excludes nonprofit organizations, certain governmental employers, and employers paying 5.4%.

[3] Taken from employee portion of unemployment tax.

[4] Portion of Stabilization Tax listed in Table 2-11.

[5] Only collected when trust fund is above specified level.

[6] The social charge rate is calculated to the nearest .01% and may not raise an employer's total rate above 6.2%.

[7] Contribution rates may not be reduced for new employers below 1.0%, nor below 5.4% for employers in category 20.

[8] Administrator shall adjust rate to substantially equal $22 million.

[9] Governmental contributory employers pay 0.09% and reimbursable employers pay 0.08%.

[10] Employers tax rate as listed in Table 2-10 is reduced (see state law for details).

[11] Applies only to experience rated employers with a reserve ratio <2.25%.

[12] Employers Replenishment Tax Rate listed in Table 2-10 is reduced by an amount equal to this tax.

Special Provisions for Financing Benefits Paid to Employees of Nonprofit Organizations, State and Local Governments, and Indian Tribes

The Reimbursement Option

As discussed in the Coverage chapter, amendments made to FUTA in 1970, 1976, and 2000 require coverage of most services performed for certain nonprofit organizations, state and local governments, and federally recognized Indian tribes. These amendments also require that states permit these entities to elect to make "payments in lieu of contributions" (more commonly called "reimbursements") to a state's unemployment fund. Prior to these amendments, states were not permitted to allow nonprofit organizations or Indian tribes to finance their employees' benefits on a reimbursable basis because of the experience-rating requirements of Federal law.

Most state laws provide that reimbursing employers will be billed at the end of each calendar quarter, or other period determined by the agency, for the benefits paid during that period attributable to service in their employ. A second method, mostly limited to nonprofit organizations, bills the nonprofit at the end of each calendar quarter, or other time period specified by the agency, at a flat rate based on a percentage of the organization's total payroll in the preceding calendar year. This method appears to be less burdensome because it spreads benefit costs more uniformly throughout the calendar year. Alabama and North Carolina mandate this second method for nonprofits, while 17 states[53] permit a nonprofit the option of choosing either method, subject to the approval of the state agency. Arkansas is the only state to extend this method beyond nonprofits. By law the State of Arkansas is required to use the first method, while nonprofit organizations and political subdivisions that choose reimbursement must use the second method.

Although states may noncharge benefits to reimbursing employers, few do. Unlike contributing employers, who share noncharged benefit costs through such devices as minimum contribution and solvency rates, a reimbursing employer will not fully pay its noncharging costs. Only one state that noncharges benefits to reimbursing employers has developed a system for having such employers bear the costs of such noncharges. In Mississippi, political subdivisions reimbursing the fund may elect to pay 0.25 percent of taxable wages as a condition of having benefits noncharged under the same conditions as contributory employers.

Some state laws permit two or more reimbursing employers jointly to apply to the state agency for the establishment of a group account to pay the benefit costs attributable to service in their employ. This group is treated as

---

[53] AK, CA, DC, ID, MD, ND, OH, PR, SC, SD, TN, UT, VT, VA, VI, WA, and WV.

a single employer for the purposes of benefit reimbursement and benefit cost allocation.

Special Provisions for State and Local Governments

Generally, state laws treat governmental entities the same as nonprofit organizations and Indian tribes for financing purposes. However, treatment of governmental entities differs in the following ways.

- The state law may designate the state as a whole as a governmental entity and choose for it the financing option. (Effectively, the state legislature elects the state's financing option.)
- Governmental entities using the contribution option must or may, depending on state law, use a method different from those applicable to other employers in the state. (Unlike nonprofit organizations and Indian tribes, the Federal experience-rating requirements do not apply to state governments and their political subdivisions.)
- A governmental entity may be liable for the full amount of extended benefits paid based on service in its employ. The Federal government does not share these costs because governmental entities do not pay the FUTA tax that pays the Federal share. (This extended benefit rule applies to Indian tribes as well.)

The following table indicates how states treat governmental entities.

California has three separate plans for governmental entities. The state is limited to contributions or reimbursement. Schools have, in addition to those two options, the option of making quarterly contributions of percent of total wages to the School Employee's Fund plus a variable local experience charge to pay for "administrative indiscretions." The Local Public Entity Employee's Fund and School Employee's Fund have been established in the state Treasury to which political subdivisions and schools, respectively, contribute a percentage of their payrolls and from which the state unemployment compensation fund is reimbursed for benefits paid.

Table 2-17. Financing provisions for governmental entities

State	State's Method Required by Law	Options in Addition to Reimbursement		State	State's Method Required by Law	Options in Addition to Reimbursement	
		Regular Contributions	Special Schedule			Regular Contributions	Special Schedule
AL	Reimbursement	X		AK		X	
AZ		X		AR		X	
CA		X	X	CO	Reimbursement	X	
CT	Reimbursement	X		DE			X
DC		X		FL		X	
GA	Contribution1	X		HI		X	
ID		X		IL2	Reimbursement	X	
IN		X		IA		X	X
KS		X	X	KY		X	
LA		X		ME	Contribution1		
MD		X		MA			X
MI		X		MN		X	
MS	Reimbursement	X	X	MO		X	
MT			X	NE		X	
NV		X		NH	Reimbursement	X	
NJ		X	X	NM	Reimbursement	X	X
NY	Reimbursement	X		NC		X	
ND		X	X	OH		X	
OK	Contribution		X	OR	Reimbursement	X	X
PA	Reimbursement	X		PR		X	
RI		X		SC		X	
SD	Reimbursement	X		TN		X	X
TX			X	UT	Reimbursement	X	

Table 2-17. (Continued)

State	State's Method Required by Law	Options in Addition to Reimbursement		State	State's Method Required by Law	Options in Addition to Reimbursement	
		Regular Contributions	Special Schedule			Regular Contributions	Special Schedule
VT3	Reimbursement	X		VA		X	
VI		X		WA	Reimbursement	X	X
WV		X		WI	Reimbursement	X	
WY		X					

[1] GA and ME - governmental entities can elect direct reimbursement.

[2] Benefits paid to state employees are financed by appropriation to the state Department of Employment Security, which then reimburses the unemployment compensation fund for benefits paid.

[3] State institutions of higher education have an option of contributions or reimbursement; all other state agencies must reimburse.

Kansas and Massachusetts have developed a similar experience-rating system applicable to governmental entities that elect the contributions method. Under this system, three factors are involved in determining rates: required yield, individual experience, and aggregate experience. In Kansas, the rate for employers not eligible for a computed rate is based on the benefit cost experience of all rated governmental employers. In this state, no employer's rate may be less than 0.1 percent. In Massachusetts, the rate for employers not eligible for a computed rate is the average cost of all rated governmental employers but not less than 1.0 percent. Massachusetts also imposes an emergency tax of up to 1.0 percent when benefit charges reach a specified level.

In Montana, governmental entities that elect contributions pay at rates ranging from 0.06 percent to 1.5 percent (in 0.1 percent intervals) on total wages. Rates are adjusted annually for each employer under a benefit- ratio formula. New employers are assigned the median rate for the first year in which they elect contributions. Governmental rates become effective July 1, rather than January 1, as is the case for the regular contribution rate system.

New Mexico permits political subdivisions to participate in a "local public body unemployment compensation reserve fund" managed by the risk management division. This special fund reimburses the state unemployment fund for benefits paid based on service with the participating political subdivision. The employer contributes to the special fund the amount of benefits paid attributable to service in its employ plus an additional unspecified amount to establish a pool and to pay administrative costs of the special fund.

North Dakota political subdivisions contribute to a special fund managed by the Office of Management and Budget. This fund reimburses the state's unemployment fund for benefits paid based on service with the participating political subdivision.

Oregon has a "local government employer benefit trust fund" to which a political subdivision may elect to pay a percentage of its gross wages. The rate is redetermined each June 30 under a benefit-ratio formula. No employer's rate may be less than 0.1 percent nor more than 5.0 percent. This special fund then reimburses the state unemployment compensation fund for benefits paid based on service with political subdivisions that have elected to participate in the special fund, repayment of advances, and any interest due because of shortages in the fund.

In Tennessee, each governmental entity that is a contributing employer will pay rates ranging from 0.3 percent to 3.0 percent determined according to its reserve ratio.

In Washington, counties, cities, and towns may elect regular reimbursement or the "local government tax." Other political subdivisions may elect either reimbursement or regular contributions. Rates are determined yearly for each employer under a reserve-ratio formula. The following minimum and maximum rates have been established: 0.2 percent and 3.0 percent. No employer's rate may increase by more than 1.0 percent in any year. At the discretion of the Commissioner, an emergency excess tax of not more than 1.0 percent may be imposed whenever benefit payments would jeopardize reasonable reserves. New employers pay at a rate of 1.25 percent for the first two years of participation.

Bonding Requirements

Since reimbursing employers pay the unemployment fund after benefits have been paid, Federal law expressly authorizes states to establish bond or other reasonable requirements to assure that, in the event the reimbursing employer ceases to exist or otherwise does not pay, the unemployment fund is not left with unreimbursed costs. The following table lists those states that have imposed bond or other deposit requirements. (Please note that this table does not necessarily reflect state law pertaining to treatment of Indian tribes.)

Table 2-18. States that require bond or deposit of employers electing reimbursement

State	Provision is:		Amount
	Mandatory	Optional	
AL	X		Percent of taxable payrolls determined by director or administrator, not to exceed the maximum percentage charged to contributing employers
AK	X		Amount determined by regulation
AR	X		Prepays estimated charges each quarter
CO		X[1]	Greater of 3 x amount of regular and ½ EB paid, based on service within part year or sum of such payments during past 3 years, but not to exceed 3.6% nor less than 0.1% of taxable payrolls
CT		X[2]	Percent of taxable payrolls not to exceed the maximum contribution rate in effect
DC		X	0.25% of taxable payroll
GA	X		2.7% of taxable payroll as of various alternative dates, or if none, as determined by the Commissioner
HI	X		0.2% of total payrolls
ID		X	Determined on basis of potential benefit cost
IA	X		Amount determined by regulation
KS		X	5.4% of taxable payrolls
KY		X[3]	2.0% of total payrolls
ME	X	X	By regulation; 5.0% of taxable wages
MD	X		2.7% of taxable wages if the organization has taxable wages less than 25 x the taxable wage base, or 5.4% of taxable wages if the organization's taxable wages equal or exceed 25 x the taxable wage base
MA		X	Percent of taxable payrolls not to exceed the maximum contribution rate in effect
MI	X[4]		4.0% of estimated annual payroll
MS		X	1.35% of taxable payrolls for nonprofit organizations and 2.0% of taxable payrolls for governmental entities
NC	X		Non-profits must keep 1.0% of prior year's taxable payroll in unemployment fund
NJ		X	Percent of taxable payrolls not to exceed the maximum contribution rate in effect
NM	X[5]		2.7% of contributions x the organization's taxable wages
OH	X		3.0% of taxable payrolls but not more than $2,000,000
OR	X		2.0% of total wages for the 4 CQs immediately preceding effective date of election to reimbursable status
PA	X		1.0% of taxable payroll for the most recent 4 CQs prior to election of reimbursable status

Table 2-18. (Continued)

State	Provision is:		Amount
	Mandatory	Optional	
PR	X		Determined by rule
RI		X	No greater than double amount of estimated tax due each month, but not less than $100
SC		X	Bond from nonprofit organizations which do not possess real property and improvements valued in excess of $2 million; regulation requires bond or deposit of minimum of $2,000 for employers with annual wages of $50,000 or less; for annual wages exceeding $50,000, an additional $1,000 bond required for each $50,000 or portion thereof
SD		X	Maximum effective tax rate x organization's taxable payroll
TX		X	Higher of 5.0% of total anticipated wages for next 12 months or amount determined by the commission
UT		X	Nonprofit employers may be required to deposit 1% of total wages paid in 4 CQs prior to demand; in the absence of 4 quarters of wages, the Division will determine the amount; deposit subject to adjustments
VA		X	Determined by commission based on taxable wages for preceding year
VI	X		1.35% of taxable payrolls
WA		X	Amount sufficient to cover benefit costs but not more than the amount organization would pay if it were liable for contributions
WI	X		4.0% of taxable payrolls of preceding year or anticipated payroll for current year, whichever is greater
WY		X	No amount specified in law

[1] Regulation states that bond or deposit shall be required if the amount is $100 or more.

[2] If agency deems necessary because of financial conditions.

[3] Bond or deposit required as condition of election unless agency determines that the employing unit or a guarantor possesses equity in real or personal property equal to at least double the amount of bond or deposit required.

[4] Applies only to nonprofit organizations that pay more than $100,000 in remuneration in a CY.

[5] Applies only to nonprofit organizations.

SECTION 3. MONETARY ENTITLEMENT

In General

This chapter deals with the monetary requirements of state UI laws, including work history, benefit amounts, and the length of time during which an individual may receive UC.

Although the states have developed many different ways to determine monetary entitlement to UC, there are also many similarities. This chapter discusses the:

- wages and employment needed in a "base period" to qualify;
- period during which UC may be collected, commonly called the "benefit year";
- amount payable for a week of total or partial unemployment;
- dependents' allowances;
- waiting periods; and
- maximum amount of regular UC an individual may receive in a benefit year.

> *Note:* Information regarding deductible income provisions is located in the nonmonetary eligibility chapter.

While most individuals are employed in the state in which they reside, many individuals regularly commute to a different state to work, work in more than one state, or move to a different state to look for new work when they become unemployed. The law of the state under which the individual claims benefits applies as it would for any other individual. Determinations on eligibility, disqualifications, and the amount and duration of benefits are made by the state in which the wages were paid. However, the process by which these individuals apply for benefits may vary. For example, the Interstate Benefit Payment Plan provides a method of filing for benefits in the state in which an individual has qualifying wages even though the individual is not physically present in that state.

Although this chapter analyzes monetary factors separately, the relationship among these factors is complex. In comparing state laws, consideration often needs to be given to these relationships.

Base Period and Benefit Year

An individual's benefit rights are determined using wages and employment during a period of time called the base period. Benefits are paid during a period of time called the benefit year. Individuals who exhaust their benefits before the end of a benefit year must wait until a new benefit year is established before they can again draw benefits.

Benefit Years

The benefit year is a 1-year or 52-week period during which an individual may receive benefits based on a previous period of employment. In all states, the beginning date of the benefit year depends on when an individual first files a "valid claim," meaning the individual meets minimal wage and employment requirements. In most states, the benefit year begins with the week in which the valid claim is filed. Exceptions are:

Table 3-1. When Benefit Year Begins - Other Than the Week a First Claim Is Filed

AR	Benefit year begins with the first day of the quarter in which a claim is first filed. As a result, the benefit "year" ranges from 40 to 52 weeks.
NY	Benefit year consists of 53 weeks beginning with the effective date of a valid claim.

Base Periods

The base period is the time period during which wages earned and/or hours/weeks worked are examined to determine an individual's monetary entitlement to benefits. Almost all states use the first four of the last five completed calendar quarters preceding the filing of the claim as their base period. Massachusetts uses the four completed calendar quarters preceding the first day of the benefit year. Minnesota uses the last four completed calendar quarters, provided the effective date of the claim is not during the month immediately following the fourth completed calendar quarter.

Because base-period employment and/or earnings are an imperfect proxy for labor market attachment, there are instances when individuals with labor market attachment are ineligible for benefits. To address this, some states developed expanded definitions of the base period.

Alternative Base Periods (ABP)

A base period consisting of the first four of the last five completed calendar quarters results in a lag of up to six months between the end of the base period and the date an individual becomes unemployed/files a claim. As a result, the individual's most recent work history is not used when making an eligibility determination. For individuals failing to qualify under the regular base period, many states use an ABP. For example, if the individual fails to qualify using wages and employment in the first four of the last five completed calendar quarters, the state will use wages and employment in the last four completed calendar quarters.

Extended Base Periods (EBP)

Several states allow individuals who have no wages in the current base period to use older wages and employment under certain conditions. These conditions typically involve illness or injury. For example, an individual who was injured on the job and who has collected workers' compensation benefits may use wages and employment preceding the date of the individual's injury to establish eligibility. (Note that some state laws may describe these base periods as "alternative" base periods.)

The following table outlines the options states use in addition to the standard base period.

Table 3-2. States with alternative and/or extended base periods

State	ABP/EBP	State	ABP/EBP
AK	ABP: Last 4 completed quarters EBP: BP extended up to 4 quarters if individual was incapable of working during the greater part of a quarter	AR	ABP: Last 4 completed quarters EBP: Up to 4 quarters if individual has insufficient wages to establish a claim because of a job-related injury for which the individual received worker's compensation
AZ	EBP: Last 4 completed quarters following previous BP when new BY overlaps preceding BY; also, first 4 of last 5 completed quarters preceding the week a compensable industrial injury began if not qualified under normal base period, if claim is filed within 2 years of beginning of disability	CA	ABP: Last 4 completed quarters
CO	ABP: Last 4 completed quarters	CT	ABP: Last 4 completed quarters EBP: Last 4 completed quarters preceding sickness or disability
DE	ABP: Last 4 completed quarters	DC	ABP: Last 4 completed quarters
GA	ABP: Last 4 completed quarters	HI	ABP: Last 4 completed quarters
ID	ABP: Last 4 completed quarters EBP: An individual who experienced a temporary total disability may elect a BP of the first 4 of the last 5 completed quarters preceding the disability if the individual filed a claim within 3 years of the disability and no later than 6 months after the end of the disability	IL	APB: Last 4 completed quarters EBP: BP extended up to 1 year if the individual received temporary total disability under a workers' compensation act or occupational diseases act
IN	EBP: Up to 4 quarters preceding the last day the individual was able to work	IA	ABP: Last 4 completed quarters EBP: BP extended 3 or more quarters if the individual received workers' compensation or weekly indemnity insurance benefits for 3 or more quarters
KS	ABP: Last 4 completed quarters	KY	EBP: BP extended up to 4 quarters if an individual, due to job- related injury or who has received workers' compensation, files a UI claim within 4 weeks after having last received workers' compensation

State	ABP/EBP	State	ABP/EBP
	EBP: Last 4 completed quarters preceding the date of qualifying injury		
ME	ABP: Last 4 completed quarters	MD	ABP: Last 4 completed quarters
	EBP: BP extended up to 4 quarters if 1 quarter has been used in a previous determination, extend the BY up to 1 week if there would otherwise be overlapping of the same quarter in 2 consecutive BPs		
MA	ABP: Last 3 quarters, plus any weeks of work in quarter in which claim is filed; individual may also elect to use this ABP if it results in a 10% or more increase in WBA	MI	ABP: Last 4 completed quarters if individual fails to meet qualifying wage requirements
	EBP: BP extended to 52 weeks if individual received compensation for temporary total disability under a workers' compensation law for more than 7 weeks in BP		
MN	ABP: First 4 of last 5 completed quarters[1]	MT	ABP: Last 4 completed quarters
	EBP: Up to 4 quarters depending on length of time an individual received compensation for temporary disability under a workers' compensation law		EBP: Up to 4 quarters preceding the disability if the claim was filed within 24 months from the date of the individual's disability
NE	ABP: Last 4 completed quarters	NV	ABP: Last 4 completed quarters
			EBP: Last 4 quarters preceding BY if 1 quarter has been used in a previous determination; extend the BY up to 1 week if there would otherwise be overlapping of the same quarter in 2 consecutive BPs
NH	ABP: Last 4 completed quarters	NJ	ABP: BP may be one of two alternatives: 1) last 4 completed quarters or 2) last 3 completed quarters, plus any weeks of work in quarter in which claim is filed
NM	ABP: Last 4 completed quarters	NY	ABP: Last 4 completed quarters

Table 3-2. (Continued)

State	ABP/EBP	State	ABP/EBP
NC	ABP: Last 4 completed quarters EBP: Up to 4 quarters, if individual has insufficient wages to establish a claim because of a job-related injury for which the individual received workers' compensation	OH	ABP: Last 4 completed quarters
OK	ABP: Last 4 completed quarters EBP: 4 quarters prior to regular base period	OR	ABP: Last 4 completed quarters EBP: BP extended up to 4 quarters if the individual is disabled for the majority of a quarter; if the individual received workers' compensation, the base year can be extended up to 4 quarters preceding the illness or injury
PA	EBP: Last 4 completed quarters immediately preceding the date of the injury if the individual was eligible for workers' compensation during the individual's current BP	PR	ABP: Last 4 completed quarters
RI	ABP: Last 4 completed quarters EBP: Individual who received workers' compensation and has requested reinstatement to a previous position that no longer exists is eligible to have base period determined as of the date of the work-related injury	SC	ABP: Last 4 completed quarters
SD	ABP: Last 4 completed quarters EBP: Individual who received temporary total disability payments under workers' compensation law may use a BP of the first 4 of the last 5 completed quarters preceding the disability if a claim is filed within 24 months of the date the disability occurred	TN	EBP: Individual who received temporary total disability payments under workers' compensation law may use a BP of the last 4 completed quarters preceding the disability

State	ABP/EBP	State	ABP/EBP
TX	EBP: If an initial claim is filed within 24 months from the date an individual's illness or injury began or occurred, the BP will be the first 4 of the last 5 completed quarters preceding the illness or injury	UT	ABP: Last 4 completed quarters EBP: First 4 of last 5 completed quarters prior to date of illness/injury; individual must have received temporary disability payments during normal BP, filed initial claim no later than 90 days after release to work and within 36 months of the date the injury/illness occurred
VA	ABP: Last 4 completed quarters	VI	ABP: Last 4 completed quarters
VT	ABP: One of two alternatives: 1) last 4 quarters or, if still ineligible 2) last 3 quarters plus any weeks of work in quarter in which claim is filed	WA	ABP: Last 4 completed quarters
WV	ABP: Last 4 completed quarters	WI	ABP: Last 4 completed quarters
WY	EBP: An individual who experienced a temporary total disability under workers' compensation may elect a BP of the last 4 completed quarters preceding the date of injury if the individual filed a claim within 3 years of the date of injury and no later than 60 days after notice of the end of the disability		

GENERAL NOTE: Information about various base periods used in MA and MN is located in paragraphs preceding this table.

[1] If the claim has an effective date during the month immediately following the last completed calendar quarter, the base period is the first 4 of the last 5 completed calendar quarters; however, the first 4 of the last 5 completed calendar quarters must be used if the individual has more wage credits in those quarters than in the last 4 completed quarters.

Qualifying Wages or Employment

All states require an individual to have earned a certain amount of wages or to have worked for a certain period of time (or both) within the base period to be monetarily eligible to receive any benefits. Most individuals qualify for benefits based on employment and wages in a single state. However, some individuals who work in more than one state will not have sufficient employment and wages in any single state to establish monetary eligibility, or would be eligible for a lower weekly benefit amount. In these situations, individuals may file a claim in one of the states where they worked, and elect to combine the employment and wages earned in one or more of the other states in which they had employment and wages to establish eligibility or to increase their weekly benefit amount. The "paying state" for a combined wage claim combines all base-period employment and wages earned under its law with employment and wages transferred from other states to determine the individual's monetary eligibility under its law. For example, if the individual has earned wages in multiple states, the individual may choose in which state to file the claim. Because of the potential of establishing more than one benefit year in more than one state, Federal regulations stipulate that employment and wages transferred from one state to a second state for use in establishing a combined wage claim in that second "paying" state cannot be used again to establish monetary eligibility. The methods that states use to determine monetary eligibility vary greatly, as described in the following text.

Methods of Qualifying

Multiple of High-Quarter Wages

Under this method, individuals must earn a certain dollar amount in the quarter with the highest earnings of their base period. Individuals must also earn total base-period wages that are a multiple of the high-quarter wages (typically 1½). For example, if an individual earns $5,000 in the high quarter, the individual must earn another $2,500 in the rest of the base period. States require earnings in more than one quarter to minimize the likelihood that individuals with high earnings in only one quarter receive benefits.

Multiple of Weekly Benefit Amount

Under this method, the state first computes the individual's weekly benefit amount. The individual must have earned an amount equal to or greater than a specified multiple of the weekly benefit amount during the base period. For example, if an individual's weekly benefit amount is $100, in a state requiring earnings equal to 40 times the weekly benefit amount, the individual will need base-period earnings of $4,000. Most states also require wages in at least two quarters. Some states have weighted schedules that require varying multiples for varying weekly benefits.

Flat Qualifying Amount

States using this method require a certain dollar amount of total wages to be earned during the base period. This method is often used by states with an annual wage requirement for determining the weekly benefit and by some states with a high-quarter-wage/weekly benefit requirement.

Weeks/Hours of Employment

Under this method, the individual must have worked a certain number of weeks/hours at a certain weekly/hourly wage.

The following table provides information on the qualifying formulas used by the states, and the minimum wages needed to qualify for benefits in each state. The amounts displayed assume level wage earnings throughout the claimant's base period.

Table 3-3. Base period wage and employment requirements for benefits

State	Qualifying Formula: Wages or Employment	Minimum Wages Needed to Qualify:	
		High Quarter	Base Period
AL	1½ x HQW in BP	N/A	>$2,314 in 2 HQs
AK	$2,500 flat amount and wages in 2 quarters of BP, at least $250 outside HQ	N/A	$2,500
AZ	1½ x HQW in BP and 390 x minimum wage in effect ($4,290) in one quarter; alternative flat-amount requirement - wages in 2 quarters of BP, wages in 1 quarter sufficient to qualify for the maximum WBA, and total BPW ≥ the taxable wage base ($7,000)	$4,290	$6,435
AR	35 x WBA in BP and wages in 2 quarters of BP	N/A	$2,835
CA	$1,300 in HQ; alternatively $900 in HQ with BPW = 1¼ x HQ	$900	$1,125

Table 3-3. (Continued)

State	Qualifying Formula: Wages or Employment	Minimum Wages Needed to Qualify:	
		High Quarter	Base Period
CO	40 x WBA or $2,500 in BP, whichever is greater	$1,084 in 2 HQs	$2,500
CT	40 x WBA in BP	N/A	$600
DE	36 x WBA in BP; if insufficient BPW, but (36 x WBA) - BPW ≤ $180, eligible for reduced WBA	N/A	$720
DC	$1,300 in one quarter, $1,950 in 2 quarters, and 1½ x HQW in BP or within $70 of meeting the 1½ HQW in BP requirement	$1,300	$1,950 in 2 HQs
FL	1½ x HQW in BP; minimum of $3,400 in BP	N/A	$3,400
GA	1½ x HQW in BP; alternatively 1/21 HQW for WBA with 40 x WBA in BP and wages in 2 quarters	$924	$1,760 in 2 HQs
HI	26 x WBA in BP and wages in 2 quarters	N/A	$130
ID	1¼ x HQW in BP and $1,872 in HQW; minimum HQW, determined on January 1, must equal 50% of state minimum wage multiplied by 520 hours (rounded to the next lower multiple of the weekly benefit multiplier)	$1,872	$2,340
IL	$1,600 flat amount with $440 outside HQ	N/A	$1,600
IN	1½ x HQW in BP, not less than $4,200 in BP, and wages totaling at least $2,500 in last 2 quarters of BP	N/A	$4,200
IA	1¼ x HQW in BP (HQW must equal 3.5% of the statewide AAW) and ½ HQW in another quarter	$1,610	$2,410
KS	30 x WBA in BP and wages in 2 quarters	$2,777	$3,540
KY	1½ x HQW in BP, 8 x WBA in last 2 quarters of BP, $1,500 in a quarter	N/A	$3,230
LA	1½ x HQW in BP	$800	$1,200
ME	2 x AWW in each of 2 different quarters and total wages of 6 x AWW in BP	$1,659 in each of 2 Qtrs	$4,976
MD	Wages in 2 quarters equal 1½ x $1,200 (established by schedule in law) and >$1,176 in HQ; alternate eligibility for a lower WBA can be established if BP wages meet a specified amount on the wage schedule	>$1,176	$1,800
MA	30 x WBA in BP and $4,700 minimum in BP	N/A	$4,700

State	Qualifying Formula: Wages or Employment	Minimum Wages Needed to Qualify:	
		High Quarter	Base Period
MI	1½ x HQW in BP and wages in 1 quarter equal to \$3,589; alternatively BPW equal to 20 times the state AWW and wages in 2 quarters	\$3,589	\$5,384
MN	5.3 percent of state AAW rounded to the lower \$100	N/A	\$2,900
MS	40 x WBA in BP, 26 x minimum WBA in HQ and wages in 2 quarters	\$780	\$1,200
MO	1½ x HQW in BP and \$1,500 in one quarter; alternatively wages in 2 quarters and BPW of 1½ x maximum taxable wage base for that year	\$1,500	\$2,250
MT	1½ x HQW in BP with total BP wages ≥7% of the AAW; alternatively total BPW ≥ 50% of AAW	\$1,926	\$2,888
NE	\$4,246 in BP, \$1,850 in HQ, \$800 in another quarter	\$1,850	\$4,246
NV	1½ x HQW in BP and \$400 in HQ; alternatively wages in 3 of the 4 quarters in the BP and \$400 in HQ	\$400	\$600
NH	\$1,400 in each of 2 quarters	\$1,400	\$2,800
NJ	20 base weeks (base week is 20% of state AWW); alternatively 1,000 times the state minimum hourly wage (\$8,500)	N/A	\$3,440
NM	Wages in 2 quarters	\$1,993	\$1,994
NY	1½ x HQW in BP; HQW equal to 221 x state minimum wage, rounded to the next lower \$100 increment	\$2,400	\$3,600
NC	6 x AWW in BP and wages in last 2 quarters	N/A	\$780 in last 2 Qtrs
ND	1½ x HQW in BP	N/A	\$2,795 in 2½ Qtrs
OH	20 weeks employment with wages in each week of at least 27.5% of the state AWW in BP and wages in 2 quarters	N/A	\$5,220
OK	1½ x HQW in BP and \$1,500 in BP; alternatively flat-amount requirement ≥\$17,600 in BP (100% state taxable wage base)	N/A	\$1,500

Table 3-3. (Continued)

State	Qualifying Formula: Wages or Employment	Minimum Wages Needed to Qualify:	
		High Quarter	Base Period
OR	1½ x HQW in BP and $1,000 in BP; alternatively flat-amount requirement 500 hours of employment in BP	$667	$1,000
PA	18 credit weeks and at least 37% BPW outside of HQ	$1,688	$2,718
PR	40 x WBA in BP and wages in 2 quarters; if fail to meet qualifying requirement for WBA computed on HQW but do meet qualifying requirement for next lower bracket, eligible for lower WBA, unlimited step-down provision; PR has a flat qualifying requirement for agricultural workers; individual's annual salary is used for agricultural workers	$77	$280
RI	1½ x HQW in BP and 200 x minimum hourly wage in 1 quarter and BP wages at least 400 x the minimum hourly wage; alternatively $1,200 x minimum hourly wage in BP	$2,100	$4,200
SC	1½ x HQW in BP and $1,092 HQW and $4,455 BPW	$1,092	$4,455
SD	$728 in HQ and 20 x WBA outside HQ	$728	$1,288
TN	40 x WBA in BP and lesser of 6 x WBA or $900 outside HQ	>$780 in each of 2 Qtrs	>$1,560 in 2 HQs
TX	37 x WBA in BP and wages in 2 quarters	N/A	$2,516
UT	1½ x HQW in BP (BPW must be 8% of state average fiscal year wages in BP, rounded to the higher $100)	$2,534	$3,800
VT	1.4 x HQW in BP (HQW will be adjusted by a percentage increase equal to the percentage increase in the state minimum wage for the prior year)	$2,734	$3,828
VA	$3,000 in 2 highest quarters of BP	N/A	$3,000 in 2 HQs
VI	1½ x HQW in BP and $858 in HQ; alternatively flat-amount requirement $858 in HQW and 39 x WBA in BP	$858	$1,287
WA	680 hours employment in BP and wages in BP or alternate BP	N/A	N/A

State	Qualifying Formula: Wages or Employment	Minimum Wages Needed to Qualify:	
		High Quarter	Base Period
WV	$2,200 flat amount and wages in 2 quarters	N/A	$2,200
WI	35 x WBA in BP with 4 x WBA outside HQ and wages in at least 2 quarters	$1,350	$1,890
WY	1.4 x HQW in BP (BPW must be ≥8% of statewide AAW rounded down to lower $50 increment – minimum HQW requirement calculated by dividing BPW by 4 and rounded down to the lower $50 increment)	$800	$3,350

GENERAL NOTE: Additional monetary requirements in some state laws result in minimum high-quarter and/or base-period wages that are higher than what the qualifying formula alone would require.

Qualifying for a Second Benefit Year

Since the standard base period established by states' laws results in a significant lag between the end of the base period and the establishment of a benefit year, an individual could conceivably use lag-period wages and employment to qualify for two consecutive benefit years during one long unemployment spell (after benefits are exhausted and the first benefit year ended). As a result, all states require individuals to earn wages after the beginning of the first benefit year. In many states, the amount an individual must earn is a multiple of the weekly benefit amount. A few states require an individual to earn wages sufficient to meet the minimum qualifying requirement. In addition, some states specify that the wages needed to requalify must be earned in covered employment.

Table 3-4. Wages needed to establish new benefit year (amount times WBA unless indicated)

State	Subsequent to Beginning of Preceding Benefit Year	Subsequent to Date of Last Valid Claim	Other	Wages Must Be in Insured Work	State	Subsequent to Beginning of Preceding Benefit Year	Subsequent to Date of Last Valid Claim	Other	Wages Must Be in Insured Work
AL	8			X	AK	8			
AZ	8				AR	8			X
CA			Equivalent qualifying wages as in preceding BY		CO	$2,000			
CT	5 or $300, whichever is greater			X	DE		10		X
DC	10				FL	3			
GA	10			X	HI	5			X
ID	6; wages must be in bona fide work				IL	3			
IN	8			X	IA	8			X
KS	8			X	KY	5			
LA	6; or 3/13th of HQW, whichever is less			X	ME	8			X
MD	10			X	MA	3			

State	Subsequent to Beginning of Preceding Benefit Year	Subsequent to Date of Last Valid Claim	Other	Wages Must Be in Insured Work	State	Subsequent to Beginning of Preceding Benefit Year	Subsequent to Date of Last Valid Claim	Other	Wages Must Be in Insured Work
MI	5				MN	5.3% AAW			X
MS	8			X	MO		5; 10 x WBA in non-covered work		X
MT	6; or 3/13th of HQW, whichever is less			X	NE			Vages in nsured work at east 6 x WBA	X
NV	3				NH	$700 during or subsequent to benefit year			X
NJ	4 weeks of employment and at least 6 x WBA in wages				NM	5			
NY	10				NC	10			X
ND		101		X	OH	3 x AWW and covered employment in 6 weeks			X
OK	10			X	OR	6			X
PA	6				PR	3; for at least one CQ, but not < $50			X

Table 3-4. (Continued)

State	Subsequent to Beginning of Preceding Benefit Year	Subsequent to Date of Last Valid Claim	Other	Wages Must Be in Insured Work	State	Subsequent to Beginning of Preceding Benefit Year	Subsequent to Date of Last Valid Claim	Other	Wages Must Be in Insured Work
RI	80 x the minimum hourly wage			X	SC	8			Insured work; must be with a single employer
SD	4			X	TN	5			X
TX	6				UT	6			X
VT	4			X	VA	30 days or 240 hours of work2			X
VI	6				WA	6			
WV	8			X	WI	8			X
WY	8								

[1] Does not apply to employment by a partnership, corporation, or limited liability company if, at the time claim is filed, ownership interest has been ceded.

[2] Must be with one employer.

Weekly Benefit Amount

After determining if an individual has sufficient wages and/or employment to qualify for benefits, it is necessary to determine the weekly benefit amount, that is, the amount payable for a week of total unemployment. As previously mentioned, UI is intended to provide partial wage replacement. For this reason, all individuals do not receive the same benefit amount. Some states replace approximately 50% of individuals' lost wages up to a certain limit (usually the average weekly wage in the state). As a result, states tend to replace a higher percentage of low-wage individuals' income than they do for high-wage individuals. Several states provide dependents' allowances. All states round weekly benefits to an even dollar amount.

States determine eligibility for benefits weekly (generally, Sunday through the following Saturday). In many states, the claim week is adjusted to coincide with the employer's payroll week when an individual files a benefit claim for partial unemployment.

Methods of Computing Weekly Benefits

As with qualifying wages, states utilize a variety of methods to determine an individual's weekly benefit amount.

High-Quarter Method

Slightly more than half of the states determine the weekly benefit amount by using the quarter in the base period with the most wages. This quarter is viewed as the period most nearly reflecting full- time work for the individual. By dividing this amount by 13 (the number of weeks in a calendar quarter) the average weekly wage is calculated. Based on the percentage of the weekly wage the state intends to replace, the weekly wage is divided and the weekly benefit amount is calculated. For example, an individual who earns $2,600 in the high quarter has an average weekly wage of $200 a week ($2,600 divided by 13). If the state replaces ½ of the average weekly earnings, the weekly benefit amount is $100. To simplify the calculations, states determine the "overall" multiple of the high-quarter wages to determine the weekly benefit amount. In the previous example, it would be 1/26 (1/13 times ½). The most common multiple used by states is 1/26. Other states that use high-quarter wages calculate the benefit as a percentage of high-quarter wages.

Since even the quarter of highest earnings may include some unemployment, some states use a fraction generating a higher weekly benefit (e.g., 1/23). Some states use a weighted schedule, which gives a greater proportion of the high-quarter wages to lower-paid individuals than to those earning more.

Multi-Quarter Method

Several states compute the weekly benefit amount as a multiple of the total or average quarterly wages paid in more than one quarter. This approach is viewed as being more likely to reflect an individual's usual full-time employment pattern since it surveys a greater period of time rather than just focusing on the quarter with highest earnings.

Annual-Wage Method

Under this method the weekly benefit is calculated as a percentage of annual wages in the base period. This approach reflects the view that annual wages determine the individual's standard of living. Some states using this method utilize a weighted schedule, which gives a larger proportion of annual wages to lower-paid individuals to determine their weekly benefit amount, other states use a flat percentage.

Weekly-Wage Method

Under this method the weekly benefit is calculated as a percentage of the individual's average weekly wages in the base period.

The following table provides information on how states calculate weekly benefit amounts, what the minimum and maximum weekly benefit amounts are, and the wages required to be eligible for the maximum weekly benefit amounts. The amounts displayed assume level wage earnings throughout the claimant's base period.

Table 3-5. Weekly benefit amounts

State	Method of Calculating and Formula	Rounding to	Weekly Benefit Amount		Minimum Wages Required for Maximum WBA	
			Minimum[1]	Maximum[1]	High quarter	Base period
AL	MQ 1/26 of average wages in 2 high quarters	Higher $	$45	$265	N/A	$13,754 in 2 quarters
AK	AW 0.9% - 2.2% BP wages + DA (see table in law)	Nearest $	$56 - $128	$370 - $442	N/A	$42,000
AZ	HQ 1/25	Nearest $	$172	$240	$5,988	$8,982
AR	MQ 1/26 of average in 4 quarters	Lower $	$81	$451	N/A	$46,904
CA	HQ 1/23-1/26 (if HQW <$1,833, see table in law; otherwise, 1/26 HQW)	Higher $	$40	$450	>$11,674	>$11,674
CO	HQ/WW Higher of: (1) 60% of 1/26 of 2 highest consecutive quarters, capped by 50% of average weekly earnings (low formula); or (2) 50% of 1/52 BP earnings, capped by 55% of average weekly earnings (high formula)	Lower $	$25	$542 (low formula) $597 (high formula)	$11,744 (low formula) N/A (high formula)	$23,487 in 2 quarters (low formula) $62,088 (high formula)
CT	MQ/HQ 1/26 of the average of the 2HQs + DA; for construction workers, 1/26 of HQW + DA	Lower $	$15 - $30	$631 - $706	$16,406 in each of 2 quarters	$32,812 in 2 quarters
DE	MQ 1/46 of wages earned in highest 2 quarters	Lower $	$20	$330	N/A	$15,180 in 2 quarters

Table 3-5. (Continued)

State	Method of Calculating and Formula	Rounding to	Weekly Benefit Amount		Minimum Wages Required for Maximum WBA	
			Minimum[1]	Maximum[1]	High quarter	Base period
DC	HQ 1/26	Lower $	$50	$438	$11,388	$17,082
FL	HQ 1/26	Lower $	$32	$275	$7,150	$10,725
GA	MQ 1/42 wages in 2 HQs; computed as 1/21 of HQW when alternative qualifying wages are used (Note: If individual would qualify for $27 - $44, the claimant's WBA is $44.)	Lower $	$44	$330	N/A	$13,860 in 2 quarters
HI	HQ 1/21	Higher $	$5	$630	$13,210	$16,380
ID	HQ 1/26	Lower $	$72	$414	$10,764	$13,455
IL	MQ 47% of the claimant's wages in highest 2 quarters divided by 26 + DA	Higher $	$51 - $77	$471 - $648	N/A	$26,013 in 2 quarters
IN	WW 47% of AWW	Lower $	$37	$390	N/A	$43,149
IA	HQ 1/19 (4 or more dependents) - 1/23 (no dependents)	Lower $	$70 - $84	$467 - $573	$10,741	$16,112
KS	HQ 4.25%	Lower $	$118	$474	$11,153	$14,220
KY	AW 1.1923% BPW	Nearest $	$39	$502	N/A	$42,062

State	Method of Calculating and Formula	Rounding to	Weekly Benefit Amount		Minimum Wages Required for Maximum WBA	
			Minimum[1]	Maximum[1]	High quarter	Base period
LA2	MQ 1/25 of the average wages in 4 quarters of BP x 1.05 x a multiple ranging from 1.03 to 1.32	Lower $	$10	$221 to $284	N/A	$22,100 to $28,400
ME	MQ 1/22 of the average of the 2 HQs + DA (see table in law)	Lower $	$75 - $112	$431 - $646	N/A	$18,964 in 2 quarters
MD	HQ 1/24 + DA (see table in law)	Higher $	$50 - $90	$430 same with or without DA	>$10,296	$15,480
MA	MQ 50% of 1/26 of total wages in 2 HQs up to 57.5% of state AWW	Lower $	$45 - $67	$795 - $1,192	N/A	$41,340 in 2 high quarters
MI	HQ 4.1% + DA	Lower $	$147 - $177	$362 same with or without DA	$8,830	$13,245
MN	HQ/WW The higher of 50% of 1/52 BPW up to 66⅔% of the state AWW, or 50% of 1/13 HQ up to 43% of the state's AWW	Lower $	$28	$462 (based on HQW) $717 (based on BPW)	$12,012 (based on HQW) N/A (based on BPW)	$12,012 (based on HQW) $74,568 (based on BPW)
MS	HQ 1/26	Lower $	$30	$235	$6,110	$9,400
MO	MQ 4.0% of the average of the 2 HQs	Lower $	$35	$320	N/A	$16,000 in 2 quarters
MT	AW/MQ 1.0% of BPW or 1.9% of wages in the 2 HQs	Lower $	$150	$527	N/A	$27,737 in 2 quarters
NE	WW ½ of AWW, may not exceed ½ of state AWW	Lower even $	$70	$426	$11,076	$11,876

Table 3-5. (Continued)

State	Method of Calculating and Formula	Rounding to	Weekly Benefit Amount		Minimum Wages Required for Maximum WBA	
			Minimum[1]	Maximum[1]	High quarter	Base period
NV	HQ 1/25	Lower $	$16	$450	$11,250	$16,875
NH	AW 1.0% - 1.1% of BPW (see table in law)	Nearest $	$32	$427	N/A	$41,500
NJ	WW 60% (base weeks' wages/number of base weeks) + DA	Lower $	$103 - $118	$696 same with or without DA	N/A	$23,200 in 20 weeks
NM	WW 53½% of AWW in HQ + DA; wages in 2 quarters of BP	Lower $	$82 - $123	$442 - $492	$10,741	$10,742
NY	HQ/MQ Wages in 4 quarters - 1/26 HQW or 1/25 if HQW ≤$3,575 Wages in 2 or 3 quarters - 1/26 average of the highest 2 quarters, unless the HQW is ≤$4,000 but >$3,575 then 1/26 HQW, and if HQW is ≤$3,575 then 1/25 HQW	Lower $	$100	$450	$11,700	$17,550
NC	MQ 1/52 of last 2 quarters	Lower $	$15	$350	N/A	$18,200 in last 2 quarters
ND	MQ 1/65 of (total wages earned in highest 2 quarters and ½ of total wages in third highest quarter)	Lower $	$43	$595	N/A	$38,675 In 2.5 quarters

State	Method of Calculating and Formula	Rounding to	Weekly Benefit Amount		Minimum Wages Required for Maximum WBA	
			Minimum[1]	Maximum[1]	High quarter	Base period
OH	WW 50% (wages in qualified weeks in BP / number of such weeks) + DA	Lower $	$130	$443 - $598	N/A	$17,720 in 20 weeks
OK	HQ 1/23	Lower $	$16	$520	$11,960	$17,940
OR	AW 1.25% BP wages	Lower $	$146	$624	N/A	$49,920
PA	HQ (4% HQW + 2) x 0.98 + DA (see table in law)	Lower $	$68 - $76	$561 - $569	$14,263	$22,641
PR	HQ 1/11 - 1/26	Lower $	$7	$133	$3,458	$5,320
RI	MQ 3.85% of average of 2 highest quarter wages + DA	Lower $	$53 - $103	$566 - $707	N/A	$29,404 2 quarters
SC	WW 50% AWW in HQ	Lower $	$42	$326	$8,476	$12,714
SD	HQ 1/26	Lower $	$28	$402	$10,452	$18,492
TN	MQ 1/26 of average of 2 HQs (see table in law)	Lower $	$30	$275	N/A	>$14,300 in 2 quarters
TX	HQ 1/25	Nearest $	$68	$507	$12,663	$18,741
UT	HQ 1/26 minus $5	Lower $	$31	$560	$14,690	$22,035
VT	MQ Wages in the 2 highest quarters divided by 45	Lower $	$68	$498	N/A	$22,410 in 2 quarters

Table 3-5. (Continued)

State	Method of Calculating and Formula	Rounding to	Weekly Benefit Amount		Minimum Wages Required for Maximum WBA	
			Minimum[1]	Maximum[1]	High quarter	Base period
VA	MQ 1/50 of 2 HQs (see table in law)	Lower $	$60	$378	N/A	>$18,900 in 2 quarters
VI	HQ 1/26	Lower $	$33	$552	$14,352	$21,528
WA	MQ 3.85% of average of 2 HQs	Lower $	$178	$749	N/A	$38,910 in 2 quarters
WV	AW 55% of 1/52 of median wages in individual's wage class (see table in law)	Lower $	$24	$424	N/A	$40,150
WI	HQ 4.0%	Lower $	$54	$370	$9,250	$12,950
WY	HQ 4.0%	Lower $	$35	$489	$12,225	$17,115

KEY: HQ = High Quarter Formula; MQ = Multi-Quarter Formula; AW = Annual Wage Formula; WW = Average Weekly Wage Formula; DA = Dependents' Allowances.

GENERAL NOTE: Since the high quarter and base period wage requirements for the minimum weekly benefit amount are the same as the wage and employment requirements to qualify for benefits, they are not repeated in this table. (See Table 3-3.) Additionally, in states where the benefit entitlement is calculated using multi-quarter, annual wage, or average weekly wage formulas, the high-quarter cell is shown as N/A as no specific level of wages is required in the high quarter pursuant to state law.

[1] When 2 WBAs are listed, higher figure includes DA. Higher figure for minimum and maximum WBAs includes DA for maximum number of dependents.

[2] Depending upon the procedure in place in a given year, different benefit multipliers are utilized. As a result, the MWBA varies from year to year and similarly the amount of BPWs necessary to receive the MWBA fluctuates.

Table 3-6. States with automatic adjustment to benefit amounts

State	Method of Computation					Percentage of State AWW		Effective Date Of New Amounts
	Annually as % of AWW in Covered Employment in:			Semiannually as % of AWW in Covered Employment in:				
	Preceding CY	12 Months Ending March 31	12 Months Ending June 30	12 Months Ending 6 Months Before Effective Date	All Industries In State	Maximum	Minimum	
AR	X					66⅔% (high formula)	12% (low formula)	July 1
CO					X	55%		July 1
CT			X			50%		1st Sunday in October
DC		X				66⅔%		January 1
HI			X			70%		January 1
ID	X					Percentage varies (52% - 60%) depending upon the base tax rate in a given year		January 1
IL	X					47%; for claimants with dependents, maximum is limited to 65.2% of state's AWW, which is based on percentage changes from year to year		January 1
IA	X					53% for claimants with no dependents; for claimants with dependents, ranges from 55% to 65%		1st Sunday in July
KS	X					60%	25% of max WBA	July 1

Table 3-6. (Continued)

State	Method of Computation					Percentage of State AWW		Effective Date Of New Amounts
	Annually as % of AWW in Covered Employment in:			Semiannually as % of AWW in Covered Employment in:				
	Preceding CY	12 Months Ending March 31	12 Months Ending June 30	12 Months Ending 6 Months Before Effective Date	All Industries In State	Maximum	Minimum	
KY	X					62%; cannot increase in any year when tax schedule increases from previous year (year-to-year increases limited depending on fund balance)		July 1
LA		X				66⅔%		September 1
ME	X					52%		June 1
MA		X				57½%		1st Sunday in October
MN	X					Higher of 50% of the individual's AWW in the BP to a maximum of 66⅔% of the state AWW; or 50% of the individual's AWW during the HQ to a maximum of 43% of the state AWW		Last Sunday in October
MT	X					67½%	20%	July 1
NV	X					50%		July 1
NJ	X					56⅔%		January 1
NM			X			53½%	10%	1st Sunday in January
NC	X					66⅔%		August 1

State	Method of Computation					Percentage of State AWW		Effective Date Of New Amounts
	Annually as % of AWW in Covered Employment in:			Semiannually as % of AWW in Covered Employment in:				
	Preceding CY	12 Months Ending March 31	12 Months Ending June 30	12 Months Ending 6 Months Before Effective Date	All Industries In State	Maximum	Minimum	
ND	X					62%; 65% of state AWW if trust fund reserves on Oct. 1 are ≥ the required amount and the state's average contribution rate is < the nationwide average for the preceding year		1st Sunday in July
OH			X			Percentage used is not specified in law		1st Sunday in January
OK	X					The greater of $197 or 60%, 57.7%, 55%, 52½% or 50% of state AWW of the second preceding CY, depending on the condition of the fund		July 1
OR	X					64%	15%	Week of July 4
PA			X1			66⅔%		January 1
PR	X					50%		July 1
RI	X					57.7%		July 1
SC	X					66⅔%		July 1
SD	X					50%		July 1
TX	X					47.6%	7.6%	October 1
UT			X			62½% minus $5		January 1
VT	X					Percentage not specified by law		1st Sunday in July

Table 3-6. (Continued)

State	Method of Computation					Percentage of State AWW		Effective Date Of New Amounts
	Annually as % of AWW in Covered Employment in:			Semiannually as % of AWW in Covered Employment in:				
	Preceding CY	12 Months Ending March 31	12 Months Ending June 30	12 Months Ending 6 Months Before Effective Date	All Industries In State	Maximum	Minimum	
VI			X			65%		January 1
WA	X					63%	15%	1st Sunday in July
WV	X					66⅔%		July 1
WY	X					55%	4%	1st Sunday in July

[1] State AWW computed using 36-month period.

Automatic Adjustments to Weekly Benefit Amounts

In those states where UI is intended to replace a specific percent of wages up to a fixed percent of the state's average weekly wage, the calculation of benefit entitlement is determined by the state's average weekly wage. Because wages increase, states recalculate the average weekly wage periodically to update the benefit schedule and continue to replace the desired percentage of an individual's lost wages. The maximum weekly benefit amount is usually more than 50 percent of the average weekly wage in covered employment within the state during a recent 1-year period. In most states, the minimum weekly benefit is an amount specified in the law. However, some states' laws link the minimum weekly benefit amount with the states' average weekly wage as well. The following table includes states with automatic adjustments to benefit amounts.

Waiting Period

Individuals who are otherwise eligible for benefits must first serve a waiting period in most states. In most states, the waiting period requirement for weeks of partial unemployment is the same as for weeks of total unemployment. The waiting period is served in or with respect to a particular benefit year. Special provisions may exist for successive benefit years. When an individual, after intervening employment, has an additional spell of unemployment that continues beyond the end of the first benefit year, the individual may not have to serve another waiting week if ~~he is~~ monetarily eligible for benefits in the second year.

Table 3-7. State initial waiting periods

State	Duration (in weeks)[1]	Becomes Compensable After:	May Be Waived Under These Circumstances
AL	1		
AK	1		
AZ	1		
AR	1		
CA	1[2]		During a state of war emergency or a state of emergency if compliance with the waiting period requirement would prevent, hinder, or delay the mitigation of the effects of a state of emergency (e.g., natural disaster)
CO	1		
CT	No waiting period		
DE	1		
DC	1		
FL	1		
GA	No waiting period		
HI	1		
ID	1		
IL	1		
IN	1[3]		For individuals who become unemployed due to employer terminating business operations within the state, declaring bankruptcy, or initiating a workforce reduction pursuant to the Federal WARN Act
IA	No waiting period		
KS	1		For individuals who become unemployed due to employer terminating business operations within the state, the employer declaring bankruptcy, or a workforce reduction that is subject to the Federal WARN Act

State	Duration (in weeks)[1]	Becomes Compensable After:	May Be Waived Under These Circumstances
KY	1	The remaining balance on claim is equal to or less than compensable amount for waiting week	
LA	1		
ME	1		
MD	No waiting period		
MA	1		No waivers though authority exists and has been used before
MI	No waiting period		
MN	1		If the individual would have been entitled to DUA but has established benefit account
MS	1		In counties or areas identified for individual assistance, if the President declares a major disaster in accordance with Stafford Act
MO	1	The remaining balance on claim is equal to or less than compensable amount for waiting week	
MT	1		
NE	1		
NV	No waiting period		
NH	1		
NJ	No waiting period		
NM	1		Natural disaster, extended benefit program
NY	1		At the direction of the Governor
NC	1		
ND	1		
OH	1		
OK	1		
OR	1		

Table 3-7. (Continued)

State	Duration (in weeks)[1]	Becomes Compensable After:	May Be Waived Under These Circumstances
PA	1		
PR	1		
RI	1		For individuals who become unemployed due to a natural disaster or state of emergency
SC	1		
SD	1		
TN	1	3 consecutive weeks of compensable unemployment immediately following a waiting period	
TX	1[3]	Receipt of benefits equaling 3 x WBA	
UT	1		If Department approval for training is granted for the first eligible week of the claim
VA	1		For an individual whose unemployment was caused by his employer terminating operations, closing its business, or declaring bankruptcy without paying the final wages earned; authorized by the Governor under an executive order
VI	1[3]		
WA	1		
WV	1		
WI	1		
WY	No waiting period		

[1] For total unemployment, partial unemployment, or in consecutive benefit years unless otherwise noted.

[2] One week waiting period is deferred if claimant is in continued claim status from a prior year's claim. The one-week waiting period must be served later in the new benefit year if there is an interruption of UI payments for one or more weeks. Also, the 1-week waiting period credit for the new benefit year may be served in the last week of the prior benefit year if the claim was exhausted prior to the last week of that benefit year.

[3] No waiting period required for new/consecutive benefit year.

Benefits for Partial Unemployment

Often, instead of being laid off, individuals may have their hours reduced during an economic downturn.

Unemployed individuals may also find short-term work while looking for a permanent, full-time job. These circumstances characterize partial unemployment. The UI system is set up to permit benefit receipt by these individuals as long as they meet all eligibility requirements. However, the weekly benefit amount payable differs.

A week of total unemployment is commonly defined as a week in which the individual performs no work and with which remuneration is not payable. In Puerto Rico, an individual is deemed totally unemployed if earnings from self-employment are less than 1½ times the weekly benefit amount or if no service is performed for a working period of 32 hours or more in a week. In a few states, an individual is considered totally unemployed in a week even though certain small amounts of wages are earned. In most states, an individual is partially unemployed in a week of less than full-time work and earnings of less than the weekly benefit amount. In some states, an individual is partially unemployed in a week of less than full-time work when less than the weekly benefit amount plus an allowance is earned, either from odd-job earnings or from any source as indicated in the following table.

The individual's benefit will generally equal the difference between the weekly benefit amount and earnings. All states disregard some earnings as an incentive to take part-time or short-term work.

When determining monetary entitlement to benefits, the state usually specifies a maximum dollar amount that can be received, usually equal to a specified number of weeks of benefits for total unemployment multiplied by the weekly benefit amount for total unemployment or a percentage of base period wages.

Consequently, a partially unemployed individual may draw benefits for a greater number of weeks than a totally unemployed individual.

Table 3-8. Partial unemployment and earnings disregarded when determining weekly benefit

State	Definition of Partial Unemployment - Week of Less Than Full-Time Work if Earnings are Less Than:	Earnings Disregarded in Computing Weekly Benefit for Partial Unemployment	State	Definition of Partial Unemployment - Week of Less Than Full-Time Work if Earnings are Less Than:	Earnings Disregarded in Computing Weekly Benefit for Partial Unemployment
AL	WBA	⅓ WBA	AK	1⅓ x WBA + $50	$50 and ¼ wages over $50
AZ	WBA	$30	AR	WBA + 40% WBA	40% WBA
CA	WBA	Greater of $25 or ¼ of wages	CO	WBA	¼ WBA
CT	1½ + basic WBA	⅓ wages; includes holiday pay in the remuneration for determining partial benefits	DE	WBA + greater of $10 or ½ WBA	Greater of $10 or ½ WBA
DC	WBA + $20	⅓ of wages + $50	FL	WBA	8 x Federal hourly minimum wage
GA	WBA	$50; excludes payments for jury service	HI	WBA	$150
ID	1½ WBA	½ WBA	IL	WBA	½ WBA
IN	WBA	Greater of $3 or 20% WBA from other than base-period employers; excludes payments for jury service	IA	WBA + $15	¼ WBA; excludes payments for jury service
KS	WBA	¼ WBA	KY	1¼ x WBA	20% wages
LA	WBA	Lesser of ½ WBA or $50	ME	WBA + $5	$100
MD	Augmented WBA	$50	MA	WBA	⅓ WBA; earnings plus WBA may not equal or exceed the individual's AWW

State	Definition of Partial Unemployment - Week of Less Than Full-Time Work if Earnings are Less Than:	Earnings Disregarded in Computing Weekly Benefit for Partial Unemployment	State	Definition of Partial Unemployment - Week of Less Than Full-Time Work if Earnings are Less Than:	Earnings Disregarded in Computing Weekly Benefit for Partial Unemployment
MI	1.6 x WBA	For each $1 earned, WBA reduced by 50 cents (benefits and earnings cannot exceed 1 3/5 WBA); earnings above 1.6 x WBA result in dollar-for-dollar reduction in WBA; if the resulting WBA is zero, weeks of benefits payable reduced by 1 week; excludes wages for on-call or training services as a volunteer firefighter if wages are <$10,000	MN	WBA	For each $1 earned, WBA reduced by 50 cents; no deduction for jury pay and wages earned for services performed in National Guard and military reserve, and as a volunteer firefighter or in ambulance services
MS	WBA	$40	MO	WBA + $20 or 20%WBA, whichever is greater	$20 or 20% WBA, whichever is greater; excludes termination pay, severance pay, and wages from service in the organized militia for training or authorized duty from benefit computation
MT	2 x WBA	¼ WBA	NE	WBA	¼ WBA
NV	WBA	¼ wages	NH	WBA	30% WBA
NJ	WBA + greater of $5 or 20% WBA	Greater of $5 or 20% WBA	NM	WBA	20%WBA; excludes payments for jury service

Table 3-8. (Continued)

State	Definition of Partial Unemployment - Week of Less Than Full-Time Work if Earnings are Less Than:	Earnings Disregarded in Computing Weekly Benefit for Partial Unemployment	State	Definition of Partial Unemployment - Week of Less Than Full-Time Work if Earnings are Less Than:	Earnings Disregarded in Computing Weekly Benefit for Partial Unemployment
NY	Benefits paid at the rate of ¼ WBA for each effective day within a week beginning on Monday (effective day defined as 4th and each subsequent day of total unemployment in a week in which claimant earns not more than $300)		NC	Week of less than 3 customary scheduled full-time days	20% WBA
ND	WBA	60% WBA	OH	WBA	20% WBA
OK	WBA + $100	$100	OR	WBA	Greater of $120 or ⅓ WBA
PA	WBA + 40% WBA	Greater of $21 or 30% WBA	PR	1½ x WBA; week in which wages or remuneration from self-employment are less than 1½ times claimant's WBA or the claimant performs no service for a working period of 32 hours or more in a week	WBA
RI1	Basic WBA	20% WBA	SC	WBA	¼ WBA
SD	WBA	¼ wages over $25	TN	WBA	Greater of $50 or ¼ WBA
TX	WBA + greater of $5 or ¼ WBA	Greater of $5 or ¼ WBA	UT	WBA	30% WBA
VT	WBA + $15 provided the claimant works less than 35 hours (35 hours is considered full-time employment)	½ of gross wages	VA	WBA	$50

State	Definition of Partial Unemployment - Week of Less Than Full-Time Work if Earnings are Less Than:	Earnings Disregarded in Computing Weekly Benefit for Partial Unemployment	State	Definition of Partial Unemployment - Week of Less Than Full-Time Work if Earnings are Less Than:	Earnings Disregarded in Computing Weekly Benefit for Partial Unemployment
VI	1⅓ x WBA + $15	¼ wages in excess of $15	WA	1⅓ x WBA + $5; weekly hours of work temporarily reduced by employer by no more than 60%	¼ wages over $5
WV	WBA + $61	$60	WI	Any week the individual receives any wages under $500 or performs services less than 32 hours; no individual may be eligible for partial benefits if the benefit payment is <$5	$30 plus 33% of wages in excess of $30 (excludes wages received as a volunteer firefighter or voluntary medical technician from benefit computation)
WY	WBA	½ WBA			

[1] Special provision for totally unemployed individuals who have days of employment between the end of the waiting period and the beginning of the first compensable week, and also for those who return to work prior to the end of a compensable week, provided they have been in receipt of benefits for at least 2 successive weeks of total unemployment. For each day of unemployment in such week in which work is ordinarily performed in the individual's occupation, one-fifth of the weekly benefit is paid, up to four-fifths of the weekly rate.

Most state laws provide that the benefit for a week of partial unemployment will be rounded to the nearest or the lower dollar. For example, in a state with a $30 earnings disregard and rounding to the nearest dollar, an individual with a $40 weekly benefit amount and earnings of $50.95 would receive a partial benefit of $19.

Dependents' Allowances

Although wages earned during the base period are the primary factor in determining the amount of the payment a claimant receives each week, some states' laws provide for a dependents' allowance above and beyond the basic benefit amount payable. The definition of dependent, for UI purposes, varies from state to state, as does the allowance granted. In general, a dependent must be wholly or mainly supported by the individual, or living with or receiving regular support from the individual.

Definition of Dependent

All states with dependents' allowances include children under a specified age. The intent is to include all children whom the individual is obligated to support. In most of these states, allowances may be paid on behalf of older children who are unable to work because of physical or mental disability. In some states, children are not the only dependents recognized, that is, spouses, parents, or siblings may also be included in the definition. The following table outlines the states that have dependents' allowances and their definition of a dependent.

Table 3-9. Definition of dependent

State	Dependent Child		Nonworking Dependent			Number of Dependents Fixed by BY	Maximum Number of Dependents
	Under 18 Unless Otherwise Noted[1]	Older Child Not Able to Work[1]	Spouse	Parent	Brother or Sister		
AK	Child must be unmarried; must have received more than half the cost of support from individual or be lawfully in the individual's custody at the time the individual claims the allowance[2]	X[2]					3
CT	21 if child is full-time student	X[3]	X				5
IL	X[2]	X[2]	Spouse must be currently ineligible for benefits in the State because of insufficient BPW				1
IA	X2	X[2]	No dependency allowance paid for any week in which spouse earns more than $120 in gross wages	X	X	X	4
ME	X[2]	X[2, 3]	No dependency allowance paid for any week in which spouse is employed full time and is contributing to support of dependents				X[4]
MD	X[2]	X[2]				X	5

Table 3-9. (Continued)

State	Dependent Child		Nonworking Dependent			Number of Dependents Fixed by BY	Maximum Number of Dependents
	Under 18 Unless Otherwise Noted[1]	Older Child Not Able to Work[1]	Spouse	Parent	Brother or Sister		
MA[5]	Child must be unmarried and, by interpretation, 24 if child is full- time student[2]	X[2, 3]				X	X[4]
MI	Must have received more than half the cost of support from individual for at least 90 consecutive days or for the duration of the parental relationship[2]	X[2, 3]	X	X[6]	X[7]	X	5
NJ	19; child must be unmarried; 22 if child is full-time student[2]	X[2, 3]	X			X	2[4]
NM	Child must also be unemancipated; child may be in legal custody of claimant pending adoption; court requires claimant to contribute to child's support and no one else is receiving benefits for that child						2
OH	Must have received more than half the cost of support from individual within 90 days prior to BYB (or duration of parental relationship, if less than 90 days)	X[2]	May not be claimed as dependent if average weekly income is in excess of 25% of the claimant's AWW			X	3

State	Dependent Child		Nonworking Dependent			Number of Dependents Fixed by BY	Maximum Number of Dependents
	Under 18 Unless Otherwise Noted[1]	Older Child Not Able to Work[1]	Spouse	Parent	Brother or Sister		
PA		X	X			X	2
RI	X[2]	X[2]				X	5

[1] In all states except MA, includes stepchild by statute.

[2] AK, IL, IA, ME, MD, MI, NJ, OH, and RI - adopted child is included by statute; MA - adopted child is included by interpretation, and legal guardians are included by statute.

[3] Full-time student included in CT, ME, MA, MI, and NJ.

[4] The dependent allowance is capped at 50% of the individual's WBA.

[5] Only dependents residing within the U.S. and its Territories and possessions.

[6] Parents over 65 or permanently disabled from gainful employment.

[7] Brother or sister under 18, orphaned, or whose living parents are dependents.

Amount of Weekly Dependents' Allowances

Table 3-10. Amount of weekly dependents' allowances

State	Weekly Allowance per Dependent	Weekly Dependents' Allowances Capped at:	Maximum Dependents' Allowance for Minimum Weekly Benefit	Maximum Dependents' Allowance for Maximum Weekly Benefit
AK	$24	$72	$72	$72
CT	$15	Lesser of WBA or $75	$15	$75
IL[1]	$26 - $178		$26	$178
IA	$3 - $14	Schedule $3 - $106	$14	$106
ME	$10	½ WBA	37	$215
MD	$8	$40	$40	same maximum WBA with or without dependents
MA	$25	½ WBA	$22	$397
MI	$6	$30	$30	same maximum WBA with or without dependents
NJ	7% of WBA for 1st dependent and 4% for each of the next 2 dependents		$15	same maximum WBA with or without dependents
NM	$25	½ WBA up to $50	$41	$50
OH	$1 - $155	Determined by schedule according to the dependency class	$0	$155
PA	$5; $3 for one other dependent	$8	$8	$8
RI	$15 or 5% of WBA up to 5 dependents	Greater of $50 or 25% of WBA	$50	$144

GENERAL NOTE: Full dependents' allowance (DA) given for weeks of partial benefits in all states with the following exceptions: MD and PA - Not more than 26 DA payments for dependents may be made in any one BY (individuals are partially unemployed if they earn less than the unadjusted WBA).

[1] IL - the amount shown is dependent child allowance; individuals without a child who have a non-working spouse receive a different amount (amounts are determined by applying the applicable dependent allowance rate (see state benefit chart)).

As with the definition of dependents, there is much variation among states concerning the amount of weekly dependents' allowance payable. However, there are some commonalities. For example, the allowance is ordinarily a fixed sum. In addition, all states have a limit on the total amount of dependents' allowance payable in any week in terms of dollar amount, number of dependents, percentage of weekly benefit amount. This limitation results in reductions, for some individuals, in the actual allowance per dependent or the maximum number of dependents on whose behalf allowances may be paid. In almost all states the number of dependents is fixed for the benefit year when the monetary determination on the claim is made. Likewise, in virtually all states, only one parent may draw allowances if both are receiving benefits simultaneously. Individuals who are eligible for partial benefits may draw dependents' allowances in addition to their basic benefits in most of the states providing for these allowances. They receive the full allowance for a week of partial unemployment. Consequently, the allowance for dependents may be greater than the basic benefit for partial unemployment. A few states permit dependents' allowances to be adjusted during the benefit year if an individual acquires additional dependents.

Maximum Benefit Entitlement

When states compute an individual's monetary eligibility for benefits, in addition to calculating the weekly benefit amount they determine the maximum benefit amount payable.

Table 3-11. Maximum benefit entitlement

State	Formula for Calculating Benefit Entitlement	Maximum Potential Benefits		
		Amounts[1]	Wage Credits Required	
			High quarter	Base period
AL	Lesser of 26 x WBA or ⅓ BPW	$6,890	N/A	$20,670
AK	Ratio of annual wages to HQW—from less than 1.5 to 3.5 or more	$9,620 - $11,492	N/A	$42,000
AZ	Lesser of 26 x WBA or ⅓ BPW	$6,240	$5,988	$18,720
AR	Lesser of 16 x WBA or ⅓ BPW	$7,216	N/A	$46,904
CA	Lesser of 26 x WBA or ½ BPW	$11,700	>$11,674	$23,400
CO	Lesser of 26 x WBA or ⅓ BPW	$14,092 (low formula)	$11,744 (low formula)	$42,276 (low formula)
		$15,522 (high formula)	N/A (high formula)	$62,088 (high formula)
CT	N/A: Uniform duration state	$16,406 - $18,356	$16,406 in each of 2 quarters	$32,812
DE	½ BPW	$8,580	N/A	$17,160
DC	N/A: Uniform duration state	$11,388	$11,388	$17,082
FL	25% BPW up to $6,325	$6,325	$7,150	$25,300
GA	Lesser of 14 - 20 x WBA or ¼ BPW	$6,600	N/A	$26,400
HI	N/A: Uniform duration state	$16,380	$13,210	$16,380
ID	Sliding scale of seasonally adjusted unemployment rates determines number of weeks	$10,764	$10,764	$38,321
IL	N/A: Uniform duration state	$12,246 - $16,848	N/A	$26,013 in 2 quarters
IN	Lesser of 26 x WBA or 28% of BP wage credits	$10,140	N/A	$43,149

State	Formula for Calculating Benefit Entitlement	Maximum Potential Benefits		
		Amounts[1]	Wage Credits Required	
			High quarter	Base period
IA	Lesser of 26 x WBA or ⅓ BPW; if laid off due to employer going out of business, ½ of wages in BP up to 39 weeks	$12,142 - $14,898	$10,741	$36,426
KS	Lesser of 26 x WBA or ⅓ BPW	$12,324	$11,153	$36,972
KY	Lesser of 26 x WBA or ⅓ BPW	$13,052	N/A	$42,062
LA2	N/A: Uniform duration state	$5,746 to $7,384	N/A	$22,100 to $28,400
ME	Lesser of 26 x WBA or ⅓ BPW	$11,206 - $16,796	N/A	$33,618
MD	N/A: Uniform duration state	$11,180 same maximum with or without DA	>$10,296	$15,480
MA	Lesser of 30 x WBA or 36% BPW (reduced to 26 x WBA if all of the local areas unemployment rate ≤5.1%)	$23,850 - $35,760	N/A	$66,250
MI	43% BPW	$7,240 same with or without DA	$8,830	$16,838
MN	Lesser of 26 x WBA or ⅓ BPW	$12,012 (based on HQW)	$12,012 (based on HQW)	$36,036 (based on HQW)
		$18,642 (based on BPW)	N/A (based on BPW)	$74,568 (based on BPW)
MS	Lesser of 26 x WBA or ⅓ BPW	$6,110	$6,110	$18,330
MO	Lesser of 20 x WBA or ⅓ BPW	$6,400	N/A	$19,200
MT	Ratio of BPW to HQW—from 1.0 to 3.5 or greater (see schedule in law)	$14,756	N/A	$48,540
NE	Lesser of 26 x WBA or ⅓ BPW	$11,076	$11,076	$33,228
NV	Lesser of 26 x WBA or ⅓ BPW	$11,700	$11,250	$35,100

Table 3-11. (Continued)

State	Formula for Calculating Benefit Entitlement	Maximum Potential Benefits		
		Amounts[1]	Wage Credits Required	
			High quarter	Base period
NH	N/A: Uniform duration state	$11,102	N/A	$41,500
NJ	Lesser of 26 x WBA or total number of weeks worked in BP x WBA	$18,096 same with or without DA	N/A	$30,160
NM	Lesser of 26 x WBA or 60% BPW	$11,492 - $12,792	$10,741	$19,154
NY	N/A: Uniform duration state	$11,700	$11,700	$17,550
NC	N/A: Uniform duration state	$7,000	N/A	$18,200
ND	Ratio of BPW to HQW—from 1.5 to 3.2	$15,470	N/A	$82,507
OH	Lesser of 26 x WBA or 20 x WBA+ WBA for each qualifying week in excess of 20 up to a maximum of 26 weeks	$11,518 - $15,548	N/A	$23,036 in 26 weeks
OK	Lesser of 26 x WBA or a variable percentage of the state's AAW for the 2nd preceding year depending upon the conditional factor in place	$11,300	$11,960	$17,940
OR	Lesser of 26 x WBA or ⅓ BPW	$16,224	N/A	$49,920
PA	An individual with at least 18 credit weeks is eligible for 26 weeks (a credit week is one in which claimant earned at least $116)	$14,586 - $14,794	$14,263	$22,641
PR	N/A: Uniform duration state	$3,458	$3,458	$5,320
RI	Lesser of 26 x WBA or 33% BPW	$14,716 - $18,382	N/A	$44,594
SC	Lesser of 20 x WBA or ⅓ BPW	$6,520	$8,476	$19,560
SD	Lesser of 26 x WBA or ⅓ BPW	$10,452	$10,452	$31,356
TN	Lesser of 26 x WBA or ¼ BPW	$7,150	N/A	$28,600

State	Formula for Calculating Benefit Entitlement	Maximum Potential Benefits		
		Amounts[1]	Wage Credits Required	
			High quarter	Base period
TX	Lesser of 26 x WBA or 27% BPW	$13,182	$12,663	$48,823
UT	27% BPW	$14,560	$14,690	$53,926
VT	Lesser of 26 x WBA or 46% BPW	$12,948	N/A	$28,148
VA	26 x WBA (see table in law)	$9,828	N/A	>$37,800
VI	Lesser of 26 x WBA or ⅓ BPW	$14,352	$14,352	$43,056
WA	Lesser of 26 x WBA or ⅓ BPW	$19,474	N/A	$58,422
WV	N/A: Uniform duration state	$11,024	N/A	$40,150
WI	Lesser of 26 x WBA or 40% BPW	$9,620	$9,250	$24,050
WY	Lesser of 26 x WBA or 30% BPW	$12,714	$12,225	$42,380

GENERAL NOTE: Since the high quarter and base period wage requirements for the minimum duration of the minimum weekly benefit amount are the same as the wage and employment requirements to qualify for benefits, they are not repeated in this table. (See Table 3-3.) Some states will extend duration under certain circumstances; see chapter 4 for additional information. Additionally, in states where the benefit entitlement is calculated using multi-quarter, annual wage, or weekly wage formulas the high quarter cell is shown as N/A as no specific level of wages is required to exist in the high quarter pursuant to state law.

[1] When 2 amounts are given, higher amount includes dependents' allowance.

[2] Depending on the procedure in place in a given year, different benefit multipliers are utilized. As a result, the maximum potential benefit payable varies from year to year and, similarly, the amount of BPWs necessary to receive the maximum potential benefit payable fluctuates.

Depending on the formula in a state's law and an individual's distribution of wages in their base period, individuals with the same total base-period wages can have different maximum potential benefit entitlement. Maximum benefit entitlement formulas are generally tied to some percentage of base period wages; however, some states use formulas that take into consideration the ratio of high-quarter wages to total base period wages. A few states' laws establish uniform durations for all individuals who meet the qualifying wage requirements.

The following table describes how each state calculates benefit entitlement and the wage credits required to qualify for the maximum duration of the maximum weekly benefit for all states. The amounts displayed assume level wage earnings throughout the claimant's base period. This table reflect only benefits available from the regular UI program. Benefits tied to extensions are addressed in chapter four.

Duration of Benefits

Duration – how long benefits may be collected – is determined by dividing the maximum benefit amount payable by the individual's weekly benefit amount. The maximum number of weeks available varies from state to state, however most states provide a maximum of 26 weeks of benefits. A few states' laws establish uniform durations of 26 weeks for all individuals who meet the qualifying wage requirements, whereas the rest of the states have variable durations. Uniform duration states are not necessarily "more generous" than the other states because many of these states have comparatively high minimum wage thresholds to qualify for all but the lowest benefit levels. Similarly, whether directly or indirectly, all uniform duration states require employment in more than one quarter for all – or most – individuals to qualify for benefits.

In variable duration states, the state calculates the maximum entitlement, then this amount is divided by the weekly benefit amount to derive the duration. In most of these states, an individual's benefits are limited to a fraction or percent of base-period wages. Some states' laws specify both the minimum and maximum duration, in weeks, along with the method of calculating benefit entitlement. Since in all of these states the maximum potential benefit may be used for weeks of total or partial unemployment, individuals can collect benefits longer than their stated duration, until they have exhausted their maximum entitlement.

Table 3-12. Duration of benefits

State	**Uniform**	**Variable Duration**			
		Weeks Based on Base-Period Wages (BPW)		Weeks based on BPW and Unemployment Rate	
		Minimum	Maximum	Minimum	Maximum
AL		15	26		
AK		16	26		
AZ		8	26		
AR		9	16		
CA		14	26		
CO		13	26		
CT	26				
DE		24	26		
DC	26				
FL				9	12-23
GA				6	14-20
HI	26				
ID				10	20-26
IL	26				
IN		26	26		
IA		8	26		
KS				10	16-26
KY		15	26		
LA	26				
ME		15	26		
MD	26				
MA		10	301		
MI		14	20		
MN		11	26		
MS		13	26		
MO		8	20		
MT		8	282		
NE		10	26		
NV		8	26		
NH	26				

Table 3-12. (Continued)

State	Uniform	Variable Duration			
		Weeks Based on Base-Period Wages (BPW)		Weeks based on BPW and Unemployment Rate	
		Minimum	Maximum	Minimum	Maximum
NJ		20	26		
NM		14	26		
NY	26				
NC	12-203				
ND		12	26		
OH		20	26		
OK		16	26		
OR		3	26		
PA		18	26		
PR	26				
RI		17	26		
SC		13	20		
SD		15	26		
TN		13	26		
TX		10	26		
UT		10	26		
VT		21	26		
VA		12	26		
VI		13	26		
WA		1	26		
WV	26				
WI		14	264		
WY		11	26		

[1] Maximum number of weeks is capped at 26 during periods of low unemployment.

[2] To qualify for 28 weeks, individual's ratio of total base-period wages to HQ wages must be at least 3.5.

[3] Number of weeks paid in a given year is dependent upon the state's unemployment rate.

[4] With some limited exceptions, individuals with significant ownership interest in family partnerships, LLCs, and corporations, and certain members of their families, are limited to 4 weeks of regular UI benefits.

Depending on the distribution of wages in the base period, individuals with the same total base-period wages can have different durations and different weekly benefit amounts. For example, individuals whose wages are concentrated largely or wholly in the high quarter will have a higher weekly benefit amount but a shorter duration.

The following Table 3-12 displays the duration of benefits available in each state. Additionally, the table indicates whether the state has a uniform duration formula or a variable duration formula.

Seasonal Employment and Benefits

Special provisions are found in several states' laws restricting the payment of benefits to individuals who earned some or a substantial part of their base-period wages from employers whose operations take place only during certain seasons of the year.

In these provisions, the term seasonal is defined either in the statute or in the rules or regulations implementing the statute in terms of the:

- industry, employer, or occupation involved;
- wages earned during the operating period of the employer or industry; and
- individual.

In most states, the designation of seasonal industries, occupations, or employers and the beginning and ending dates of their seasons is made in accordance with a formal procedure, following action initiated by the UI agency or upon application by the employers or individuals. Typically this involves hearings and presentation of supporting data. It is possible for state law to allow an employer classified as a seasonal employer to request to not to be treated as a seasonal employer.

In other states, a seasonal pursuit, industry, or employer is defined as one in which, because of climatic conditions or the seasonal nature of the employment, it is customary to operate only during a regularly recurring period or periods of less than a specified number of weeks: 16 weeks in Massachusetts; 26 weeks in Colorado, Indiana, Michigan, Oklahoma, and Tennessee; 26 weeks in Maine (except for seasonal lodging facilities, variety stores, or trading posts, restaurants, and camps, where a period of less than 26 weeks applies); 36 weeks in North Carolina; and 40 weeks in Ohio.

Table 3-13. Seasonal wage credits available only during season

AR	Off-season wages of (a) less than 30 times the weekly benefit amount, if individual's seasonal wages were earned in an industry with an operating period of 2-6 months; or (b) less than 24 times the weekly benefit amount, if seasonal wages were earned in an industry with an operating period of 7-8 months	AZ	For employment in transient lodging only; no benefits based on seasonal wages during the off-season if unemployment is due to substantial slowdown in operations	CO	Some seasonal wages in operating period of seasonal industry
IN	Some seasonal wages in operating period of seasonal employer	ME	Some seasonal wages in operating period of seasonal employer	MA	Some seasonal wages in operating period of seasonal industry
MI	Wages must be within seasonal period of 26 weeks or less; designation of employment as seasonal is voluntary	MS	Off-season wages of (a) less than 30 times the weekly benefit amount, if individual's seasonal wages were earned in a cotton ginning industry or professional baseball with an operating period of 6-26 weeks; or (b) less than 24 times the weekly benefit amount, if seasonal wages were earned in a cotton ginning industry or professional baseball with an operating period of 27-36 weeks	NC	25% or more of base- period wages earned in operating period of seasonal employer
OH	Some seasonal wages earned in operating period of seasonal employer	PA	Seasonal wages for less than 180 days of work in operating period; applies only if reasonable assurance of reemployment exists	SD	Some wages earned in operating period of seasonal employer
TN	Wages must be 26 consecutive weeks or less and for a seasonal employer as defined by the state				

In general, restrictions on the payment of benefits to individuals employed during the operating periods of these seasonal industries fall into one of two groups.

The most frequent restriction provides that wage credits earned in seasonal employment are available for payment of benefits only for weeks of unemployment in the benefit year that fall within the operating period of the employer or industry where they were earned. Wage credits earned in non-seasonal work or in employment with a seasonal employer outside the operating period are available for payment of benefits at any time in the benefit year. The states with this type of provision are listed in the following table, together with the definitions of "seasonal worker" to whom the restrictions apply.

Other states have established differing seasonal provisions, which are listed in the following table.

Table 3-14. Other seasonal provisions

DE	Individual with 75% or more of base-period earnings in seasonal employment – defined as the processing of agricultural or seafood products – will be eligible only if the individual had been employed in the corresponding month of the base period
WV	Individual working less than 100 days in seasonal employment is not eligible unless the individual has non-seasonal employment earnings of at least $100
WI	Individual working less than 90 days for a seasonal employer is not eligible unless the individual is paid wages of $500 or more by at least one other employer

Deductions and Withholding from Benefits

Under Federal law, benefits must be paid to an individual as a matter of right and may not be intercepted to satisfy debts or other obligations. However, Federal law provides some exceptions to this requirement discussed in the following text.

Overpayments

All states reduce benefits otherwise payable to recover earlier UI overpayments. See Chapter 6 for more information on this topic.

Child Support

Federal law requires states to deduct child support obligations from benefits only when the obligations are enforced by the state child support agency.

Overissuances of Food Stamps

If the individual owes an uncollected overissuance of food stamps, a state's UI agency may deduct such amount from benefits payable. The following table indicates which state laws provide for these deductions. However, not all of these states necessarily make these deductions; it depends on whether the state UI and food stamp agencies have entered into agreements.

Table 3-15. States with authority to deduct food stamp overissuances

Alabama	Arizona	Arkansas	Colorado	Delaware
Georgia	Hawaii	Illinois	Iowa	Kansas
Louisiana	Maine	Massachusetts	Missouri	Montana
Nebraska	New Hampshire	New Jersey	New Mexico	New York
Oklahoma	South Dakota	Tennessee	Texas	Utah
Vermont	Virgin Islands	Virginia	Wyoming	

Income Tax

Federal law requires states to offer individuals the opportunity to voluntarily have Federal income tax withheld from benefits at the rate of 10 percent. Federal law also permits states to withhold state and local income tax from benefits. The following table indicates which states offer individuals the opportunity to have state (and/or local) income taxes withheld.

Table 3-16. Withholding state and local income tax at claimant option

State	State	Local	State	State	Local	State	State	Local	State	State	Local	State	State	Local
AZ	X		CO	X		CT	X	X	DE	X		DC	X	X
GA	X		HI	X	X1	ID	X		IL	X		IA	X	
KS	X	X	KY	X		ME	X	X	MD	X		MA	X	
MI	X2		MN	X		MS	X	X	NE	X		NM	X	X
NY	X	X	NC	X		ND	X		OK	X2		OR	X	
RI	X		SC	X		UT	X		VT	X		WV	X	
WI	X													

GENERAL NOTE: AK, FL, NV, SD, TX, WA, and WY have no state income tax.

[1] Local income taxes deducted and withheld from the individual's UI for other states and localities.

[2] If Federal taxes are elected to be withheld from benefits, then state taxes will be withheld as well.

Healthcare Coverage

Illinois and Oklahoma authorize the deduction of health insurance premiums from the UI weekly benefit amount if the individual so elects, provided that the state has an approved health care plan for unemployed individuals. However, neither state has implemented this authority. Massachusetts has a health insurance program for unemployed individuals; however, it is unrelated to the UI program.

SECTION 4. EXTENSIONS AND SPECIAL PROGRAMS

In General

The previous chapter included a discussion of duration of benefits concerning the regular UI program. However, extensions of UI benefits are available under certain circumstances. In addition, some programs provide benefits under conditions when UI is not normally payable. This chapter covers these special programs. In particular, it discusses:

- the federal-state Extended Benefits (EB) program;
- special Federal extension programs;
- state additional benefits (AB) programs;

- Trade Readjustment Allowances (TRA);
- Disaster Unemployment Assistance (DUA);
- Short-Time Compensation (STC or worksharing); and
- Self-Employment Assistance (SEA).

Federal-State Extended Benefits (EB)

Since 1970, Federal law has provided for payment of EB during periods of high and rising unemployment in a state.

Triggers for EB

The following "triggers" are used to determine whether EB is payable in a particular state:

- Mandatory – A state must pay up to 13 weeks of EB if the insured unemployment rate (IUR) for the previous 13 weeks is at least 5% and is 120% of the average of the rates for the corresponding 13-week period in each of the two previous years. (The IUR is the ratio of the number of individuals collecting regular UI to the number of individuals who could potentially collect UI if they lost their jobs.)
- Optional – A state may pay up to 13 weeks of EB if the IUR for the previous 13 weeks is at least 6%, regardless of the experience in the previous years.
- Optional – A state may pay up to 13 weeks of EB if the average total unemployment rate (TUR), seasonally adjusted, for the most recent three months is at least 6.5% and is 110% of the rate for the corresponding three-month period in either or both of the two previous years. If such rate is at least 8.0% and is 110% of the rate for the corresponding three-month period in either or both of the two previous years, the duration increases from 13 to 20 weeks. (The TUR is the ratio of the total number of all unemployed persons to the civilian labor force.)

Table 4-1. States with optional triggers for EB

State	Uses 6% IUR Option	Uses 6.5% TUR Option	State	Uses 6% IUR Option	Uses 6.5% TUR Option
AL	X		NH		X
AK	X	X	NJ	X	X
AZ	X		NM	X	
CA	X		NC	X	X
CO	X		OH	X	
CT	X	X	OR	X	X
DC	X		PA	X	
ID	X		RI	X	X
IL	X		SC	X	
IN	X		TN	X	
KS	X	X	TX	X	
ME	X		VT	X	X
MD	X		VA	X	
MN	X	X	WA		X
MO	X		WV	X	
NV	X		WI	X	

Financing of EB

Under permanent law, half of the sharable benefits paid are financed by the Federal government from Federal Unemployment Tax Act (FUTA) revenues. (If the state already provides for duration of over 26 weeks for regular UI, the Federal government will also share in the cost of any weeks beyond 26.) The Federal share of EB will be reduced if a state has no waiting week, permits payment of the waiting week at any time, or does not round benefits down to the lower dollar. No Federal sharing is available for EB costs attributable to employment with state and local governmental entities or federally recognized Indian tribes. (These entities do not pay the FUTA tax, which finances the Federal share of EB.)

Special Qualifying Requirements

Generally, state law applies to the payment of EB. However, some special qualifying requirements exist.

- An individual must have 20 weeks of covered work or the equivalent in covered wages (which exceed 1½ times high-quarter wages or 40 times the weekly benefit amount) in the base period.
- An individual claiming EB who fails to make "a systematic and sustained" work search or to apply for or accept "suitable work" is not entitled to EB until the individual has been employed during at least four weeks and has earned a total of four times the individual's weekly EB amount. Suitable work is defined as "any work within such individual's capabilities."
- Any disqualification for voluntarily quitting work, committing misconduct, or refusing suitable work must be purged through subsequent employment.

Table 4-2. EB monetary requirement used in states where regular UI minimum qualifying formula does not satisfy 20-week requirement*

State	20 Weeks	Exceeds 40 x WBA	Exceeds 1½ HQW
AK		X	X
AZ		X	X
AR	X	X	X
CA		X	X
DE		X	
DC			X
HI	X	X	X
ID	X	X	X
IL			X
IN			X
IA			X
KS			X
ME			X
MD			X
MA	X	X	X
MN		X	
MT	X	X	X
NE			X
NV	X	X	X
NH		X	
NJ		X	
NM			X
NY			X

State	20 Weeks	Exceeds 40 x WBA	Exceeds 1½ HQW
NC	X	X	X
OK			X
OR		X	
PA			X
PR		X	
RI		X	X
TX		X	X
VT		X	
VA	X	X	
VI			X
WA		X	X
WV		X	
WI		X	
WY			X

* See Table 3-3 for information on qualifying requirements for regular UI benefits.

Reductions in Amount of EB

EB paid on interstate claims is limited to two weeks unless both agent and liable states are in an EB period. Also, individuals who received TRA before EB triggered on in a state will have their EB entitlement reduced by the number of weeks of TRA received. In addition, some states reduce the EB amount payable to an individual during a period in which Federal sharing of the cost of EB is reduced pursuant to a sequester order.

Special Federal Extension Programs

In addition to the permanent EB program, Congress has, from time to time, enacted temporary programs extending unemployment compensation benefits. The most recent such program was Emergency Unemployment Compensation 2008 (EUC08). This program provided weeks of 100 percent federally financed compensation to eligible individuals in all states and some additional weeks for individuals in "high unemployment" states.

Table 4-3. Special federal extension programs enacted by Congress

Name	Effective Dates
Temporary Unemployment Compensation (TUC)	6/58 to 6/59
Temporary Extended Unemployment Compensation (TEUC)	4/61 to 6/62
Temporary Compensation (TC)	1/72 to 3/73
Federal Supplemental Benefits (FSB)	1/75 to 1/78
Federal Supplemental Compensation (FSC)	9/82 to 6/85
Emergency Unemployment Compensation (EUC)	11/91 to 4/94
Temporary Extended Unemployment Compensation (TEUC)	3/02 to 3/04
Emergency Unemployment Compensation (EUC08)	7/08 to 01/14

State Additional Benefits (AB)

A number of states have provisions for extending the potential duration of benefits during periods of high unemployment for individuals in approved training who exhaust benefits, or for a variety of other reasons. Although some state laws call these programs "extended benefits," this publication uses the term "additional benefits" to avoid confusion with the federal-state EB program.

The following table includes information about states that have AB programs. Caution should be taken in using the following table because: 1) some AB programs may be subject to annual legislative appropriations, meaning they may not be in effect; and 2) short-term AB programs will not be included if their legislative authorization expired prior to publication. Enactment of the American Recovery and Reinvestment Act of 2009 (Public Law 111-5) resulted in changes to laws in some states seeking to modernize their unemployment compensation programs. Please note that the following table does not align with the requirements established by Public Law 111-5.

Table 4-4. States with additional benefits (AB) programs

State	Name of Extension	Duration	To Whom/When Payable	Miscellaneous
AK	Supplemental State Benefits	13 weeks	Exhaustees of regular UI who satisfy the requirements for receipt of regular benefits and are ineligible for extended benefits solely because they do not meet EB earnings requirement of 40 x WBA or 1.5 HQW	Permanent
CA	Extended Duration Benefits	13 weeks	Exhaustees who are not entitled to regular benefits, if they meet applicable eligibility requirements for regular benefits, are not subject to disqualification, and are not under a disqualification for regular benefits	Triggers if IUR equals or exceeds 6%
	California Training Benefits (CTB)	Up to 52 x WBA, less regular UI and any extensions paid	Individuals who lack competitive job skills and who are enrolled in approved training for a demand occupation; individual must apply for or inquire about CTB program no later than the 16th week of receiving UI benefits	Permanent
CT	Additional Benefits	13 weeks	Individuals who are not entitled to benefits under the federal-state EB program that week	Triggers if an EB period is in effect
GA	Training Extension	14-20 weeks, less any deductible income	Individuals who are separated from a declining occupation and have exhausted all rights to regular unemployment compensation, including extensions, and who are enrolled in and making satisfactory progress in an approved training program that prepares individuals for entry into a high- demand occupation	Permanent TUR for most recent 3 months must > 11%

Table 4-4. (Continued)

State	Name of Extension	Duration	To Whom/When Payable	Miscellaneous
HI	Additional Unemployment Compensation	13 weeks	Unemployed as a result of natural or man-made disaster, as declared by the Governor; must exhaust regular UI, not qualify for UI monetarily, or be self-employed	Must be approved by Governor
IA	Extended Benefits	13 weeks	If unemployed due to last employer going out of business, wage credits are recomputed up from ⅓ of wages for insured work to ½	Permanent
	Training Extension	26 weeks	Individuals who are separated from a declining occupation and have exhausted all rights to regular unemployment compensation including extensions, and who are enrolled in and making satisfactory progress in an approved training program that prepares individuals for entry into a high- demand occupation	Permanent
ID	Training Extension	26 weeks	Individuals who are separated from a declining occupation and have exhausted all rights to regular unemployment compensation including extensions, and who are enrolled in and making satisfactory progress in an approved training program that prepares individuals for entry into a high- demand occupation	Permanent
KS	Training Extension	26 weeks	Individuals who are enrolled in and making satisfactory progress in an approved training program	Claimants in shared work program may not qualify for additional benefit for 2 years after

State	Name of Extension	Duration	To Whom/When Payable	Miscellaneous
				training benefits expire
MD	Training Extension	26 weeks	Individuals who are enrolled in and making satisfactory progress in an approved training program; payments limited to 1 year following end of benefit year	Permanent
MA	Training Extension	26 weeks	Attendees in an approved training course who, in opinion of Commissioner, will be aided in finding appropriate employment; only paid while attending such course and only if not eligible for Trade Readjustment Assistance, exhausted all rights to regular UI and EB, and has no rights to benefits under any other state or Federal law	Determined by Commissioner
	Lockedout Workers	26 weeks	Individuals eligible due to an employer's lockout; extension limited to lesser of 26 weeks or the period of the lockout	Permanent
ME	Dislocated Worker Benefits	26 weeks	Must meet the definition of "dislocated worker" and be attending training approved by the UI Commission; must exhaust all rights to regular UI and EB, and have no rights to benefits under any other state or Federal law	Permanent
MI	Extended Training or Retraining Benefits	18 weeks	Must be in approved training, and is separate from TRA	Optional – not currently in effect
MN	Additional Benefits	13 weeks	If individual was laid off from main BP employer; that employer had 100 or more workers; employer laid off at least 50% of workforce; employer has no intentions of rehiring individual; individual exhausted regular UI;	Permanent – Determined by Commissioner

Table 4-4. (Continued)

State	Name of Extension	Duration	To Whom/When Payable	Miscellaneous
			and facility is located in county with unemployment rate at least 10% from 3 months before to 3 months after layoff; individuals who have stopped working because of a lockout are eligible if the lockout is in active progress	
MT	Additional Training Benefits	26 weeks	Individuals who are separated from a declining occupation and have exhausted all rights to regular unemployment compensation including extensions, and who are enrolled in and making satisfactory progress in an approved training program that prepares individuals for entry into a high- demand occupation	Permanent
NE	Training Extension	26 weeks	Individuals who are separated from a declining occupation and have exhausted all rights to regular unemployment compensation including extensions, and who are enrolled in and making satisfactory progress in an approved training program that prepares individuals for entry into a high- demand occupation	Permanent
NJ	Additional Benefits During Training	26 weeks	Dislocated workers unlikely to return to previous employment because opportunities in the job classification are impaired due to substantial reduction in employment at worksite; training must be for a labor demand occupation and must be approved	Permanent

State	Name of Extension	Duration	To Whom/When Payable	Miscellaneous
NY	Additional Training Benefits	104 effective days	Exhaustees of regular UI benefits and, if in effect, any other extended benefits, provided that entitlement to a new benefit claim cannot be established; individual must be in approved training, separate from TRA	Permanent – Subject to availability of funds
OR	Supplemental Benefits – Dislocated Worker Program	1-26 weeks	Eligible dislocated workers who are ineligible to receive extended benefits or additional benefits, and who are demonstrating satisfactory progress and attendance in the approved training	Permanent – Additional eligibility requirements apply
	Additional Benefits	Up to 25% of most recent regular UI claim	Exhaustees of regular UI benefits who continue to meet eligibility requirements for regular UI benefits and are not eligible for any other unemployment benefits including any federal extensions; payable for weeks not within an EB period, not within a federal extension period, and when IUR equals or exceeds 4.5%	Permanent
PR	Additional Benefits	(20 x WBA plus 32 x additional WBA) less max. potential benefits payable in last BY	Individuals displaced due to technological progress and/or the permanent disappearance of an industry, establishment, or occupation; not for seasonal unemployment	Permanent – Secretary determines if special unemployment situation exists
VT	Training Extension	26 weeks	Individuals who are separated from a declining occupation and have exhausted all rights to regular unemployment compensation including extensions, and who are enrolled in and making satisfactory progress in an approved training program	Permanent

Table 4-4. (Continued)

State	Name of Extension	Duration	To Whom/When Payable	Miscellaneous
			that prepares individuals for entry into a high- demand occupation	
WA	Training Benefits Program	52 x WBA less regular UI and EB paid	Unemployed individuals who are disabled, low-income, members of the Washington National Guard, or recently discharged from the military, and in need of full-time training in a demand occupation	Permanent – Training benefits not payable for weeks more than 2 years beyond end of benefit year of regular claim
WI	Wisconsin Supplemental Benefits	8 weeks	Individual who has exhausted benefits; Wisconsin supplemental benefit period occurs when IUR is 4% and TUR is 5%	Governor can elect to run this program or allow payment through federal-state EB program

Trade Readjustment Allowances (TRA)

The Trade Act of 1974, as amended, provides for adjustment assistance to individuals who are unemployed or underemployed because of the adverse effect of increased imports, as a result of trade arrangements permitted under the Act, or because of shifts in production outside the United States. Trade adjustment assistance (TAA) provided by the Act consists of trade readjustment allowances (TRA), relocation and job search allowances, and subsistence and transportation allowances during periods of approved training.

The Secretary of Labor has entered into agreements with state agencies whereby the agencies will act as agents for the Federal government in paying TRA and other allowances to eligible individuals. Payments and administrative costs are paid for with Federal funds.

Certification Process

Individuals are certified as eligible to apply for TAA if a group of three or more workers, an employer, a certified or recognized union or duly authorized representative, or a state workforce official petitions the Secretary of Labor for a determination of eligibility to apply for TAA and the Secretary determines that the importation of competitive foreign products or shifts in production outside the United States contributed importantly to the loss of employment at the firm mentioned in the petition.

Qualifying Requirements

To qualify for TRA, the individual must have had at least 26 weeks of employment with wages of at least $30 a week within the 52-week period ending with the week of the individual's total or partial separation from adversely affected employment. Along with other requirements to receive TRA payments, the individual must be participating in an approved training program unless it is determined that training is not feasible or appropriate.

Duration

Basic TRA is payable at the state UI rate over a 104-week eligibility period beginning with the first week after the individual's most recent TRA qualifying separation from employment. Basic TRA provides 52 weeks of income support less the UI entitlement in the trade-qualifying UI benefit period (generally 26 weeks of UI). Individuals may be eligible for an additional 65-78 weeks for a total of 130 weeks of income support if they are participating in approved training. For additional information on the Trade Readjustment Assistance program go to: http://www.doleta.gov/tradeact/.

Subsistence and Transportation Allowances

An adversely affected individual may receive TRA while participating in approved training. Individuals may also receive subsistence and transportation allowances while attending training at a facility that is not within commuting distance of their residence.

Relocation Allowances

Relocation allowances are payable to totally separated individuals who have no reasonable expectation of securing suitable work in the area in which they live, and who have a bona fide offer of suitable work in the area to which they wish to relocate. Relocation allowances consist of a lump sum payment of up to 90 percent (not to exceed $1,250) of the allowable expenses incurred in moving the individuals, their families, and their household effects to the location of their new jobs.

Job Search Allowances

Job search allowances are payable to totally separated individuals who have no reasonable expectation of securing suitable work in the area in which they live, and who have a reasonable expectation of securing suitable employment in the area of the proposed job search. Job search allowances consist of up to 90 percent of the cost of the necessary expenses incurred in the job search, not to exceed $1,250, under a single certification.

Disaster Unemployment Assistance (DUA)

The Robert T. Stafford Disaster Relief and Emergency Assistance Act authorizes the President to provide to any individual unemployed as a result of a major disaster such assistance as the President deems appropriate while the individual is unemployed. Among the types of assistance available as a result of a presidentially declared disaster is DUA – a payment made by state UI agencies under agreements with the Secretary of Labor. Funds for both DUA benefits and administrative costs are provided by the Federal Emergency Management Administration to the Secretary of Labor who, in turn, makes them available to the states.

Eligibility

In general, Federal regulations provide that certain individuals living or working in areas affected by a major disaster who are unemployed because of the disaster are eligible for DUA though they are not eligible for UI benefits or other wage replacement payments (e.g., the self-employed). Applications for DUA must be filed within 30 days of the Governor's announcement of a disaster in the state; the unemployment must be directly caused by the disaster; and, in general, individuals must be able and available for suitable work.

Disaster Assistance Period

The disaster assistance period – the period during which DUA is payable – begins with the first week following the date the major disaster began. DUA is available to an individual during this period as long as unemployment caused by the disaster continues or until he or she is reemployed in a suitable position, but no longer than 26 weeks after the major disaster is declared.

Weekly Assistance Amount

In most of the jurisdictions that operate a UI program the weekly DUA amount is computed in accordance with the applicable state law formula used to compute the weekly amount under the state's regular unemployment insurance program except that if the individual's weekly amount is less than 50 percent of the state's average weekly payment of regular compensation in the state, the individual will be entitled to 50 percent of the average weekly payment of regular compensation in the state.

In Guam and the Northern Mariana Islands, the weekly DUA amount is the average of the payments of regular compensation made under all state laws referred to in 20 CFR 625.2(r)(1)(i) for weeks of total unemployment in the first 4 of the last 5 completed calendar quarters immediately preceding the quarter in which the major disaster began. In American Samoa, Marshall Islands, Micronesia, and the Trust Territory of the Pacific Islands (Palau), the weekly DUA amount is the agreed-upon amount to approximately 50% of the area-wide average of the weekly wages paid to individuals in the major disaster area in the quarter immediately preceding the quarter in which the major disaster began.

Deductions

The DUA payable to an individual for a week is reduced by the amount of any of the following that an applicant has received for the week or would receive for the week if he or she filed a claim: 1) any compensation or insurance from any source for loss of wages due to illness or disability; 2) supplemental unemployment benefits pursuant to a collective bargaining agreement; 3) workers' compensation by virtue of death of head of household; and 4) the amount of retirement pension or annuity under a public or private retirement plan or system if such amount is deductible under the state UI law. In addition, the weekly DUA amount is reduced by the amount of wages that the individual earns in a week as determined by applying to the wages the earnings allowance for partial or part-total unemployment prescribed by the applicable state's UI law.

Short-Time Compensation (STC)

Like the partial benefit provisions of state UI laws, STC programs, also known as worksharing or shared work, allow an individual who is employed for a portion of the week to collect UC. Under STC, an employer elects to avoid layoffs by reducing the number of regularly scheduled hours of work for all, or a group of, individuals during disruptions to a firm's regular business activity. Whereas partial benefit formulas look at individuals' earnings, STC looks at the hours of work and provides individuals a pro-rata share of weekly benefits based on the reduction in weekly hours of work.

Most states do not allow seasonal employees to participate in an employer's STC plan. Several states require that employers be current in filing reports and paying contributions as a condition of participation. Many states require the union to agree to an STC plan if the employer is unionized.

The definition of STC was modified by the Middle Class Tax Relief and Job Creation Act of 2012. States are not required to enact an STC program; however, states may not operate an STC program that does not conform to this definition.

Table 4-5. States with worksharing programs

State	Period of Approved Plan	Required Reduction of Work	Maximum Number of Weeks Payable
AZ	1 year	At least 10% but not more than 40%	26 weeks (limitation does not apply if state IUR consisting of the week and the preceding 12 weeks is ≥ 4%)
AR	12 months or date in plan, whichever is earlier	Not less than 10%, but not more than 40%	25 weeks
CA1	6 months	At least 10%	No limit on weeks, but total paid cannot exceed 26 x WBA
CO	12 months or less	At least 10% but not more than 40%	18 weeks
CT	26 weeks (with 26-week extension possible)	Not less than10%, but not more than 60%	26 weeks
DC2	12 months	At least 20%, but not more than 40%	50 weeks (with 2-week extension possible)
FL	12 months	Not less than 10%, but not more than 40%	26 weeks
IA	52 weeks	Not less than 20%, but not more than 50%	26 weeks
IL2	12 months	Not less than 20%, but not more than 60%	52 weeks
KS	12 months	Not less than 20%, but not more than 40%	26 weeks
ME	12 months	Not less than 10%, but not more than 50%	52 weeks
MD	6 months	At least 20%, not to exceed to 50%	26 weeks
MA	52 weeks	Not less than 10%, but not more than 60%	52 weeks
MI	52 weeks	Not less than 15% and no more than 45%	No limit on weeks, but total paid cannot exceed 20 x WBA
MN	At least 60 days, but not more than 1 year	Not less than 20%, but not more than 50%	52 weeks
MO	12 months	Not less than 20%, but not more than 40%	52 weeks
NE	12 Months	Not less than 10%, but not more than 60%	52 weeks
NH	26 weeks	Not less than 10%, but not more than 50%	26 weeks
NJ	12 months	Not less than 10%	26 weeks

Table 4-5. (Continued)

State	Period of Approved Plan	Required Reduction of Work	Maximum Number of Weeks Payable
NY		Not less than 20%, but not more than 60%	26 weeks
OH	52 weeks	Not less than 10%, but not more than 50%	26 weeks
OR	Not more than 1 year	At least 20%, but not more than 40%	52 weeks
PA3	52 weeks	Not less than 20%, but not more than 40%	52 weeks
RI	12 months	Not less than 10%, but not more than 50%	52 weeks
TX	12 months	At least 10%, but not more than 40%	26 weeks
VT	6 months or date in plan, whichever is earlier	Not less than 20%, but not more than 50%	26 weeks
WA	12 months or date in plan, whichever is earlier	Not less than 10%, but not more than 50%	No limit on weeks, but total paid cannot exceed maximum entitlement
WI	6 months in any 5-year period within the same work unit	Not less than 10%, but not more than 50%	No limit on weeks, but total paid cannot exceed maximum entitlement

[1] STC benefits shall not be payable on any type of extended claim.
[2] Not operational prior to promulgation of regulations, currently no regulations for this program exist.
[3] Program expires February 16, 2021.

Under the definition in FUTA, employers must submit an STC plan to the state for approval. The employer's plan must be consistent with employer obligations under applicable Federal and state laws. Further, the affected employees' (also known as "affected unit") workweeks must have been reduced by at least 10 percent, and by not more than the percentage, if any, that is determined by the state to be appropriate, but in no case more than 60 percent. Individuals receiving STC payments meet the UC availability for work and work search test requirements by being available for their customary workweek as required by state law. Moreover, the STC plan must provide that employers will maintain (to the same extent as for other employees not participating in the STC program) certain specified health benefits and retirement benefits for employees in the affected unit, despite the reduced hours. In addition, the plan may provide that workers in the affected unit may participate in employer-sponsored or Workforce Innovation and Opportunity Act funded training if approved by the UI agency.

Self-Employment Assistance (SEA)

SEA programs help unemployed individuals create their own jobs by starting small businesses. To be eligible for SEA payments, individuals must be:

- Eligible for UI;
- Engaged on a full-time basis in activities relating to the establishment of a business and becoming self-employed;
- Identified as likely to exhaust their benefits; and
- Participating in self-employment activities including entrepreneurial training, business counseling, and technical assistance.

The authorizing Federal law provides that no more than five percent of individuals receiving regular UI benefits under a state program may participate in the SEA program. Individuals enrolled in the SEA program will receive weekly allowances. These allowances are the same as the individual's regular unemployment weekly benefit amount. Participants actively engage full-time in activities relating to the establishment of a business and becoming self-employed, and are considered to be unemployed. Provisions of state law relating to availability for work, search for work, and refusal to accept work do not apply.

The Middle Class Tax Relief and Job Creation Act of 2012, enacted on February 22, 2012, amended Federal law to extend the SEA program to the long-term unemployed receiving benefits under the Emergency Unemployment Compensation (EUC) and Extended Benefits (EB) programs if state law permits.

Table 4-6. States with sea programs

Delaware	Louisiana (Authority in law, but program not active)	Maine
Mississippi	New Hampshire	New Jersey
New York (expires 12/7/2019)	Oregon	Pennsylvania
Rhode Island		

SECTION 5. NONMONETARY ELIGIBILITY

In General

Along with monetary requirements, each state's UI law requires individuals to meet nonmonetary requirements. Federal law mandates some of these requirements. The general rule is that individuals must have lost their job through no fault of their own and must be able to work, available for work, and actively seeking work. By examining the individual's current attachment to the labor force, these provisions delineate the type of risk covered by UI law – primarily, unemployment caused by economic conditions.

Usage Note: There is often a distinction between issues that result in disqualification and issues that result in weeks of ineligibility. A disqualified individual has no right to benefits until s/he requalifies, usually by obtaining new work or by serving a set disqualification period. In some cases, benefits and wage credits may be reduced. An ineligible individual is prohibited from receiving benefits until the condition causing the ineligibility ceases to exist. Eligibility issues are generally determined on a week-to-week basis.

This chapter is organized from the perspective of an individual experiencing the claims process. First, the state would determine if there are any issues related to the individual becoming unemployed. Second, issues concerning week-to-week eligibility would be explored, as would any refusals of suitable work. Third, the state would examine whether the individual received any "deductible income" causing a reduction in benefits payable.

Separations from Employment

Voluntarily Leaving Work

Since the UI program is designed to compensate wage loss due to lack of work, voluntarily leaving work without good cause is an obvious reason for disqualification from benefits. All states have such provisions.

In most states, disqualification is based on the circumstances of separation from the most recent employment. These disqualification provisions may be phrased in terms such as "has left his most recent work voluntarily without good cause." In a few states, the agency looks to the causes of all separations within a specified period. An individual who is not disqualified for leaving work voluntarily with good cause is not necessarily eligible to receive benefits. For example, if the individual left because of illness or to take care of a family member who is ill, the individual may not be able to work or available for work. This ineligibility would generally last only until the individual was again able and available.

Good Cause for Voluntarily Leaving

In all states, individuals who leave their work voluntarily must have good cause if they are not to be disqualified.

In many states, good cause is explicitly restricted to good cause connected with the work, attributable to the employer, or involving fault on the part of the employer. However, in a state where good cause is not explicitly linked to the work, the state may interpret its law to include good personal cause or it may limit it to good cause related to work. Since a state law limiting good cause to the work is more restrictive, it may contain specific exceptions that are not necessary in states recognizing good personal cause. (For example, an explicit provision not disqualifying an individual who quits to accompany a spouse to a new job might not be necessary in a state that recognizes good personal cause; it would be necessary in a state restricting good cause to that related to the work.)

The following table reflects states that restrict good cause for quitting due to reasons connected to the work.

Table 5-1. Voluntarily leaving - must be connected to work

State	Basis	State	Basis	State	Basis	State	Basis
AL	L	AZ	L	AR	L	CO	L
CT	L	DE	L	DC	L	FL	L
GA	L	ID	L, R	IL	L	IN	L
IA	L	KS	L	KY	L	LA	L
ME	L, R	MD	I	MA	L	MI	L
MN	L	MO	L	MT	L, R	NE	L
NH	L	NJ	L, R	NM	L	NC	L
ND	L	OK	L	PR	I	SC	I
SD	I	TN	L	TX	L	VT	L
WA	L	WV	L	WI	I	WY	L

KEY: L = law R = regulation I = interpretation.

Wisconsin does not disqualify an individual who accepts work that could have been refused with good cause and then terminates with good cause within the first 30 calendar days after starting the job.

The following tables indicate common “good cause” provisions. Other provisions are discussed in the text following the tables. Note that domestic violence provisions are found in Table 5-4 and are not part of the more general category of “sexual or other harassment” displayed in Table 5-2 below. Please note that the following tables are intended to provide a general overview of voluntary leaving provisions in the states; they are not meant to be exhaustive. Please consult the appropriate state statute, regulation, or policy for more specific information. Please note that NC law does not include any of these provisions.

Table 5-2. Good personal cause - general provisions

State	To Accept Other Work	Compulsory Retirement	Sexual or Other Harassment	Individual's Illness
AL	L		L1	L
AK	L2	I	I	I
AZ	R	R3	R	R
AR			L	L
CA	R	L, R	L	R
CO	L2	L	L	L
CT	L2	R	R	R, I4
DE		I	I	L
DC			R	R4
FL	L2	I		L
GA	I	I3	R5	R4, 5
HI	R	R	L	I
ID	L, R	L, R	L	L, R
IL	L	I	L	L4
IN	L	L	L	L
IA	L	R	I	L
KS	L	L	L	L
KY	L	I	I1	I4
LA	I2	I	I	
ME	L, R	L, R	R	L, R4
MD		I3	I	L4
MA	L	L	L	I
MI	L	I3	I	L4
MN	L	I	L	I
MS	I	L3	L	I
MO	L2		I	I
MT		L, R	L, R6	L, R
NE	L2	L3	L	L
NV	L	I3	I	I
NH	L, R2	I	I	L4, R
NJ	R	I3	I	R
NM	L	L	L, R	L
NY	I	I	I	I
ND	L2		L	L
OH	L2	I	I	I
OK		I	I	L
OR	R2	I3	I5	I4, 5
PA	I	I	I5	I5
PR	I	I	I	I
RI	I	I3	L	I

Table 5-2. (Continued)

State	To Accept Other Work	Compulsory Retirement	Sexual or Other Harassment	Individual's Illness
SC		I	I	
SD	L2	I	I	L
TN		L3	L	L4
TX	L	I	L	L
UT	R	I3	R	R
VT	I7	I3	I	
VA	L2	I	L5	L5
VI	I	I	I	I
WA	L4	I	L, R	L4
WV			I	L
WI	L	L	L	L
WY				L

KEY: L = law, R = regulation, I = interpretation or policy.

[1] AL and KY - only if the sexual harassment occurred on the job.

[2] State has specific requirements related to the pay, hours, or type of work the individual quit to accept; when new work must begin; or other requirements related to either the new or old job.

[3] Separations due to compulsory retirement addressed under misconduct section of the rules; separations considered a discharge for reasons other than misconduct.

[4] Requires illness be related to work; physician recommendation/certification and/or failure of the employer to provide accommodations; or other specific limitation.

[5] Requires employer notification or pursuit of reasonable alternatives/adaptations prior to leaving.

[6] If individual or individual's child is a victim of sexual assault or stalking, and individual quit to protect self or child from sexual assault or stalking.

[7] Only if the new job never materializes due to lack of work.

Table 5-3. Good personal cause - to join the armed forces

AK	I	AZ	R	CO	I	GA	I	HI	I
ID	L	IN	L	IA	R	KS	L	ME	I
MA	I	MI	I	MN	I	MO	I1	NV	I
NM	L, R	NY	I	OH	L2	OR	I3	PA	I
RI	I	TN	L	UT	I	VI	I	WA	L

KEY: L = law, R = regulation, I = interpretation or policy

[1] Only if the military pay is more remunerative.

[2] If individual is inducted into armed forces within 30 days after separation, or 180 days after separation if date of induction is delayed solely at the discretion of the armed forces.

[3] If the offer of work is definite, begins in shortest time reasonable, is reasonably expected to continue, and pays more than previous employment or WBA.

The table above shows states whose law, regulation, or policy addresses separation from employment to join the armed forces.

Table 5-4. Good Personal Cause - Domestic Violence

AK	L	AZ	L	AR	L	CA	L
CO	L1	CT	L	DE	L	DC	L
GA	L	HI	L	IL	L	IN	L
IA	I	KS	L	ME	L, R	MD	L
MA	L	MN	L1	MS	R	MT	L
NE	L	NV	L	NH	L, R	NJ	L, R
NM	L	NY	L	NC	L	ND	L
OK	L	OR	L, R	PA	I	PR	I
RI	L	SC	L	SD	L	TX	L
UT	I	VI	L	WA	L	WI	L
WY	L						

KEY: L = law, R = regulation, I = interpretation or policy.

[1] Includes immediate family member.

Table 5-5. Good personal cause - to perform marital, domestic, or filial obligations

State	Basis	Cause Must Be Illness or Disability of Immediate Family Member	State	Basis	Cause Must Be Illness or Disability of Immediate Family Member
AK	R	X	AZ	R	
AR	L	X1	CA	L, R	X2
CO	L	X3	CT	L	X
DE	L	X	DC	L	X
HI	L	X	IL	L	X2
KS	I		ME	L, R	X2
MA	I	X	MN	L	X2, 4
NV	L	X4	NH	L	X
NY	L, I	X5	OH	L	
OK	L	X	OR	L	X4
PA	I	X4	RI	L	X
SC	L	X	TX	L	

Table 5-5. (Continued)

State	Basis	Cause Must Be Illness or Disability of Immediate Family Member	State	Basis	Cause Must Be Illness or Disability of Immediate Family Member
UT	I		VA	I	X2, 4
VI	L		WA	L	X2, 4
WV6	L		WI	L	X2

KEY: L = law, R = regulation, I = interpretation or policy

[1] Includes pregnancy.

[2] Must discuss quit with employer and attempt to retain employment relationship; see state laws for more specific requirements.

[3] Includes provisions regarding employer's medical leave policies and the Family Medical Leave Act.

[4] All reasonable alternatives to quitting must have been pursued.

[5] Quit is acceptable if individual is unable to accept a particular shift as a result of undue family hardship.

[6] Quit is acceptable if due to shift change resulting in loss of child care (individual must be available for full-time work on original shift).

Good Cause and Quit to Follow Spouse

Most states have provisions for individuals who quit as a result of a need to accompany a spouse due to a change in the spouse's employment. Many states require the new location have an impractical commute to be considered good cause and some specify requirements to define impractical commute. Several states have provisions related to military spouses but state laws vary regarding the circumstances when the spouse of a service member is eligible for benefits. See a state's law for specific eligibility factors.

Other Good Cause Provisions

Several states specify by statute that an individual has good cause in various circumstances relating to work separations that, by statute, require a determination that the individual left with good cause. Examples of reasons that may constitute good cause include:

- transportation difficulties;
- a permanent change in the work conditions that have a negative impact on the employee, including a reduction in pay or a requirement to relocate;

- accepting a voluntary lay off when a an employer announces a planned layoff;
- certain circumstances related to part-time employment; or
- to attend approved training.

Good Cause - Relation to Other Laws

Some states define good cause provisions related to other laws. Examples of these types of provisions include leaving work as a result of:

- hazardous work conditions;
- being asked to perform an illegal act or violate an ordinance or statute; or
- being deprived of equal employment opportunities based on bona fide occupational qualifications.

Good Cause and Labor Arrangements

Several state laws explicitly address separations that occur under collective bargaining agreements. Separation situations where individuals would not be disqualified under a collective bargaining agreement vary by state, but may include:

- accepting a layoff under certain circumstances;
- electing to be laid off in place of a worker with less seniority;
- being placed on a referral list or accepting a referral to another employer from the individual's hiring hall; or
- an employer's breach of a collective bargaining agreement.

Good Cause and Suitable Work

Some states have provisions that do not disqualify an individual for refusing an offer of work when the work is determined to not be suitable employment for the individual. An individual is not required to accept work that is less favorable than previous work, so suitability, in general, is defined in relation to the individual's work history, commuting distance, etc. Good cause can also be defined in relation to labor standards such as general labor market conditions (prevailing wages for the locality). State law should be consulted to determine how good cause related to suitable work is defined. Examples of situations where an individual would not be disqualified include:

- leaving work to accept a better job such as a job that increases wages or is closer to home;
- when an individual accepts new work that would have been determined unsuitable and leaves the job within a specified number of days or weeks;
- leaving work determined to be unsuitable to attend approved training; or
- leaving due to a violation of the work agreement or a change in the work conditions that are less favorable.

Good Cause and Jobs for Temporary Service Employers

Several states' laws provide that, if an employee of a temporary service employer fails to be available for future assignments upon completion of the current assignment, such individual shall be deemed to have voluntarily left employment without good cause connected to the work.

Table 5-6. States with Temporary Workers Provisions

States Where Failure to Contact Employer Upon Completion of Assignment is Deemed VQ							
AL	R	AZ	R	AR	L	CO	L
DE	L	FL	L	GA	L	HI	I
ID	L, R	IN	L	IA	L	KS	L
KY	L	LA	L, I	MA	L	MI	L
MN	L	MO	L	NE	L	NJ	R
NY	I	ND	L	OK	L	PA	I
PR	I	RI	L	SC	R	SD	I
TN	I	TX	L	UT	I	WV	I

KEY: L = law, R = regulation, I = interpretation.

These states require the employer to provide employees with notice that the employee must notify the temporary service upon the completion of an assignment and that failure to do so may result in benefit denial.

Period of Disqualification

In most states, the disqualification lasts until the individual is again employed and earns a specified amount of wages. In Alaska and Colorado, the disqualification is a fixed number of weeks (in Colorado, only for separations from the most recent employer); the longest period in either of these states is 10 weeks. Nebraska has a disqualification of 13 weeks. Maryland and North Carolina impose fixed duration disqualifications for certain conditions.

Reduction of Benefit Rights

Table 5-7. Voluntarily leaving - disqualification

State	Benefits Postponed for:		Amount of Benefits Reduced
	Number of Weeks	Weeks and/or Wages to Requalify [1]	
AL		10 x WBA[2]	6-12 x WBA
AK	W + 5[2, 3]		3 x WBA
AZ		5 x WBA	
AR		At least 30 days of covered work	
CA		5 x WBA	
CO	WF + 10		Wage credits from employer removed from the claim (applies to all BP employers)
CT		10 x WBA[4]	
DE		4 weeks of work and 4 x WBA	
DC		10 weeks of work and wages equal to 10 x WBA[3]	
FL		17 x WBA[2]	
GA		10 x WBA[5]	
HI		5 x WBA	
ID		14 x WBA	
IL		Wages equal to WBA in each of 4 weeks	

Table 5-7. (Continued)

State	Benefits Postponed for:		Amount of Benefits Reduced
	Number of Weeks	Weeks and/or Wages to Requalify [1]	
IN		Wages in each of 8 weeks and wages ≥ 8 x WBA	By 25%
IA		10 x WBA[2]	
KS		3 x WBA	
KY		10 weeks of covered work and wages equal to 10 x WBA[2]	
LA		10 x WBA[2]	
ME		4 x WBA[2, 4]	
MD	W + 5-10[2, 3]	15 x WBA[2, 3]	
MA	X[2]	8 weeks of work and wages of 8 x WBA	
MI		12 x WBA	
MN		One-half of amount required to establish benefit account[6]	
MS		8 x WBA	
MO		10 x WBA[2]	
MT		Wages equal to 6 x WBA[3]	
NE	13 [2, 7]	4 x WBA	Equal[7]
NV		Wages equal to WBA in each of 10 weeks[4]	
NH		5 weeks of work in each of which earned 20% more than WBA[8]	
NJ		8 weeks of work and wages equal to 10 x WBA	
NM		5 x WBA in covered work	
NY		3 days work in each of 5 weeks and 10 x WBA	
NC	X[3]	10 x WBA earned in at least 5 weeks[3]	X[3]
ND		8 x WBA	
OH		6 weeks in covered work and wages equal to 27.5% of AWW[2, 9]	
OK		10 x WBA	
OR		4 x WBA	8 x WBA
PA		6 x WBA	
PR		4 weeks of work and wages equal to 10 x WBA	
RI		8 x WBA	
SC		8 x WBA	Equal
SD		6 weeks in covered work and wages equal to WBA in each week[2]	

State	Benefits Postponed for:		Amount of Benefits Reduced
	Number of Weeks	Weeks and/or Wages to Requalify [1]	
TN		10 x WBA[2]	
TX		6 weeks of work or wages equal to 6 x WBA[7]	
UT		6 x WBA[2]	
VT	X[10]	6 x WBA	
VA		30 days or 240 hours of work[2]	
VI		4 weeks of work and 4 x WBA	
WA		7 weeks and earnings in bona fide work of 7 x WBA	
WV		At least 30 working days of covered employment	Equal
WI	X[10]	7 weeks and 14 x WBA	Wage credits from employer removed from the claim
WY		8 x WBA	

KEY: W = Week of separation, WF = Week of filing "Equal" indicates reduction equal to WBA multiplied by number of weeks of disqualification.

[1] Minimum employment or wages to requalify for benefits.

[2] Separation preceding the most recent separation may be considered under the following circumstances. AL - if last employment not considered bona fide work; AK, FL, IA, MD, MA, MO, OH, and UT - when employment or time period subsequent to separation does not satisfy potential disqualification; LA - disqualification applicable to base period or last employer; ME - disqualification applicable to most recent previous separation if last work was a voluntary quit and was not in usual trade or was intermittent; VA - disqualification applicable to last 30-day or 240-hour employer; DC, SD, and WV - if employment was less than 30 days unless on an additional claim; KY and NE - reduction or forfeiture of benefits applicable to separations from any base-period employer; TN - any employer with whom the individual earned 10 x WBA (disqualification does not apply if individual quit to join the armed forces).

[3] AK - disqualification is terminated if individual returns to work and earns at least 8 x WBA; MT - disqualification is terminated after individual attends school for three consecutive months and is otherwise eligible; MD - the duration disqualification imposed unless a valid compelling or necessitous circumstance exists; NC - the agency may reduce permanent disqualification to five weeks, with a corresponding reduction in total benefits; if an employer gives notice of future work separation, disqualification of four weeks imposed if individual establishes good cause for his or her failure to work out the notice.

[4] ME - disqualified for duration of unemployment and until individual earns 6 x WBA if voluntarily retired; NV - disqualified for W+4 to enter self employment, and for 10 weeks to seek better employment; CT - voluntary retiree disqualified for the duration of unemployment and until 40 x WBA is earned.

[5] Individual must work for a liable employer and become unemployed through no fault of his or her own.

[6] $2,400 in 4-quarter base period or 5.3 percent of state's AAW rounded down to next lower $100, whichever is higher.

[7] NE - a disqualification for the week of separation plus two weeks if individual leaves to accept a better job; TX - disqualification begins with week following filing of claim.

[8] Requirement to earn requalifying wages does not apply to individuals who become unemployed after leaving work to accept better employment.

[9] If individual left work for compelling domestic circumstances, can requalify by earning the lesser of ½ of AWW or $60 in covered employment.

[10] VT - disqualified for 1-6 weeks if individual left work due to health reasons; in WI - disqualification for week of termination + 4 weeks if individual refuses transfer to a job paying less than 2/3 of wage rate.

In some states, in addition to the postponement of benefits, benefit rights are reduced, usually equal in extent to the weeks of benefit postponement imposed as described in the table above.

Discharge for Misconduct Connected with the Work

Discharge for misconduct (which may be called a discharge for "just cause" or "a disqualifying act") provisions for disqualification follow a pattern similar to that for voluntary leaving. Many states provide for greater disqualification in the case of discharge for dishonesty or a criminal act, or other acts of aggravated misconduct. (See section on "Disqualifications for Gross Misconduct.")

In some states, the definition of misconduct is expanded to include specific offenses or circumstances.

Some of the areas addressed more specifically in state laws include:

- violations related to an attendance policy, or chronic or excessive absenteeism or tardiness;
- violations of an employer rule or policy;
- participation in an illegal strike as determined under state or Federal laws, without good cause or notice to the employer;
- damage to an employer's or a customer's property;
- conduct that neglects or endangers the health and safety of others;
- violation of a state standard or regulation, loss or failure to obtain or maintain a license or certification that is a requirement of the position, or failure to maintain standards of the profession;
- falsification of an employment application or any other documentation provided to the employer; or
- absence from work due to incarceration or violation of a law related to employment.

Detailed interpretations of what constitutes misconduct have been developed in each state's benefit decisions. In determining what constitutes misconduct, many states rely on the definition established in the 1941 Wisconsin Supreme Court Case, Boynton Cab Co. v. Neubeck, 237 Wis. 249, 296 N.W. 636 (1941):

> "Misconduct . . . is limited to conduct evincing such willful or wanton disregard of standards of behavior which the employer has the right to expect of his employee, or in carelessness or negligence of such degree as to manifest an equal culpability, wrongful intent or evil design, or to show an intentional and substantial disregard of the employer's interest or of the employee's duties and obligations to his employer."

Kentucky law provides that a legitimate activity in connection with labor organizations or failure to join a company union shall not be construed as misconduct.

Wyoming law provides that misconduct does not include ordinary negligence in isolated instances, good faith errors in judgment or discretion, or inefficiency or failure in good performance as the result of inability or incapacity.

Illegal Drug and Alcohol Provisions

The following table includes information about states with provisions in their UI law dealing specifically with alcohol and/or illegal drugs, and testing for alcohol or illegal drugs.

Disqualification for discharge for misconduct, as for voluntary leaving, is usually based on the circumstances of separation from the most recent employment. However, as indicated in the following table, a few state laws require consideration of the reasons for separation from employment other than the most recent.

Federal law permits cancellation of wage credits for only three reasons: misconduct in connection with the work, fraud in connection with a claim, or receipt of disqualifying income. The severity of the cancellation penalty depends mainly on the presence or absence of additional wage credits during the base period. If the wage credits canceled extend beyond the base period for the current benefit year, the individual may not be monetarily eligible in the subsequent benefit year.

Table 5-8. States with drug and/or alcohol provisions

State	Workers Will Be Disqualified:
AL	For testing positive for illegal drugs after being warned of possible dismissal, for refusing to undergo drug testing, or for knowingly altering a blood or urine specimen
AK	For reporting to work under the influence of drugs/alcohol, consumption on the employer's premises during work hours, or violation of employer's policy as long as policy meets statutory requirements
AZ	For refusing to undergo drug or alcohol testing, or having tested positive for drugs or alcohol
AR	For drinking on the job or reporting for work while under the influence of intoxicants, including a controlled substance; if discharged for testing positive for an illegal drug
CA	For chronic absenteeism due to intoxication, reporting to work while intoxicated, using intoxicants on the job, or gross neglect of duty while intoxicated, when any of these incidents is caused by an irresistible compulsion to use intoxicants; also disqualified if individual quit for reasons caused by an irresistible compulsion to use intoxicants
CT	If discharged or suspended due to being disqualified from performing work under state or Federal law for which hired as a result of a drug or alcohol testing program mandated and conducted by such law
FL	For drug use, as evidenced by a positive, confirmed drug test
GA	For violating an employer's drug-free workplace policy
IL	For consuming alcohol or illegal drugs, non-prescribed prescription drugs, or using an impairing substance in an off-label manner on the employer's premises during working hours in violation of the employer's policies, or showing up to work impaired during normal working hours
KY	For reporting to work under the influence of drugs/alcohol, or consuming them on employer's premises during working hours
State	Workers Will Be Disqualified:
LA	For the use of illegal drugs, on or off the job
MI	For illegally ingesting a controlled substance on the employer's premises, for refusing to submit to a drug test that was required to be administered in a nondiscriminatory manner, or for testing positive on a drug test that was administered in a nondiscriminatory manner
MO	For any drug/alcohol use; positive pre-employment drug/alcohol test is considered misconduct
NH	For intoxication or use of drugs that interferes with work
OK	For refusing to undergo drug or alcohol testing, or having tested positive for drugs or alcohol

State	Workers Will Be Disqualified:
OR	For failure or refusal to take a drug or alcohol test as required by employer's written policy; being under the influence of intoxicants while performing services for the employer; possessing a drug unlawfully; testing positive for alcohol or an unlawful drug in connection with employment; or refusing to enter into/violating terms of a last-chance agreement with employer; not disqualified if participating in a recognized rehabilitation program within 10 days of separation
PA	For failure to submit to and/or pass a drug test conducted pursuant to an employer's established substance abuse policy, provided that the drug test is not requested or implemented in violation of the law or of a collective bargaining agreement
SC	For failure or refusal to take a drug test or submitting to a drug test which tests positive for illegal drugs or legal drugs used unlawfully
WV	For reporting to work in an intoxicated condition or under the influence of any controlled substance without a valid prescription; for being intoxicated or under the influence of any controlled substance without a valid prescription while at work; for manipulating a sample or specimen to thwart a lawfully required drug or alcohol test; for refusal to submit to random drug testing for employees in safety-sensitive positions
VA	For drug use, as evidenced by a positive, confirmed USDOT qualified drug screen conducted in accordance with the employer's bona fide drug policy

Period of Disqualification

Some states have a variable disqualification for discharge for misconduct. In some states the range is small, in others, the range is large. Some states provide a fixed disqualification, and others disqualify for the duration of the unemployment or longer. Some states reduce or cancel all of the individual's benefit rights. Some states provide for disqualification for disciplinary suspensions.

Table 5-9. Discharge for misconduct - disqualification

State	Includes Other Than Last Employer	Benefits Postponed for:		Benefits Reduced or Canceled	Disqualification for Disciplinary Suspension
		Number of Weeks	Duration of Unemployment Until Requalify[1]		
AL	X[2]		10 x WBA	Equal	W + 1-3
AK		W + 5[3]		3 x WBA	Same as discharge for misconduct
AZ			5 x WBA		

Table 5-9. (Continued)

State	Includes Other Than Last Employer	Benefits Postponed for:		Benefits Reduced or Canceled	Disqualification for Disciplinary Suspension
		Number of Weeks	Duration of Unemployment Until Requalify[1]		
AR			30 days covered employment		Lesser of duration of suspension or 8 weeks
CA			5 x WBA		
CO		WF + 10		Equal	
CT			10 x WBA		Same as discharge for misconduct
DE			4 weeks of work and 4 x WBA		
DC	X[2]	WF + 7[3]	8 weeks of work and 8 x WBA	8 x WBA	
FL	X[2]	W + 1-52[3]	17 x WBA		Duration
GA			10 x WBA	Equal	Same as discharge for misconduct
HI			5 x WBA		
ID	X[2]		14 x WBA		
IL			Wages equal to WBA in each of 4 weeks		
IN			Wages in each of 8 weeks and wages ≥ 8 x WBA	25%, only one reduction during benefit year	
IA			10 x WBA		Same as discharge for misconduct
KS			3 x WBA		
KY			10 weeks of covered work and wages equal to 10 x WBA		
LA			10 WBA		
ME			8 x WBA		Duration or until earns 4 x WBA

State	Includes Other Than Last Employer	Benefits Postponed for:		Benefits Reduced or Canceled	Disqualification for Disciplinary Suspension
		Number of Weeks	Duration of Unemployment Until Requalify[1]		
MD	X[2]	W + 10-15			Same as discharge for misconduct
MA	X[2]		8 weeks of work and wages of 8 x WBA		
MI			17 x WBA		
MN			One-half of amount required to establish benefit account[4]		Duration
MS			8 x WBA		
MO	X[2]		6 x WBA for each disqualifying separation		Same as discharge for misconduct
MT			Wages equal to 8 x WBA		
NE	X[2]	14		Equal	
NV			Wages equal to WBA in each of 15 weeks		
NH			5 weeks work in each of which earned 20% more than WBA		Duration
NJ	X[2]	W + 5			Same as discharge for misconduct
NM			5 x WBA in covered work		
NY			3 days work in each of 5 weeks and 10 x WBA		

Table 5-9. (Continued)

State	Includes Other Than Last Employer	Benefits Postponed for:		Benefits Reduced or Canceled	Disqualification for Disciplinary Suspension
		Number of Weeks	Duration of Unemployment Until Requalify[1]		
NC		X[3]	10 x WBA in at least 5 weeks	X3	
ND	X[2]		10 x WBA		Duration
OH	X[2]		6 weeks in covered work plus wages equal to 27.5% of state AWW		Duration
OK			10 x WBA		
OR			4 x WBA	8 x WBA	Same as discharge for misconduct
PA			6 x WBA		Same as discharge for misconduct
PR			4 weeks of work and wages equal to 10 x WBA		Same as discharge for misconduct
RI	X[2]		8 x WBA		Same as discharge for misconduct
SC		WF + 20[5]		Equal	
SD	X[2]		6 weeks in covered work and wages equal to WBA each week		Same as discharge for misconduct
TN	X[2]		10 x WBA		
TX			6 weeks of work or wages equal to 6 x WBA		
UT	X[2]		6 x WBA in covered work		
VT		WF + 6-15			
VA	X[2]		30 days or 240 hours of work		Duration
VI			4 weeks of work and 4 x WBA		Same as discharge for misconduct
WA			10 weeks and earnings in bona fide work 10 x WBA		Same as discharge for misconduct

State	Includes Other Than Last Employer	Benefits Postponed for:		Benefits Reduced or Canceled	Disqualification for Disciplinary Suspension
		Number of Weeks	Duration of Unemployment Until Requalify[1]		
WV	X[2]	W + 6		Equal[6]	
WI			7 weeks elapsed and 14 x WBA	Benefit rights based on any work involved canceled	
WY			12 x WBA		

KEY: W = Week of discharge or week of suspension, WF = Week of filing

"Equal" indicates a reduction equal to the WBA multiplied by the number of weeks of disqualification.

[1] Minimum employment or wages to requalify for benefits and separated through no fault of his or her own.

[2] Disqualification pertains only to last separation unless indicated. AL - the preceding separation may be considered if last employment is not considered bona fide work; FL, ID, MD, MA, MO, OH, RI, and UT - a previous employer may be considered if the work with the separating employer does not satisfy a potential disqualification; VA - disqualification is applicable to last employing unit for which individual has worked 30 days or 240 hours and all subsequent employers; DC, SD, and WV - disqualification is applicable to last 30-day employing unit on new claims and to most recent employer on additional claims; ND - any employer with whom the individual earned 8 x WBA; NE - reduction or forfeiture of benefits applicable to separations from any base-period employer; NJ - provided the period of disqualification has not elapsed prior to the date of claim.

[3] AK - the disqualification is terminated if individual returns to work and earns 8 x WBA; DC - disqualification is terminated if either condition is satisfied; FL - both the term and the duration-of-unemployment disqualifications are imposed; NC - the agency may reduce permanent disqualification to time certain, but not less than five weeks; when permanent disqualification changed to time certain, benefits are reduced by an amount equal to the number of weeks of disqualification x WBA. Also, an individual will be disqualified for substantial fault on the part of the individual that is connected with work but not rising to the level of misconduct. The disqualification will vary from 4-13 weeks depending on the circumstances.

[4] $2,400 in 4-quarter base period or 5.3 percent of state's AAW rounded down to next lower $100, whichever is higher.

[5] Partial ineligibility of 5 to 19 weeks, plus waiting week, if individual is discharged for cause other than misconduct. Duration of ineligibility period determined in each case according to the seriousness of the cause for discharge.

[6] Benefit reduction is restored if individual returns to covered employment for at least 30 days within BY.

Disqualification for Gross Misconduct

Some states provide greater disqualifications for certain types of misconduct. For purposes of this section, all of these greater disqualifications will be considered disqualifications for "gross misconduct" even if the state's law does not specifically use this term.

States define gross misconduct in terms such as:

- Discharge for dishonesty or an act constituting a crime or a felony in connection with the work, if the individual is convicted or signs a statement admitting the act.
- Discharge for a dishonest or criminal act in connection with the work.
- Discharge for dishonesty, intoxication (including a controlled substance), or willful violation of bona fide written rules or customs of the employer including those pertaining to safety, harassment, unprofessional conduct, or insubordination.
- Assault or threatened assault upon supervisors, coworkers, or others at the work site.
- Assault, bodily injury, property loss or damage amounting to at least $2,000, theft, sabotage, embezzlement, or falsification of employer's records.
- Being placed on a disciplinary suspension.
- Any act that would constitute a gross misdemeanor or felony.
- Theft, fraud, intentional damage to property, intentional infliction of personal injury, or any conduct that constitutes a felony. Gross misconduct also includes the use of, or impairment from, alcohol or drugs by an individual while working, or a positive breath alcohol test or chemical test administered pursuant to specific requirements.
- Conviction of a felony or misdemeanor in connection with work.
- Assault, theft, or willful destruction of property.

Table 5-10. States with gross misconduct provisions - disqualification

State	Includes Other Than Last Employer	Benefits Postponed For:			Benefits Reduced or Canceled
		Fixed Number of Weeks	Variable Number of Weeks	Duration of Unemployment Until Requalify	
AL	X[1]			10 x WBA[1]	Wages earned from employer involved canceled
AK		52		20 x WBA	
AR				Wages in 2 quarters for insured work totaling not less than 35 x WBA	
CO		26			Equal
DC				10 weeks of work and wages equal to 10 x WBA	
FL			Up to 52	17 x WBA	
IL					All prior wage credits canceled2
IN					All prior wage credits canceled2
IA					All prior wage credits canceled
KS				8 x WBA	All prior wage credits canceled
LA	X1			10 x WBA1	Wages earned from employer involved canceled1
ME				Greater of $600 or 8 x WBA	
MD				25 x WBA3	
MI	X1	261		In each of 13 weeks, earnings at least 1/13 of minimum qualifying high quarter amount4	
MN				8 x WBA	Wages earned from employer involved canceled

Table 5-10. (Continued)

State	Includes Other Than Last Employer	Benefits Postponed For:			Benefits Reduced or Canceled
		Fixed Number of Weeks	Variable Number of Weeks	Duration of Unemployment Until Requalify	
MO	X1			6 x WBA for each disqualifying separation1, 5	Optional5
MT		12 months			Equal
NE					All prior wage credits canceled
NV					Benefit rights based on any work involved canceled6
NH			W + 4-266	5 weeks work in each of which earned 20% more than WBA	All prior wage credits canceled
NJ	X1			8 weeks of covered work and wages equal to 10 x WBA	Wages earned from employer involved canceled
NY	X1	12 months1			Wages earned from employer involved canceled
ND		12 months			
OH	X1				Benefit rights based on any work involved canceled1
OR					All prior wage credits canceled
SC				8 x WBA	Optional equal
UT		W + 51			All wage credits from the separating employer are canceled
VT				6 x WBA	Wages earned from employer canceled
WA					Greater of all hourly wage credits from employer involved or 680 hours of wage credits, canceled

State	Includes Other Than Last Employer	Benefits Postponed For:			Benefits Reduced or Canceled
		Fixed Number of Weeks	Variable Number of Weeks	Duration of Unemployment Until Requalify	
WV	X1			30 days in covered work	

KEY: W = Week of discharge, WF = Week of filing

[1] AL - disqualification applies to other than most recent separation from bona fide work only if employer files timely notice alleging disqualifying act; LA, MI, and MO - disqualification is applicable for all base-period employers; OH - applies if unemployed because of dishonesty or felony in connection with employment; NY - no days of unemployment deemed to occur for following 12 months if individual is convicted or signs statement admitting felonious act in connection with employment; WV - reduction or forfeiture of benefits is applicable to either most recent work or last 30-day employing unit; NJ - any base period employer.

[2] IL - wage credits are cancelled if gross misconduct constitutes a felony or theft and is admitted by the individual or has resulted in conviction in a court of competent jurisdiction; IN - same applies if gross misconduct constitutes a felony or misdemeanor.

[3] Has provision for aggravated misconduct, which consists of either physical assault, property loss, or damage so serious and with malice that the gross misconduct penalty is not sufficient. Disqualification is duration of unemployment and earnings of at least 30 x WBA.

[4] Or individual must file a continued claim in each of 13 weeks and certify as to satisfaction of all usual weekly eligibility requirements.

[5] Option taken by the agency to cancel all or part of wages depends on seriousness of misconduct. The only wage credits canceled are those based on work-connected misconduct.

[6] NH - if discharged for arson, sabotage, felony, assault causing bodily injury, criminal threatening, or theft equal to or greater than $250, all prior wage credits are canceled; NV - if individual is discharged and admits in writing or under oath, or is convicted for assault, arson, sabotage, grand larceny, embezzlement, or wanton destruction of property in connection with work, wage credits from that employer are canceled.

Disqualification for Fraud and Misrepresentation

In addition to assessments and prison time, individuals may be disqualified from benefits. The provisions for disqualification for fraud and misrepresentation follow no general pattern. In a few states there is a more severe disqualification when the fraudulent act results in payment of benefits. In others, it is more severe when the individual is convicted.

In a few states, the disqualification is not imposed unless the individual is convicted while in other states, the individual is not subject to an administrative disqualification if penal procedures have been undertaken or if the benefits are being or have been recovered.

Some states include a statutory limitation on the period within which a disqualification for fraudulent misrepresentation may be imposed (see footnote 3 in Table 5-11). The length of the period is usually two years. In a few states, the period runs from the date of the offense to the filing of a claim for benefits. In these states, the disqualification can be imposed only if the individual files a claim for benefits within two years of the date of the fraudulent act.

In many states, the penalty for disqualification for fraud or misrepresentation is, as would be expected, more severe than the ordinary disqualification provisions. In some states, the disqualification is for at least a year; in others, it may last longer. The provisions are difficult to compare because some disqualifications start with the date of the fraudulent act, while others begin with the discovery of the act, the determination of fraud, the date on which the individual is notified to repay the sum so received, or the date of conviction by a court. Some begin with the filing of a first claim, while others are for weeks that would otherwise be compensable.

The disqualification provisions are, moreover, complicated by tie-in with recoupment provisions and by retroactive imposition.

As following table shows, the cancellation of wage credits in many states means the denial of benefits for the current benefit year or longer. A disqualification for a year means that wage credits will have expired, in whole or in part, depending on the end of the benefit year and the amount of wage credits accumulated for another benefit year before the fraudulent act. Thus, future benefits are reduced as if there had been a provision for cancellation. In other states with discretionary provisions or shorter disqualification periods, the same result will occur for some individuals. In many states, as noted in the table below, the agency may deny benefits until the benefits obtained through fraud are repaid although some states impose a time limit for the denial. In some states, an individual may qualify after a specified period of time and repayment is made through an offset of the benefits.

Table 5-11. Disqualification for fraud

State	Duration of Disqualification	Benefits Reduced or Canceled
AL	52 weeks for 1st offense and 104 weeks for 2nd and subsequent offenses	4 x WBA to maximum benefit amount payable in BY[1]
AK	W + 6 – 52	X[1]
AZ	Until total amount of overpayment and all penalties and interest have been recovered or otherwise satisfied in compliance with a civil judgment[2, 3]	X[1]
AR	W + 13; additional 3 weeks for each week of fraud[2, 3]	Benefits canceled in BY in which fraud occurred
State	Duration of Disqualification	Benefits Reduced or Canceled
CA	If convicted, 52 weeks[2, 3, 4]	X[1]
CO	4 - 104 weeks	X[1]
CT	Full amount of overpayment must be repaid	Mandatory equal reduction
DE	W + 51	X[1]
DC	All or part of remainder of BY and for 1 year commencing with the end of such BY[1]	X[1]
FL	1 - 52 weeks and until fraudulent overpayments are repaid in full[2]	X[1]
GA	Remainder of current quarter and next 4 quarters[3]	Mandatory equal reduction[3]
HI	24 months[2, 3]	X[1]
ID	W + 52; amounts fraudulently received, plus penalty and interest, must be repaid[2, 3]	X[1]
IL	W + 6 weeks; if additional offenses, up to[2, 3]	
IN	Up to current BY	All wage credits prior to act canceled
IA	Up to current BY[2]	Mandatory equal reduction
KS	5 years after act committed or after 1st day following last week for which benefits were paid, whichever is later	X[1]
KY	Unreported earnings: W + additional weeks based on amount of unreported earnings (up to 52 W); nondisclosure of info other than wages: W + 26[2]	X[1]
LA	For remainder of BY after commission of fraudulent act and then continuing for 52 weeks following determination of fraud	X[1]
ME	6 months - 1 year; for 3rd occurrence disqualification determined by the Commissioner[2]	
MD	All benefits and interest repaid[2]	X[1]
MA	A compensable week for each week overpaid	25% of WBA
MI	Current BY and until such amounts are repaid or withheld[2, 3]	All base period wages canceled; benefits canceled in BY in which fraud occurred
MN	13 - 104 weeks	X[1]

Table 5-11. (Continued)

State	Duration of Disqualification	Benefits Reduced or Canceled
MS	W + up to 52 weeks; first overpayment results in 6 weeks for each fraudulent week; any additional overpayment results in 12 weeks for each fraudulent week	X
MO	Up to current benefit year +5	All or part of wage credits prior to act canceled
MT	1 - 52 weeks and until benefits are repaid2	
NE	Up to current benefit year +5	All or part of wage credits prior to act canceled
NV	W + 1 - 52 or until sum equal to all benefits received or paid plus any interest, penalties, or costs related to that sum is repaid, whichever is longer; period of disqualification will be fixed according to the circumstances in each case[6]	X[1]
NH	4 - 52 weeks; if convicted, 1 year after conviction; and until benefits are repaid or withheld[2]	Mandatory equal reduction
NJ	1 year[2]	X[1]
NM	Not more than 52 weeks[2]	X[1]
NY	4 - 80 days for which otherwise eligible[2, 3]	Mandatory equal reduction
NC	52 weeks[2]	X[1]
ND	W + 5[1]	X[1]
OH	Amount of fraudulent benefits must be repaid, and individual held ineligible for 2 otherwise valid weekly claims for each weekly claim canceled	2 penalty weeks are served for each week in which fraud occurred
OK	W + 51[2, 3]	BP or BY may not be established during period
OR	52 weeks; if convicted, until benefits are repaid or withheld[2, 3, 5]	If convicted, all wage credits prior to conviction canceled[6]
PA	2 weeks plus 1 week for each week of fraud or, if convicted of illegal receipt of benefits, 1 year after conviction and until benefits are withheld or repaid[3]	X1
PR	W + 51 provided that criminal procedures have not been filed against individual[2, 3]	
RI	If convicted, 1 year after conviction	X[1]
SC	W + 10 - 52[2]	X[1]
SD	Benefits denied for weeks of compensable unemployment from and after the discovery date of fraud, until benefits are repaid	X[1]
TN	W + 4 - 52[2]	X[1]
TX	Current BY	Benefits or remainder of BY canceled

State	Duration of Disqualification	Benefits Reduced or Canceled
UT	W + 13 - 49, and until benefits received fraudulently are repaid	X[1]
VT	If not prosecuted, until amount of fraudulent benefits are repaid or withheld + 1 - 26 weeks[2, 3]	X[1]
VA	W + 52; if convicted, 1 year after conviction, or until repaid[2, 3]	X[1]
VI	W + 51[2, 3]	X[1]
WA	Week of fraudulent act + 26 weeks following filing of 1st claim after determination of fraud for 1st offense; plus additional 52 weeks for 2nd offense; plus additional 104 weeks for 3rd and subsequent offenses[3]	X[1]
WV	W + 52[2]	
WI	Each week of fraud	1 - 4 x WBA[1]
WY	W + 51[2]	

GENERAL NOTE: W = week in which act occurs plus the indicated number of consecutive weeks following.

[1] Before disqualification period ends, wage credits may or will have expired in whole or in part depending on disqualification imposed and/or end of BY.

[2] HI, ID, IL, IA, MD, MT, NH, NM, OK, PR, SC, VA, and WV - period of disqualification is measured from date of determination of fraud; ME and NC - mailing date of determination; VT - date of redetermination of fraud; AR - date of delivery or mailing of determination; AZ - date of claim or registration for work; CA - week determination is mailed or served, or any subsequent week for which individual is first otherwise eligible for benefits, or if convicted, week in which criminal complaint is filed; FL, NY, and TN - waiting or compensable week after its discovery; OR - as determined by agency; KY, MI, and NJ - date of discovery of fraud; VI - determination mailed or delivered; WY - week of fraud or week following the date notice is mailed.

[3] Has a statutory limitation.

[4] Disqualification of 2 - 15 weeks if no benefits paid; 5 - 15 weeks if benefits received;. Director may extend the period of ineligibility for an additional period not to exceed eight additional weeks for successive disqualification; disqualification may be served concurrently with a disqualification imposed for any of the three major causes if individual registers for work for such week as required under latter disqualifications.

[5] MO, NE, and OR - cancellation of all wage credits means that period of disqualification will extend into second BY, depending on amount of wage credits for such year accumulated before fraudulent claim.

[6] May be waived for good cause, or if the individual adheres to an authorized repayment schedule designed to repay benefits, penalties, and interest within 18 months.

Drug Testing as a Condition of Eligibility

The Middle Class Tax Relief and Job Creation Act of 2012 (Public Law 112-96) amended Federal law to permit states to conduct drug testing on individuals applying for benefits if the individual was discharged from employment for unlawful drug use, or if the only suitable work available to the individual is in an occupation that regularly conducts drug testing. States are permitted to deny benefits to individuals who test positive for drugs under these circumstances. Three states have enacted such laws, the implementation of which is subject to applicable Federal law.

Mississippi permits drug testing on individuals as a condition of eligibility for benefits if the individual was discharged because of unlawful drug use or if s/he is seeking suitable work only in an occupation that requires drug testing. Individuals may be denied benefits based on the results of these drug tests, but may end the disqualification period early by submitting acceptable proof of a negative drug test result from an approved testing facility. Texas permits drug testing, as a condition of eligibility for benefits, on individuals for whom suitable work is available only in an occupation that regularly conducts pre-employment drug testing.

Wisconsin enacted legislation requiring the establishment of rules for a drug testing program for controlled substances, including rules identifying occupations for which drug testing is regularly conducted in the state.

Labor Disputes

Unlike many other eligibility provisions, those related to labor disputes do not question whether the unemployment is incurred through fault on the part of the individual worker. The denial is always a postponement of benefits; there is no reduction or cancellation of benefit rights. In almost all states, the denial period is indefinite and geared to the continuation of the dispute-induced work stoppage or to the progress of the dispute.

Definition of Labor Dispute

State laws use different terms to describe labor disputes. In addition to labor dispute, these terms include trade dispute, strike, "strike and lockout," or "strike or other bona fide labor dispute." Except for Alabama, Arizona, Colorado, and Minnesota, state laws do not define these terms. Some states exclude the following from their denials.

- Employer lockouts.
- Disputes resulting from the employer's failure to conform to the provisions of a labor contract.
- Disputes caused by the employer's failure to conform to any state or federal law relating to wages, hours, working conditions, or collective bargaining.
- Disputes where the employees are protesting substandard working conditions.

Location of the Dispute

Usually an individual is not denied benefits unless the labor dispute is in the establishment in which the individual was last employed. A few states deny individuals at any other premises operated by the employer, under certain circumstances.

Period of Denial

In most states, the denial period ends when the "stoppage of work because of a labor dispute" ends or the stoppage ceases to be caused by the labor dispute. In some states, the denial period lasts while the labor dispute is in "active progress." In others, the denial period lasts while the individual's unemployment is a result of a labor dispute.

A few state laws allow individuals to terminate the denial period by showing that the labor dispute (or the stoppage of work) is no longer the cause of their unemployment.

- In Indiana, the denial ends following termination of employment with the employer involved in the dispute.

- In Michigan, the denial ends if an individual works in at least two consecutive calendar weeks and earns wages in each week of at least the weekly benefit amount based on employment with the employer involved in the labor dispute.
- In Missouri, the denial ends following the bona fide employment of the individual for at least the major part of each of two weeks.
- In New Hampshire, the denial ends two weeks after the dispute has ended even if the stoppage of work continues.
- In Maine, Massachusetts, New Hampshire, and Utah an individual may receive benefits if, during a stoppage of work resulting from a labor dispute, he or she obtains employment with another employer and earns a specified amount of wages. However, wages earned with the employer involved in the dispute cannot be used to determine eligibility while the stoppage of work continues.
- In contrast, some states' laws extend the denial for the period of time necessary for the employer to resume normal operations (Arkansas, Colorado, North Carolina, and Tennessee). Others extend the denial period to shutdown and start-up operations (Michigan and Virginia).
- In New York, an individual is denied for seven consecutive weeks due to unemployment because of a strike, lockout, or concerted activity not authorized or sanctioned by the collective bargaining unit in the establishment where such individual was employed.

Exclusion of Individual Workers

Most states provide that individual workers are not denied benefits under the labor dispute provisions if they and others of the same grade or class are not participating in the dispute, financing it, or directly interested in it. The following table provides information regarding denials related to labor disputes.

Table 5-12. Labor disputes - duration of denial

State	During Stoppage of Work	While Dispute Is in Active Progress	Other
AL		X	
AK	X		
AZ			X1
AR			X
CA		X	
CO			X
CT			X1
DE	X		
DC		X	
FL		X	
GA	X2		
HI	X		
ID			X1
IL	X		
IN			X3
IA	X		
KS	X		
KY		X	
LA		X	
ME	X		
MD	X		
MA	X2		
MI			X
MN		X	
MS	X		
MO	X		
MT			X1
NE	X		
NV		X	
NH	X		
NJ	X2		
NM			X1
NY			X
NC			X
ND			X1
OH			X1
OK	X		
OR		X	
PA	X		
PR	X		

Table 5-12. (Continued)

State	During Stoppage of Work	While Dispute Is in Active Progress	Other
RI			X1
SC		X	
SD			X1
TN		X	
TX	X3		
UT	X		
VT	X		
VA		X	X
VI		X	
WA			X1
WV	X2		
WI		X	
WY	X		

[1] As long as unemployment is caused by the existence of a labor dispute.

[2] Disqualification ceases: GA - when operations have been resumed but individual has not been reemployed; MA - within one week following termination of dispute if individual is not recalled to work; NJ – unless the employer hires a replacement and does not allow employee to return during 30-day waiting period; WV - if the stoppage of work continues longer than four weeks after the termination of the labor dispute, there is a rebuttable presumption that the stoppage is not due to the labor dispute and the burden is on the employer to show otherwise.

[3] IN and TX - as long as unemployment is caused by work stoppage that exists because of labor dispute; failure or refusal to cross picket line or to accept and perform available and customary work in the establishment constitutes participation and interest.

Table 5-13. Labor disputes - exclusions

	Disputes Excluded if Caused by:			Workers Not Denied if Neither They Nor Any of the Same Grade or Class Are:		
	Employer's Failure to Conform to:		Lockout			
State	Contract	Labor Law		Participating In Dispute	Financing Dispute	Directly Interested in Dispute
AL						
AK	X	X		X		X
AZ	X	X		X	X	X
AR			X	X		X
CA			X			
CO			X[1]	X	X	X

	Disputes Excluded if Caused by:			Workers Not Denied if Neither They Nor Any of the Same Grade or Class Are:		
	Employer's Failure to Conform to:		Lockout			
State	Contract	Labor Law		Participating In Dispute	Financing Dispute	Directly Interested in Dispute
CT			X	X	X	X
DE			X			
DC			X	X		X
FL			X	X	X	X
GA			X	X	X	X
HI				X		X
ID				X	X2	X
IL			X[1]	X	X	X
IN				X	X	X
IA				X	X	X
KS				X[3]	X	X[3]
KY			X			
LA			X	X[2]		X[2]
ME	X	X	X	X	X	X
MD			X	X	X	X
MA			X	X	X	X
MI			X[4]			
MN	X	X	X	X[5]		X[5]
MS			X	X		X
MO				X	X	X
MT		X		X	X	X
NE				X	X	X
NV				X	X	X
NH	X	X		X	X	X
NJ	X		X[6]	X	X	X
NM				X		X
NY			X[7]			
NC						
ND				X		X
OH			X[1]	X[1]		
OK			X	X		X
OR	X		X	X[1]	X	X
PA			X	X		X
PR				X		X
RI			X	X[2]	X[2]	X[2]
SC				X	X[2]	X
SD			X	X	X	X
TN			X	X[1]		
TX			X	X[3]	X[3]	X[3]

Table 5-13. (Continued)

State	**Disputes Excluded if Caused by:** Employer's Failure to Conform to: Contract	Labor Law	Lockout	**Workers Not Denied if Neither They Nor Any of the Same Grade or Class Are:** Participating In Dispute	Financing Dispute	Directly Interested in Dispute
UT		X[1]	X			X
VT			X[1]	X[2]	X[2]	X[2]
VA				X	X	X
VI			X	X		X
WA				X	X	X
WV	X[8]		X	X	X	X
WI			X			
WY				X	X	X

[1] Dispute is not disqualifying: CO - unless the lockout results from demands of employees, as distinguished from an employer effort to deprive the employees of some advantage they already possess; OH - if the individual was laid off and not recalled prior to the dispute, if separated prior to the dispute, or if obtained bona fide job with another employer while the dispute was in progress; IL - if the recognized or certified collective bargaining representative of the locked out employees refuses to meet under reasonable conditions with the employer to discuss the lockout issues, or there is a final adjudication under the NLRA that during the lockout period such representative has refused to bargain in good faith with the employer over the lockout issues, or if the lockout resulted as a direct consequence of a violation by such representative of the provisions of an existing collective bargaining agreement; OR - if the individual was laid off prior to the dispute and did not work more than seven days during the 21 calendar days immediately prior to the dispute, or if his or her position was filled and the individual unilaterally abandons the dispute to seek reemployment with the employer; TN - if the individual was indefinitely separated prior to the dispute and otherwise eligible; UT - if the employer was involved in fomenting the strike; VT - if the employer brought about the lockout to gain concessions from the employees.

[2] Applies only to individual, not to other workers of the same grade or class.

[3] As long as unemployment is caused by work stoppage that exists because of labor dispute; failure or refusal to cross picket line or to accept and perform available and customary work in the establishment constitutes participation and interest.

[4] Only if unemployment is caused by lockout in another, functionally integrated U.S. establishment of the same employer.

[5] Disqualification limited to one week for individuals neither participating in nor directly interested in dispute.

[6] Individuals locked out of employment by their employer can collect benefits if they were not on strike immediately prior to the lockout and are directed by their union leadership to work under the preexisting terms and conditions of employment.

[7] If not participating and not employed by an employer that is involved in the industrial controversy that caused their unemployment, or not in a bargaining unit involved in the industrial controversy that caused their unemployment.

Nonseparations

Ability to Work

Only minor variations exist in state laws setting forth the requirements concerning ability to work. A few states specify that an individual must be physically able, or mentally and physically able to work. Evidence of ability to work is the filing of claims and registration for work at a public employment office, required under most state laws. Missouri goes one step further requiring, by law, every individual receiving benefits to report in person to the nearest office at least once every four weeks.

Several states have added a provision that no individual who has filed a claim and has registered for work shall be considered ineligible during an uninterrupted period of unemployment because of illness or disability, provided no work, which is suitable but for the disability, is offered and refused. These provisions are not to be confused with the special programs in six states for temporary disability benefits.

Availability for Work

Availability for work is often translated to mean being ready, willing, and able to work. Meeting the requirement of registration for work at a public employment office is considered as some evidence of availability. Nonavailability may be evidenced by substantial restrictions upon the kind or conditions of otherwise suitable work that an individual can or will accept, or by the refusal of a referral to suitable work made by the employment service, or of an offer of suitable work made by an employer.

The availability-for-work provisions are more varied than the ability-to-work provisions. Some states provide that an individual must be available for work; some for suitable work; and others for work in the individual's usual occupation or for which the individual is reasonably fitted by training and experience.

The following table indicates the states in which individuals are not ineligible due to illness or disability (occurring after the claim is filed and after registering for work) as long as no refusal of suitable work occurs after the beginning of the illness or disability.

Table 5-14. States with Special Provisions for Illness or Disability

Alaska[1]	Delaware	Hawaii	Idaho[2]
Massachusetts[3]	Nevada	North Dakota[4]	Tennessee
Vermont			

[1] Waiver may not exceed six consecutive weeks

[2] Only if no suitable work was available that would have paid wages greater than one-half of the individual's WBA

[3] Provision applicable for three weeks only in a benefit year

[4] Only if illness not covered by workers' compensation

Vacation

Georgia, Indiana, and West Virginia specify the conditions under which individuals on vacation are deemed unavailable or unemployed. Georgia limits to two weeks in any calendar year the period of unavailability of individuals who are not paid while on a vacation provided in an employment contract or by employer-established custom or policy. Mississippi considers an individual unavailable for work during a holiday or vacation period. In North Carolina, no individual shall be considered available for work for any week, not to exceed two weeks in any calendar year, in which the unemployment is due to a vacation. In Indiana, an individual is not considered unemployed if he or she is on a vacation week and is receiving, or has received, remuneration from the employer for that week. In addition, Indiana considers individuals to be employed if they are on a vacation week and have not received remuneration from the employer for that week because of a written contract between the employer and its workers, or because of the employer's regular vacation policy and practice (this provision applies only if the individual has reasonable assurance of employment available with the employer after the vacation period ends).

In Nebraska and New Jersey, no individual is deemed unavailable for work solely because he or she is on vacation without pay if the vacation is not the result of the individual's own action as distinguished from any collective bargaining or other action beyond the individual's control. Under New York law, an agreement by an individual or the individual's union or representative to a shutdown for vacation purposes is not in itself considered a withdrawal from the labor market or unavailability during the time of such vacation shutdown.

Other provisions relating to eligibility during vacation periods, although not specifically stated in terms of availability, exist in Virginia, where individuals are eligible for benefits only if they are not on a bona fide paid vacation; Washington provides that a cessation of operations by an employer for the purpose of granting vacations shall not be construed to be a voluntary quit or voluntary unemployment. Tennessee does not deny benefits during unemployment caused by a plant shutdown for vacation, provided the individual does not receive vacation pay. However, individuals who receive regular wages for a vacation under terms of a labor- management agreement will have their weekly benefit amount reduced by the amount of the wages received, but only if work will be available for the individuals with the employer at the end of the vacation period.

Nebraska provides that an individual is considered employed when wages are received for a specific time in which the vacation is actually taken during a time of temporary layoff or plant shutdown; vacation pay is prorated in an amount reasonably attributable to each week claimed and considered payable with respect to that week.

In Minnesota, vacation pay will not delay unemployment benefit eligibility to an applicant who has been indefinitely laid off due to lack of work as a result of adverse trade impacts and is not expected to be recalled within six months by the employer from which the applicant was laid off. This section does not apply to seasonal workers nor does it apply to temporary, indefinite, or seasonal separations.

Locality

Alabama, Michigan, Ohio, and South Carolina require that individuals be available for work in the locality where their base-period wages were earned, or in a locality where similar work is available or where suitable work is normally performed. Illinois and Utah consider individuals to be unavailable if, after separation from their most recent work, they move to and remain in a locality where opportunities for work are substantially less favorable than those in the locality they left. Oregon, Utah, and Virginia consider individuals unavailable for work if they leave their normal labor market area for the major portion of a week unless the individuals can establish that they conducted a bona fide search for work in the labor market area where they spent the major part of the week.

In Wisconsin, an individual is not considered available for work in any week they are in a country other than the United States or Canada for more than 48 hours, unless the individual has authorization to work in that country and there is a reciprocal agreement with that country concerning the payment of unemployment benefits. In Utah, an individual located in a foreign country for three or more days of a week and who is otherwise eligible for benefits is only eligible to receive benefits for that week if the individual is legally authorized to work in the foreign country, and the state and the foreign country have entered into a reciprocal agreement concerning the payment of unemployment benefits.

Availability during Training

FUTA requires, as a condition for employers in a state to receive credit against the Federal tax, that all state laws provide that compensation shall not be denied to an otherwise eligible individual for any week during which the individual is attending a training course with the approval of the state agency. Also, all state laws must provide that trade allowances not be denied to an otherwise eligible individual for any week during which the individual is in training approved under the Trade Act of 1974 because of leaving unsuitable employment to enter such training. In addition, the state law must provide that individuals in training not be held ineligible or disqualified for being unavailable for work, for failing to make an active search for work, or for failing to accept an offer of, or for refusal of, suitable work.

Federal law does not specify the criteria that states must use in approving training. Although some state laws have set forth the standards to be used, many do not specify the types of training that are approvable. Generally, approved training is limited to vocational or basic education training, thereby excluding regularly enrolled students from collecting benefits under the approved training provision.

Some states, in addition to providing regular benefits while the individual attends an industrial retraining or other vocational training course, provide for an extended duration of benefits while the individual remains in training/retraining. See Chapter 4 concerning programs for extended duration.

While in almost all states the participation of individuals in approved training courses is voluntary, in the District of Columbia and Washington an individual may be required to attend such training under certain circumstances.

In Oregon, individuals who do not attend their approved training during a particular week will be required to meet regular eligibility requirements for that week.

Availability for Part-Time Work

Many states require individuals to be available for full-time work. Other states allow individuals to be available for part-time work under certain conditions. The following table indicates those states paying benefits to workers who seek only part-time employment. Please note that considerable differences may exist between states with entries in the same column.

Michigan and West Virginia require that an individual be available for full-time work. Pennsylvania considers an individual ineligible for benefits for any week in which his or her unemployment is due to failure to accept an offer of suitable full-time work to pursue seasonal or part-time work. New Hampshire requires that an individual be available for and seek temporary work, whether full-time or part-time, if permanent work for which the individual is qualified is not immediately available within the individual's labor market area, if the individual is reasonably expected to be recalled in 4 to 26 weeks, and if the wages, hours, and other conditions of the temporary work are not substantially less favorable than those prevailing for similar temporary or permanent work in the locality.

Table 5-15. States with availability of part-time workers provisions States that pay benefits to part-time workers under certain conditions

State	If Otherwise Eligible	Claim Based on Part-Time Work, or History of Part- Time Work	Medical Restrictions or Restrictions Due to Disabilities	Other
AR	I	L		
CA		L		
CO		L, R		
CT			L, R	
DE		L1		Good Cause – I
DC				Good Cause – I
FL		I		
GA		L1		
HI		L		
IL			R	Only if part-time work is suitable because of circumstances beyond individual's control – R
ID		L1		
IA		L, R		
KS		L1, I		
LA		I		
ME		L, R	L, R2	L, R2
MD		L1		
MA		R	R	
MN		L		
MT		L	R	
NE		L1		
NV		R	I	I3
NH		L	L	R4
NJ		L, R		
NM	L, R3			L, R5
NY		L		
ND		I		
OH		I		
OK		L1		
OR			R	
PA	I6			
PR		I		
SC		L1		

State	If Otherwise Eligible	Claim Based on Part-Time Work, or History of Part- Time Work	Medical Restrictions or Restrictions Due to Disabilities	Other
SD		L1		
UT			R	
VT		I		
VA			I	
VI	L			
WA		L, R		
WY		R	R	

KEY: L = law, R = regulation, I = interpretation

[1] DE - if individual is willing to work at least 20 hours per week, is available for the number of hours comparable to part-time work in base period, or is available for the hours comparable to his or her work at the time of most recent separation; GA, ID, and NM - if individual is willing to work at least 20 hours per week; KS and OK - provided the individual is available for the number of hours per week that are comparable to part-time work experience in base period; MD - provided that the individual worked at least 20 hours per week in part-time work for a majority of the weeks of work in the base period and is in a labor market in which a reasonable demand exists for part-time work; NE - provided that the majority of weeks of work in the base period included part-time work and that the individual is available for at least 20 hours of work per week; SC and SD - provided the majority of weeks of work in the base period include part-time work.

[2] When majority of weeks in base period were full-time but individual is only able, available and seeking part-time work due to own or immediate family member's illness or disability, or when necessary for safety or protection of individual or immediate family member, including protection from domestic abuse.

[3] Student provision applies to high school students who can only work part-time while attending school.

[4] In certain circumstances, if individual is the only adult suitable to care for a child.

[5] Only for individuals who attend school full time and are actively seeking at least part-time work, and for whom school attendance was not a factor in separation from work.

[6] The Superior Court has stated that the availability requirement is met as long as an individual is ready, willing, and able to accept some substantial and suitable work.

Note: Since most state laws do not specify whether the individual must be available for full-time or part-time work, the previous table should be used with caution.

Actively Seeking Work

In addition to registration for work at a local employment office, all states, whether by law or practice, require that an individual be actively seeking work or making a reasonable effort to obtain work. The Middle Class Tax Relief and Job Creation Act of 2012 (Public Law 112-96) added an explicit statutory requirement to Federal law that individuals must be able to work, available for work, and actively seeking work to be eligible for regular unemployment compensation. The following table contains information on work search requirements and the necessity of searching for full-time or part-time work, by state. In some states, the required number of employer contacts may vary under certain circumstances, for example, during an EB period or depending on rural or urban area. Please note that this table is intended to provide a general overview of work search requirements in the states; it is not meant to be exhaustive. Please consult the appropriate state statute, regulation, or policy for more specific information on work search requirements.

Because states may not deny benefits to an individual in approved training, all states provide an exemption from the requirements to be able and available for work and conducting an active work search for any week the individual is in approved training. In addition, most states allow work search exemptions if the worker is union-attached and finds work through the union hall, though some states place a time limit on this exemption. Most states allow a work search exemption if a separation is classified as a temporary lay-off and there is a reasonable expectation that the worker will return to work soon. Other work search exemptions include that the worker has a specified start date for new employment, has jury duty, is an STC participant, has a compelling personal reason, is in a labor dispute with the employer, is the victim of domestic violence, or labor market or other information indicates no suitable employment.

The vast majority of states allow claimants to contact potential employers in person, over the telephone, through standard mail, through electronic means like fax or email, by filling out on-line applications, submitting resumes on-line, or through an employment agency. Additionally, several states allow for more varied forms of employer contact including: responding to job advertisements, uploading a resume to an on-line job market website, attending a job fair, taking a civil service test, participating in state reemployment services, or registering with a private employment services organization. In some states, union members are required to register with their appropriate local union hall.

Table 5-16. Work search requirements

State	Basis	Number of Employers Contacts Required per Week	Part-Time Work Search Acceptable
AL	L & R	≥1	
AK	L, R, & I	1 – 21	X
AZ	L, R, & I	42	
AR	L & R	≥21	X3
CA	L, R, & I	Agency determined	
CO	L & R	1 - 51, 4	X3
CT	L, R, & I	≥3	
DE	L & R	≥1 new	X2
DC	L & R	≥2	X
FL	L & R	≥3 - rural area, ≥5 - urban area4	X3
GA	L, R, & I	≥3 new	X3
HI	L & R	≥3	X3
ID	L & R	≥24	X3
IL	L, R, & I	Quality not quantity	X3
IN	L & I	≥3	
IA	L, R, & I	≥25	X3
KS	L, R, & I	14	X3
KY	L & I	Unspecified – reasonable person	
LA	L, R, & I	3 - new, 1 - union members	
ME	L & R	≥1	
MD	L, R, & I	≥2 new	X3
MA	L & I	≥36	X2
MI	L & I	≥2	
MN	L, R, & I	Unspecified	X3
MS	L & R	3	
MO	L & I	2 – 31	

Table 5-16. (Continued)

State	Basis	Number of Employers Contacts Required per Week	Part-Time Work Search Acceptable
MT	L & R	≥1 new2	
NE	R & I	≥ 52, 4	X3
NV	L & I	3 – 51	X3
NH	L, R, & I	Unspecified – reasonable person	X
NJ	R	≥34	X3
NM	L & R	≥2	X3
NY	L & R	≥34	X3
NC	L	≥3	
ND	L	4	X3
OH	L & I	2	X3
OK	L, R, & I	≥24	X3
OR	L, R, & I	52	X
PA	L & R	2 applications and 1 search activity5	X2
PR	L	1	X3
RI	L, R, & I	≥3	
SC	L	≥42, 4	X3
SD	L, R, & I	24	X3
TN	L & R	≥34	
TX	L, R, & I	37	
UT	L, R, & I	4	
VT	L, R, & I	3	X
VA	L, R, & I	≥2	X
VI	R	≥3	
WA	L & R	≥34	X3
WV	L,R, & I	Unspecified1	
WI	L&R	≥47	
WY	L&R	≥2	X3

KEY: L = law, R = regulation, I = interpretation or policy

[1] Dependent on geography, labor market, union hall membership, or other factor.

[2] Limitations or specific requirements apply.

[3] Part-time work history required.

[4] May use employment services registration, access reemployment services, jobseeking workshop, or participate in job search activities. **NE** and **SC** require at least one contact through the state system.

[5] May be adjusted.

[6] Domestic violence accommodations.

[7] Agency may increase or direct.

Table 5-17. Work search - reporting and monitoring

State	Basis	Claimant Reporting of Work Search Activities		Frequency of Monitoring
		Frequency	Method of Reporting	
AL	L & R	Weekly	Eligibility review	Random eligibility review
AK	L, R, & I	Weekly	Paper, phone, or internet	At random by Quality Control Unit
AZ	L, R, & I	Weekly	Paper or internet	Each weekly claim
AR	L & R	Weekly	Phone or paper	Random audit
CA	L, R, & I	Upon request	Interview	Eligibility review
CO	L & R	Bi-weekly	Part of continued claim process	Random or targeted audits
CT	L, R, & I	Weekly	Part of audit	Random or targeted audits
DE	L & R	Weekly	Part of weekly claim	Random audits
DC	L & R	With continued claim	Part of continued claim	Through normal BAM compliance
FL	L & R	Bi-weekly with continued claim	Part of continued claim	Random weekly audits
GA	L, R, & I	Weekly	Online or fax	Unspecified
HI	L & R	Weekly	Telephone survey questions	Incomplete work search triggers REA or eligibility review
ID	L & R	Weekly	Online with continued claim	Random or targeted audits
IL	L, R, & I	Upon request	In writing	Unspecified
IN	L & I	Weekly	With weekly claim	Unspecified
IA	L, R, & I	Able to report with continued claim, but not required	Upon request	During REA assessment and BAM audits
KS	L, R, & I	Weekly	Upon request	BAM audits
KY	L & I	Weekly	Upon request	Random eligibility review
LA	L, R, & I	Eligibility review every 6 weeks	Upon request	Eligibility review every 6 weeks
ME	L & R	Mandatory contact log upon request	Mandatory contact log upon request	Random audits or BAM audits
MD	L, R, & I	Weekly	Upon request	Random telephone interview
MA	L & I	Weekly	Upon request	Random audit or REA
MI	L & I	Monthly	Online, mail, in-person	Random audit by BAM staff
MN	L, R, & I	Upon request	Online	Random audit/ worker profiling
MS	L & R	Weekly	Online	Random audit
MO	L & I	Weekly	Online, phone, or mail	Weekly and random eligibility reviews
MT	L & R	Weekly	Weekly claim	Random audits and BAM
NE	R & I	Weekly	Online	Random audit

Table 5-17. (Continued)

State	Basis	Claimant Reporting of Work Search Activities		Frequency of Monitoring
		Frequency	Method of Reporting	
NV	L & I	Weekly	Contact log	REA, random audit
NH	L, R, & I	Weekly	Part of weekly claim	REA or eligibility review
NJ	R	Bi-weekly	Telephone, online, or by mail.	Random weekly audits, BAM
NM	L & R	Weekly	Upon request	Random audit
NY	L & R	Weekly	Upon request	Random audit
NC	L	Weekly	Upon request	Unspecified
ND	L	Weekly (online) monthly (by other means)	Online or in event of eligibility review every 4 weeks	Random audit
OH	L & I	Weekly	With continued claim	Random audit and BAM
OK	L, R, & I	Weekly	Upon request by mail, fax, or online	Random audit
OR	L, R, & I	Weekly	With continued claim	REA
PA	L & R	Weekly	Upon request	Random audit
PR	L	Weekly	Upon request	Unspecified
RI	L, R, & I	Weekly	Upon request	Random audits and REA
SC	L	Weekly	Upon request	Eligibility review
SD	L, R, & I	Weekly	With continued claim	Random weekly audit
TN	L & R	Weekly	Upon request	Random weekly audits
TX	L, R, & I	Weekly	Upon request	Random audits
UT	L, R, & I	Weekly	With weekly continued claim	Random audits, REA, and worker profiling
VT	L, R, & I	Weekly	With weekly continued claim, online	Random audits
VA	L & R	Weekly	With weekly continued claim	Random audit
VI	R	Weekly	Upon request	Random audit
WA	L & R	Weekly	Upon request	Random audit and upon request
WV	L, R, & I	Weekly	Upon request	Random audit and REA screening
WI	L & R	Weekly	Upon request	Random audits
WY	L & R	Weekly	Upon request	State reviews a randomly chosen 2-week log of the first 4 weeks claimed

KEY: L = law, R = regulation, I = interpretation or policy; BAM = Benefit Accuracy Measurement; REA = Reemployment Eligibility Assessment.

Refusal of Work

All state laws address refusal of suitable work, though they vary concerning the extent of the disqualification imposed. FUTA provides that all state laws must also consider the labor market and certain labor standards. Specifically, benefits will not be denied to an otherwise eligible individual for refusing to accept new work if:

- the position offered is vacant due directly to a strike, lockout, or other labor dispute;
- the wages, hours, or other conditions of the work offered are substantially less favorable to the individual than those prevailing for similar work in the locality; or
- as a condition of being employed the individual would be required to join a company union, or to resign from or refrain from joining any bona fide labor organization.

Criteria for Suitable Work

All states look at whether the work refused was suitable. When state laws list the criteria for suitability, they usually address the degree of risk to an individual's health, safety, and morals; the individual's physical fitness, prior training, experience, and earnings; the length of unemployment and prospects for securing local work in a customary occupation; and the distance of the available work from the individual's residence. Delaware and New York make no reference to the suitability of work offered but provide for disqualification for refusals of work for which an individual is reasonably fitted. South Carolina specifies that whether work is suitable must be based on a standard of reasonableness as it relates to the particular individual involved.

Connecticut does not deem work suitable if, as a condition of being employed, the individual would be required to agree not to leave the position if recalled by his or her previous employer. In Louisiana, an individual may refuse work if the remuneration from the employer is below 60 percent of the individual's highest rate of pay in the base period. In Wisconsin, an individual has good cause during the first six weeks of unemployment for refusing work at a lower grade of skill or significantly lower rate of pay than one or more recent jobs. New Hampshire requires that for work to be deemed suitable, the hourly rate when multiplied by 40 must be equal to or greater than 150 percent of the individual's weekly benefit amount.

Distance

In Alabama and West Virginia, no work is unsuitable because of distance if it is in substantially the same locality as the last regular employment which the individual left voluntarily without good cause connected with the employment. In Indiana, work under substantially the same terms and conditions under which the individual was employed by a base-period employer, which is within the individual's prior training, experience, and physical capacity to perform, is suitable work unless a bona fide change in residence makes such work unsuitable because of the distance involved. Delaware, New York, and Ohio provide that no refusal to accept employment shall be disqualifying if it is at an unreasonable distance from the individual's residence or the expense of travel to and from work is substantially greater than that in the former employment, unless provision is made for such expense.

Personal/Family Reasons

Maine does not impose a disqualification for refusal of suitable work if an individual refuses a position on a shift, the greater part of which falls between midnight and 5 a.m., and the individual is prevented from accepting the job because of family obligations. Maine also excludes from suitable work a job the individual previously vacated if the reasons for leaving have not been removed or changed; in addition, if an individual has refused work for a compelling reason, the disqualification will be terminated when the individual is again able and available for work. New Hampshire does not disqualify an individual who is unable to accept or unavailable for suitable, permanent full-time work in a given shift if the individual is the only available adult to care for an ill, infirm, or physically or mentally disabled family member. In addition, New Hampshire does not impose a disqualification for refusing to accept new work if the individual is unable to accept work during the hours of a particular shift because of the family obligations previously described.

Union/Collective Bargaining Issues

Ohio and New York do not consider suitable any work that an individual is not required to accept pursuant to a labor-management agreement. Illinois does not disqualify an individual for refusing new work if the position offered is a transfer to other work offered to the individual by the employing unit under the terms of a collective bargaining agreement or pursuant to an established employer plan, program, or policy, when the acceptance of such other work by the individual would require the separation from that work of another individual currently performing it. Iowa does not disqualify an individual for failure to apply for or accept suitable work if the individual left work in lieu of exercising a right to bump or oust an employee with less seniority. In Oregon, an individual will not be disqualified for refusal of suitable work if the employer unilaterally modified the amount of wages agreed upon by the individual's collective bargaining unit and the employer. In Pennsylvania, an individual will not be disqualified for refusal of suitable work when the work is offered by his or her employer, and the individual is not required to accept the offer pursuant to terms of a union contract, agreement, or an established employer plan, program, or policy. In New York, an individual not subject to recall or who does not obtain employment through a union hall and is still unemployed after receiving 10 weeks of benefits is required to accept employment that the individual is capable of doing, provided the employment would result in a quarterly wage not less than 80 percent of the high quarter in the base period or the wages prevailing for similar work in the locality, whichever is less.

Drug Testing Issues

In a few states an individual is considered to have refused an offer of suitable work if an employer withdraws an offer of work after the individual tests positive for drugs after a drug test given on behalf of the prospective employer as a condition of an offer of employment, or if the individual refuses, without good cause, to submit to a drug test required by the prospective employer as a condition of an offer of employment.

Duration of Unemployment

A few states provide for changing the definition of suitable work as the duration of the individual's unemployment grows. The suitability of the offered wage is the factor states have chosen to alter. For example, Florida requires the agency, in developing rules to determine the suitability of work, to consider the duration of the individual's unemployment and the wage rates available. In addition, Florida law specifies that, after an individual has received 25 weeks of benefits in a single year, suitable work will be a job that pays the minimum wage and is 120 percent or more of the individual's weekly benefit amount.

Idaho law merely requires individuals to be willing to expand their job search beyond their normal trade or occupation and to accept work at a lower rate of pay to remain eligible for benefits as the length of their unemployment grows. Utah considers all earnings in the base year, not just earnings from the most recent employer, in the determination of suitable work and specifies that the agency will be more prone to consider work suitable the longer the individual is unemployed and less likely to secure local work in his or her customary occupation. Wyoming applies the refusal-of-suitable work disqualification if, after four weeks of unemployment, the individual fails to apply for and accept suitable work other than in his or her customary occupation offering at least 50 percent of the compensation earned in his or her previous occupation.

Georgia specifies that, after an individual has received 10 weeks of benefits, no work will be considered unsuitable if it pays wages equal to at least 66 percent of the individual's highest quarter earnings in the base period and is at least equal to the Federal or state minimum wage.

Iowa law specifies that work is suitable if it meets the other criteria in the law and the gross weekly wage of the offered work bears the following relationship to the individual's high-quarter average weekly wage: 1) 100 percent during the first five weeks of unemployment; 2) 75 percent from the 6th through the 12th week of unemployment; 3) 70 percent from the 13th through the 18th week of unemployment; and 4) 65 percent after the 18th week of unemployment. No individual, however, is required to accept a job paying below the Federal minimum wage. Tennessee uses a similar percentage reduction system for suitable wage but the numbers of weeks required for each period of unemployment are different.

After 10 weeks of unemployment, Maine no longer considers the individual's prior wage in determining whether work is suitable. After eight weeks of unemployment, Mississippi law specifies that work is suitable if the offered employment pays the minimum wage or higher and the wage is that prevailing for the individual's customary occupation or similar work in the locality. Montana, after 13 weeks of unemployment, specifies that a suitable work offer need only include wages equal to 75 percent of the individual's earnings in his or her previous customary insured work, but not less than the Federal minimum wage. After 10 weeks of unemployment, North Carolina considers any employment offer paying 120 percent of the individual's weekly benefit amount to be suitable work. North Dakota law specifies that after an individual has received 18 weeks of benefits, suitable work will be any work that pays wages equal to the maximum weekly benefit amount, providing that consideration is given to the degree of risk involved to the individual's health, safety, morals, and physical fitness, and the distance of the work from his or her residence.

In Michigan, an individual will be denied benefits for refusing an offer of suitable work paying at least 70 percent of the gross pay rate received immediately before becoming unemployed, but, after an individual has received 50 percent of his or her benefit entitlement for the year, work will not be considered unsuitable because it is outside the individual's training or experience, or because of pay rate as long as the pay rate meets or exceeds the minimum wage, is at least the prevailing mean wage for similar work in the locality, and the pay rate is 120 percent or more of the individual's weekly benefit amount.

Period of Disqualification

Some states disqualify for a specified number of weeks any individual who refuses suitable work, while other states postpone benefits for a variable number of weeks.

More than half of the states disqualify, for the duration of the unemployment or longer, individuals who refuse suitable work. Most of these states specify an amount that the individual must earn or a period of time the individual must work to remove the disqualification.

Of the states that reduce potential benefits for refusal of suitable work, the majority provide for reduction by an amount equal to the number of weeks of benefits postponed.

Table 5-18. Refusal of Suitable Work - Disqualification

State	Benefits Postponed for:		Benefits Reduced
	Number of Weeks	Weeks and/or Wages to Requalify [1]	
AL	W + 1 - 10		
AK	W + 5		3 x WBA
AZ		8 x WBA	
AR		At least 30 days of covered work	
CA	W + 1 - 9[2]		
CO	W + 20		Equal
CT		6 x WBA	
DE		4 weeks of work and 4 x WBA	
DC		10 weeks of work and wages equal to 10 x WBA	
FL	W + 1 - 5[3]	17 x WBA[3]	Optional
GA		10 x WBA[4]	
HI		5 x WBA	
ID		14 x WBA	
IL		Wages equal to WBA in each of 4 weeks	
IN		Wages in each of 8 weeks and wages ≥ 8 x WBA	1st refusal - 75%; 2nd - 85%; 3rd - 90%

State	Benefits Postponed for:		Benefits Reduced
	Number of Weeks	Weeks and/or Wages to Requalify [1]	
IA		10 x WBA	
KS		3 x WBA	
KY		10 weeks of covered work plus 10 x WBA	
LA		10 x WBA	
ME		10 x WBA	
MD	W + 5 - 10[3]	10 x WBA	
MA	W + 7		Up to 8 weeks
MI	W + 13		Equal in current BY[3]
MN	W + 7		
MS	W + 1 - 12		
MO		10 x WBA	
MT		6 x WBA	Equal
NE	12		Equal
NV		Wages equal to WBA in each week up to 15	
NH		5 weeks of covered work with earnings equal to 20% more than WBA in each week	
NJ	W + 3		
NM		5 x WBA	Equal
NY		10 x WBA	
NC	X[5]	10 x WBA earned in at least 5 weeks	X5
ND		10 x WBA	
OH		6 weeks in covered work + wages equal to 27.5% of state AWW	
OK		10 x WBA[6]	
OR		4 x WBA	8 x WBA
PA		X[7]	
PR		4 weeks of work and wages equal to 10 x WBA	
RI		8 x WBA	
SC		8 x WBA	
SD		6 weeks of covered work and wages equal to WBA in each week	
TN		10 x WBA in covered work	
TX		6 weeks of work or wages equal to 6 x WBA (applies to any refusal within BY)	
UT		6 x WBA	
VT		6 x WBA	
VA		30 days or 240 hours of work	
VI		4 weeks of work and 4 x WBA	
WA		7 weeks and earnings in bona fide work of 7 x WBA	

Table 5-18. (Continued)

State	Benefits Postponed for:		Benefits Reduced
	Number of Weeks	Weeks and/or Wages to Requalify [1]	
WV	W + 4[8]		Equal
WI		6 x WBA	
WY		8 x WBA	

KEY: W = Week of refusal "Equal" indicates reduction equal to WBA multiplied by number of weeks of disqualification.

[1] Minimum employment or wages required to requalify for benefits.

[2] CA - must be weeks in which individual meets reporting and registration requirements. Also, agency may add 1-8 weeks for successive disqualification.

[3] FL - both term and duration of unemployment disqualifications are imposed. Aliens who refuse resettlement or relocation employment are disqualified 1-17 weeks, or reduction by not more than five weeks. MI - individual may be eligible for benefits in subsequent benefit year based on base period wages earned subsequent to refusal. MD - either disqualification may be imposed at discretion of agency.

[4] Individual must work for a liable employer and become unemployed through no fault of his or her own.

[5] Disqualification may run into next benefit year which begins within 12 months after end of current year. Also, a permanent disqualification may be reduced to a time certain disqualification, but not less than five weeks, with a corresponding reduction in benefits (weeks of disqualification x WBA).

[6] An individual who refuses an offer of work due to illness, death of a family member, or other circumstances beyond the individual's control will be disqualified for the week of occurrence.

[7] Until an individual obtains work not of a casual or temporary nature; however, if work refused was casual or temporary, then disqualification is for an equal period of time.

[8] Plus such additional weeks as offer remains open.

Special Groups

All state laws contain provisions addressing special groups of workers. FUTA requires the denial of benefits under certain circumstances to professional athletes, some aliens, and certain school personnel, while it also prohibits states from denying benefits solely on the basis of pregnancy or the termination of pregnancy. Like the FUTA provisions, most of these special provisions restrict benefits more than the usual disqualification provisions.

Students

Most states exclude from coverage service performed by students for educational institutions. In addition, many states have special provisions limiting the benefit rights of students who have had covered employment. In some of these states, the disqualification is for the duration of the unemployment; in others, it is during school attendance or during the school term.

Many states disqualify individuals during school attendance and some states extend the disqualification to vacation periods.

School Personnel

FUTA requires states to deny benefits to instructional, research, or principal administrative employees of educational institutions between successive academic years or terms if the individual performed such instructional, research, or administrative services in the first year or term and has a contract or reasonable assurance of performing such services in the second year or term.

FUTA also requires states to deny benefits to instructional, research, or principal administrative employees of educational institutions who perform services in regular but non-successive years or terms (for example, only the first semester of each academic year). These individuals are not eligible for compensation based on such services during the entire period between the regular but non-successive academic years or terms. This between terms denial also applies to vacation or holiday periods within school years or terms.

FUTA permits a state, at its option, to deny benefits between successive academic years or terms to other employees of a school or of an educational service agency who perform services for or on behalf of an educational institution if the individual performed services (other than the three types previously described) during the year or term and has a reasonable assurance or a contract to perform services in the second year or term. The option for denial of benefits also applies to vacation or holiday periods within school years or terms. However, FUTA requires states to pay benefits retroactively to school personnel performing these "other" services if they were given reasonable assurances of reemployment but were not, in fact, rehired when the new school term or year began.

Professional Athletes

FUTA requires states to deny benefits to an individual between two successive sport seasons if substantially all of the individual's services in the first season consist of participating in or preparing to participate in sports or athletic events and the individual has a reasonable assurance of performing similar services in the second season. The term "athlete" may include ancillary personnel involved with the team or event such as managers, coaches, and trainers employed by professional teams, and referees and umpires employed by professional leagues or associations. Whether the denial is extended to these other groups is a state option.

Aliens

FUTA requires denial of benefits to certain aliens. Benefits may not be paid based on service performed by an alien unless the alien is one who: 1) was lawfully admitted for permanent residence at the time the services were performed and for which the wages paid are used as wage credits; 2) was lawfully present in the United States to perform the services for which the wages paid are used as wage credits; or 3) was permanently residing in the United States "under color of law," including one lawfully present in the United States under provisions of the Immigration and Nationality Act. (Note that aliens must also be legally authorized to work to be considered available for work.)

To avoid discriminating against certain groups in the administration of this provision, Federal law requires that the information designed to identify ineligible aliens must be requested of all individuals. Whether or not the individual is in satisfactory immigration status is determined by a preponderance of the evidence.

Table 5-19. Treatment of students

State	Disqualified for Leaving Work to Attend School	Disqualified or Ineligible While Attending School	State	Disqualified for Leaving Work to Attend School	Disqualified or Ineligible While Attending School
AL	Yes	Yes, ineligible if school hours overlap normal work hours	AK	Yes, if leaving skilled work or not attending approved training	Yes, unless student pursued an academic education for a school term and worked 30 hours a week, and the academic schedule did not preclude full-time work in the student's occupation, and if the student was laid off[1]
AZ	Yes, unless leaving to resume approved training or if work hinders the student from making satisfactory progress in approved training	Yes, unless there is a pattern of concurrent, full-time work and full-time school attendance for the nine-month period before the filing of an initial claim for UI benefits, and the student has not left or refused full-time work, or reduced the hours of work to part-time to attend school	AR	Yes	Yes, except while attending a vocational school for a demand occupation and other training as long as the student is making reasonable efforts to obtain employment and doesn't refuse suitable work
CA	Yes, except if attending union apprenticeship school or approved for training benefits	Yes, ineligible unless student has a part-time seek-work plan or is available for full-time work in labor market during school[1]	CO	Yes1	No, provided school attendance does not interfere with ability to accept suitable work[1]
CT	Yes[1]	Yes, ineligible except student who becomes unemployed while attending school if work search is restricted to employment that does not conflict with regular class	DE	Yes	No, if student determined to be primarily a worker who happens to attend school

Table 5-19. (Continued)

State	Disqualified for Leaving Work to Attend School	Disqualified or Ineligible While Attending School	State	Disqualified for Leaving Work to Attend School	Disqualified or Ineligible While Attending School
		hours and if student was employed on a full-time basis during the 2 years prior to separation while in school[1]			
DC	Yes	No, provided school is not an undue restriction on availability	FL	Yes	No, provided school attendance does not interfere with availability to accept suitable work
GA	Yes, unless Trade Act training	No, provided school attendance does not interfere with availability to work, and the student is actively seeking work	HI	Yes	Yes, must be available for work and willing to quit school, except for approved training.
ID	Yes	Yes, unless attending approved training[1]	IL	Yes, unless Trade Act training	Yes, ineligible when principal occupation is student unless attends approved training[1]
IN	Yes, unless Trade Act training	No, provided school attendance does not interfere with availability to accept work, and the student is actively seeking work	IA	Yes	No, eligible if school attendance does not interfere with ability to accept suitable work
KS	Yes, unless Trade Act training	Yes, disqualified, including vacation periods, unless full-time work is concurrent with school attendance, or school schedule does not affect availability for work[1]	KY	Yes	No, provided school attendance does not interfere with ability to accept suitable work

State	Disqualified for Leaving Work to Attend School	Disqualified or Ineligible While Attending School	State	Disqualified for Leaving Work to Attend School	Disqualified or Ineligible While Attending School
LA	No	Yes, ineligible, including vacation periods, unless student loses job while in school and is available for suitable work[1]	ME	Yes	Yes, disqualified unless student is available for full-time work while in school, or would leave school for full-time work, or is in approved training
MD	Yes[1]		MA	Yes	No, provided industrial or vocational training is found to be necessary to obtain suitable work; must be full-time and less than one year in length2
MI	Yes1	Yes, ineligible unless student agrees to quit school/change class schedule to accept work, or is in approved training	MN	Yes, unless entering approved training	Yes, ineligible unless willing to quit school, except for approved training[1]
MS	Yes	No, provided school hours do not interfere with availability for full-time work	MO	Yes	Yes, ineligible if there is a significant restriction on availability; some part-time students may be eligible; does not apply to Trade Act
MT	No	No, provided that student can demonstrate that s/he meets general eligibility requirements	NE	Yes	Yes, disqualified unless major part of BPW were for services performed while attending school[1]

Table 5-19. (Continued)

State	Disqualified for Leaving Work to Attend School	Disqualified or Ineligible While Attending School	State	Disqualified for Leaving Work to Attend School	Disqualified or Ineligible While Attending School
NV	Yes, unless approved training or high school student who must legally attend school	No, if school attendance does not interfere with ability to seek and accept suitable work	NH	Yes	No, provided student is available for and seeking permanent full-time work during all the shifts and all the hours there is a market for his or her services
NJ	Yes, except for approved training	Yes, disqualified, including vacation periods, unless student earned wages sufficient to qualify for benefits while attending school[1]	NM	Yes	Yes, unless the student is able, available and seeking at least part- time work, or in approved training[1]
NY	No	No, provided school attendance does not interfere with availability to accept work, and the student is actively seeking work	NC	No	No, unemployed individual not necessarily unavailable for or unable to work while attending school and not ineligible solely on basis of attending school
ND	No	Yes, disqualified unless major part of BPW were for services performed while attending school[1]	OH	Yes, unless Trade Act training	No, if becomes unemployed while attending school, BPW were at least partially earned while attending school, meets availability and work search requirements, and if available for suitable employment on any shift[1]

State	Disqualified for Leaving Work to Attend School	Disqualified or Ineligible While Attending School	State	Disqualified for Leaving Work to Attend School	Disqualified or Ineligible While Attending School
OK	No	No, provided student offers to quit school, adjust class hours, or change shifts to secure employment[1]	OR	Yes, unless required by law to attend school2	No, provided school attendance does not interfere with availability to seek and accept suitable work
PA	Yes, unless Trade Act training and job paid less than 80% of Trade Act job and was at lesser skill level	No, provided able and available for suitable work (does not have to be full-time work)	PR		
RI	Yes, unless Trade Act training	Yes, disqualified unless hours of school do not interfere with hours of work in student's occupation	SC	Yes	No, not disqualified if student offers to quit school, adjust class hours or change shifts to secure employment; must make a work search each week
SD	Yes	Yes, ineligible if determined principally occupied as a student	TN	No	No, unless school attendance interferes with availability for suitable work
TX	Yes[1]	Yes, eligible if willing to quit school or change class schedule to accommodate full-time work[1]	UT	Yes[2]	No, disqualified when school attendance is a restriction to availability for full-time suitable work, unless in an approved training program[2]
VT	Yes	Yes, if claim is based on part-time employment and student remains available for part-time work while attending school	VA	Yes[3]	Yes, unless attendance would limit availability for only one of multiple shifts in usual occupation

Table 5-19. (Continued)

State	Disqualified for Leaving Work to Attend School	Disqualified or Ineligible While Attending School	State	Disqualified for Leaving Work to Attend School	Disqualified or Ineligible While Attending School
VI	No	No	WA	Yes, unless approved apprentice training or Trade Act training	Yes, disqualified if registered at a school that provides instruction of 12 or more hours per week, unless in approved training or demonstrates evidence of availability for work[1]
WV	Yes, unless previously enrolled in approved training[1]	No, provided student is in approved vocational training or if student is willing to drop or rearrange classes if suitable work were offered	WI	Yes, unless Trade Act training	Yes, unless student is available for full-time first shift work
WY	Yes, unless previously enrolled in approved training	Yes, disqualified unless major part of BPW were for services performed while attending school			

NOTE: Unless otherwise indicated, state is applying its voluntary quit or availability provisions

[1] State statutes specifically mention students.

[2] Regulations specifically mention students.

[3] Based upon case law; includes rebuttable presumption that graduate students working only between semesters quit to return to school.

Deductible Income

Almost all state laws provide that an individual will not receive UI for any week during which the individual is receiving or is seeking benefits under any Federal or other state UI law. A few states specifically mention benefits under the Federal Railroad Unemployment Insurance Act. Under most of the laws, no disqualification is imposed if it is finally determined that the individual is ineligible under the other law. The intent is to prevent duplicate payment of benefits for the same week. These disqualifications apply only to the week in which or for which the other payment is received.

Most states have statutory provisions that an individual is ineligible for any week during which the individual receives or has received certain other types of remuneration, such as wages in lieu of notice, dismissal wages, worker's compensation, holiday and vacation pay, back pay, and benefits under a supplemental unemployment benefit plan. In many states, if the payment is less than the weekly benefit amount, the individual receives the difference; in other states, no benefits are payable for a week of such payments regardless of the amount of payment. A few states provide for rounding the resultant benefits, like payments for weeks of partial unemployment, to half dollar or full dollar amounts.

Wages in Lieu of Notice and Dismissal Payments

A considerable number of states consider wages in lieu of notice to be deductible income. Many states have the same provision for receipt of dismissal payments as for receipt of wages in lieu of notice. The state laws use a variety of terms such as dismissal allowance, dismissal payments, dismissal wages, separation allowances, termination allowances, severance payments, or some combination of these terms. In many states, all dismissal payments are included as wages for contribution purposes, as they are under FUTA. Other states exclude dismissal payments that the employer is not legally required to make. To the extent that dismissal payments are included in taxable wages for contribution purposes, individuals receiving such payments may be considered not unemployed, or not totally unemployed, for the weeks concerned.

However, under rulings in some states, individuals who received dismissal payments have been held to be unemployed because the payments were not made for the period following their separation from work but, instead, with respect to their prior service.

Workers' Compensation Payments

Nearly half of the state laws list workers' compensation under any state or Federal law as disqualifying income. Some disqualify for the week concerned; others consider workers' compensation to be deductible income and reduce unemployment benefits payable by the amount of the workers' compensation payments. A few states reduce the unemployment benefit only if the workers' compensation payment is for temporary partial disability.

Vacation Pay, Holiday Pay, and Back Pay

Many states consider individuals receiving vacation pay as not eligible for benefits; several states hold individuals eligible for benefits if they are on vacation without pay through no fault of their own. In practically all states, as under FUTA, vacation pay is considered wages for contribution purposes – in a few states, in the statutory definition of wages; in others, in official explanations, general counsel or attorney general opinions, interpretations, regulations, or other publications of the state agency. Thus, an individual receiving vacation pay equal to his or her weekly benefit amount would, by definition, not be unemployed and would not be eligible for benefits. Some of the explanations point out that vacation pay is considered wages because the employment relationship is not discontinued, and others emphasize that an individual on vacation is not available for work. Vacation payments made at the time of severance of the employment relationship, rather than during a regular vacation shutdown, are considered disqualifying income in some states only if such payments are required under contract and are allocated to specified weeks; in other states, such payments, made voluntarily or in accordance with a contract, are not considered disqualifying income.

Retirement Payments

FUTA requires states to reduce the weekly benefit amount of any individual by the amount, allocated weekly, of any "governmental or other pension, retirement or retired pay, annuity, or any other similar periodic payment which is based on the previous work of such individual...." This requirement applies only to payments made under a plan maintained or contributed to by a base-period or chargeable employer that affected eligibility for or increased the amount of the retirement pay. States are permitted to reduce benefits on less than a dollar-for-dollar basis by taking into account the contributions made by the individual to the plan in question. (This effectively means the FUTA requirement is limited to 100 percent employer-financed pensions.) Also, the requirement applies only to those payments made on a periodic (as opposed to lump-sum) basis. As a result, states may choose from a variety of options in creating a retirement pay provision. FUTA also prohibits reductions for pensions, retirement or retired pay, annuity, or other similar payment not includible in the gross income of the individual because it was part of a rollover distribution.

Effect of Social Security Payments

Social Security payments are sometimes treated differently from retirement payments in general. In Minnesota, the amount of UI compensation is reduced by 50 percent if the claimant is collecting Social Security, unless the base period wages were earned while the claimant was already qualified to receive Social Security benefits. Separate from Social Security payments are Social Security Disability Insurance (SSDI) payments. In some states individuals that receive SSDI are held ineligible or have those payments treated as deductible income.

Table 5-20. States with wages in lieu of notice and dismissal payments provisions

State	Wages	Dismissal	State	Wages	Dismissal	State	Wages	Dismissal
AK	R	R	AZ	D (not considered unemployed)		AR	D	D
CA	R: By interpretation		CO	R	L: Benefits postponed for number of weeks equal to total amount of additional remuneration divided by usual weekly wage	CT	D	D: Not applicable to severance or accrued leave pay based on service for the Armed Forces
DE		R	DC		R	FL	R	D1
GA	D	D	IL	R: By regulation		IN	R: Excludes greater of first \$3 or 1/5 WBA from other than base-period employer	
IA	R	R	KS		R	KY	R	
LA	R	R: But not less than 1 week for each week a base- period employer provided severance pay equaling or exceeding WBA	ME	R	R	MD	R	
MA	D		MI	R	R	MN	R	R
AK	R	R	AZ	D (not considered unemployed)		AR	D	D
MO	R		NE	D	D	NV	D	D
NH	R	R	NJ	D		NM	R: By regulation	
NY		R^2	NC	D	D	OH	R	R: Not applicable to severance or accrued leave pay based on service for the Armed Forces

State	Wages	Dismissal	State	Wages	Dismissal	State	Wages	Dismissal
PA		R[3]	RI		D[4]	SD	R	R
TN	D	D[5]	TX	D	D	UT	R	R
VT	D	D	VA	R	R: Only when allocated by the employer to specific pay periods	WA	R	R[6]
WV	D		WI		R: Only when allocated by close of week, payable at full applicable wage rate, and individual had notice of allocation[7]	WY	D	D

R = weekly benefit reduced by weekly prorated amount of the payment D = all benefits denied for the week of receipt

[1] Number of weeks of disqualification equals amount of severance pay divided by individual's AWW received from employer that paid severance pay, rounded down to nearest whole number, beginning with week of separation.

[2] Does not apply during any weeks in which the initial payment of dismissal pay is made more than 30 days from the last day of the individual's employment.

[3] WBA reduced by amount of severance pay attributed to the week. Amount of severance pay attributed shall be an amount not less than zero determined by subtracting, from total amount of severance pay, 40 percent of AAW as calculated as of June 30 immediately preceding calendar year in which benefit year begins.

[4] Severance pay shall be allocated on a weekly basis from last day worked for a period not to exceed 26 weeks. If employer does not specify set number of weeks, severance pay shall be allocated using individual's WBA.

[5] Benefits denied if severance package from employer is equal to the salary individual would have received if individual was working.

[6] Previously accrued compensation except severance pay, when assigned to a period of time by collective bargaining or trade practices; negotiated settlements or proceeds given for early termination of an employment contract.

[7] Individual is ineligible for benefits for any week in which s/he receives 32 hours or more of termination pay totaling over $500, by itself or in combination with wages.

Table 5-21. States with workers' compensation provisions

State		State		State		State		State	
AL	R	CA	R	CO	R	CT	D	DE	R
FL	R	GA	D	ID	R	IL	R	IA	R
KS	D	LA	R	MA	D	MN	R	MO	R
MT	D	NE	R	NV	D	NH	R	NY	R
OH	R	RI	R	SD	R	TN	D	TX	D
UT	D	VT	D	VA	R	WA	D	WV	D
WI	R								

R = weekly benefit reduced by weekly prorated amount of the payment D = all benefits denied for the week of receipt.

Table 5-22. States with holiday pay, back pay, and vacation pay provisions

State	Holiday	Back Pay	Vacation	State	Holiday	Back Pay	Vacation
AL		D		AK	R	R: Employer withholds amount of benefits paid and remits to UI agency	R
AR	R: WBA minus holiday pay in excess of 40% of WBA		R: WBA minus vacation pay in excess of 40% of WBA	CA	R	R	
CO	Treated as wages in the week in which the holiday occurred	R: Employer withholds amount of benefits paid and remits to UI agency	D	DE		R	

State	Holiday	Back Pay	Vacation	State	Holiday	Back Pay	Vacation
DC		Employer withholds amount of benefits paid and remits to UI agency		GA		Employer withholds amount of benefits paid and remits to UI agency	D
HI	R	R	R: If continued attachment to employer	ID	R	R/D: Depending on amount	D
IL	R	R: When individual is reinstated after suspension/dis- charge and receives full compensation for period if charges reversed	R	IN	R: Excludes greater of first $3 or 1/5 WBA from other than BP employer	R: Excludes greater of first $3 or 1/5 WBA from other than BP employer; employer with- holds amount of benefits paid and remits to UI agency	R: Excludes greater of first $3 or 1/5 WBA from other than BP employer
IA			R: If employer designates a specific vacation period, benefits are reduced for that period of time; if not, reduction is limited to 1 week	KS	R	D: Employer withholds amount of benefits paid and remits to UI agency	R
KY		R: Benefits will be reduced 100% for overpayments caused by back pay award		LA			R

Table 5-22. (Continued)

State	Holiday	Back Pay	Vacation	State	Holiday	Back Pay	Vacation
ME	R	R[1]	R[2]	MD	R: Not applicable to pay attributable to any period outside the terms of an employment agreement, which specifies scheduled vacation or holiday periods		R: Not applicable to pay attributable to any period outside the terms of an employment agreement, which specifies scheduled vacation or holiday periods
MA	D			MI	R	R	R
MN	R: 55% deducted as long as amount is less than WBA	R	R: Only applies if temporary or seasonal layoff, not if permanent separation	MS		D: Employer withholds amount of benefits paid and remits to UI agency	
MO	Reportable during week of holiday	R: Employer withholds amount of benefits paid and remits to UI agency	R	NE			D

State	Holiday	Back Pay	Vacation	State	Holiday	Back Pay	Vacation
NV	Treated as wages the week in which it is paid	D: Employer withholds amount of benefits paid and remits to UI agency	D	NY	D	R	D
NM		R: By regulation		NC		D: Employer withholds amount of benefits paid and remits to UI agency	
ND	Reportable during week of holiday	Not reportable	Reportable when received unless individual takes vacation prior to layoff	OH			R
OR	May be deductible depending on circumstances		May be deductible depending on circumstances	PA	R	R	R: Only deductible if individual has a return to work date
PR			R	RI			R
SD	R			TN		R	
UT	R	R	R	VT		R	R
VA	Reportable during week of holiday	R	R	WA	R: If assigned to the week claimed rather than accrued	Employer withholds amount of benefits paid and remits to UI agency	R: If assigned to the week claimed rather than accrued

Table 5-22. (Continued)

State	Holiday	Back Pay	Vacation	State	Holiday	Back Pay	Vacation
WV	D	D	D: Except if individual is totally unemployed and if pay is accumulated prior to unemployment	WI	R: Only when allocated by close of such week, payable at full wage rate, and individual has notice[2]		R: Only when allocated by close of such week, payable at full wage rate, and individual has notice[3]
WY	D: Allocated to week the holiday occurs	R	D				

R = weekly benefit reduced by weekly prorated amount of the payment D = benefits denied for the week of receipt

[1] If a payment, which is awarded or authorized by the National Labor Relations Board, a court, or any other administrative agency of government for any settlement of a dispute, is for, or equivalent to, wages for a specific period of time, then that payment will be considered wages with respect to the week or weeks covered by the award, providing the individual receives the back payment.

[2] Individual is ineligible for benefits for any week in which the individual receives 32 hours or more of sick pay, holiday pay, or vacation pay totaling over $500, by itself or in combination with wages.

[3] Individual is ineligible for benefits for any week in which the individual receives vacation pay in an amount exceeding the equivalent of four weeks' wages. However, if total amount of vacation pay is less than WBA, WBA will be reduced by the amount of vacation pay received.

Table 5-23. Effect of retirement payments

State	Deducts All BP Employer Pensions (51 States)	Considers Employee Contributions To Pensions	Excludes Pensions Not Affected By BP Work	State	Deducts All BP Employer Pensions (51 States)	Considers Employee Contributions To Pensions	Excludes Pensions Not Affected By BP Work
AL	X	X	X	AK	X	X	X
AZ	X	X	X	AR	X	X	
CA	X	X	X	CO	X		
CT	X	X	X	DE	X	X	
DC	X	X		FL	X	X	X
GA	X	X	X	HI	X	X	X
ID	X[1]	X		IL	X[2]	X	
IN	X[3]			IA	X[1, 2]	X	X
KS	X	X	X	KY	X	X	X
LA	X			ME	X	X	X
MD	X[4]	X		MA	X	X	X
MI	X	X	X	MN	X		
MS	X			MO	X		X
MT	X	X	X	NE	X	X[5]	
NV	X	X	X	NH	X	X	X
NJ	X	X	X	NM	X	X	
NY	X	X	X	NC	X		
ND	X	X	X	OH			
OK	X[5, 6]		X	OR	X	X	
PA	X	X	X	PR	X	X	X
RI	X	X	X	SC	X	X	
SD	X	X		TN	X	X	X
TX	X	X		UT	X		X
VT		X		VA	X[2]		
VI	X			WA	X	X	X
WV	X		X	WI	X	X	X
WY	X	X					

[1] Only if 100 percent funded by employer.

[2] Deducted if base-period or chargeable employer.

[3] No deduction if individual uses distribution from pension, retirement, or annuity plan to satisfy a severe financial hardship resulting from an unforeseeable emergency that is due to events beyond individual's control.

[4] Excludes lump sums paid at time of layoff or shutdown of operations.

[5] By regulation.

[6] If individual is receiving monthly retirement payments that are required to be deducted from unemployment benefits, 7/30 of the monthly retirement payment will be deducted from each week of benefits.

Supplemental Unemployment Payments

A supplemental unemployment payment plan is a system whereby, under a contract, unemployed individuals receive payments from an employer-financed trust fund. The purpose is to provide the individual, while unemployed, with a combined UI and supplemental unemployment benefit payment amounting to a specified proportion of his or her weekly earnings while employed.

There are two major types of such plans: 1) those of the Ford-General Motors type, under which the individual has no vested interest and is eligible for payments only if s/he is laid off by the company; and 2) those under which the individual has a vested interest and may collect if s/he is out of work for other reasons, such as illness or permanent separation.

All states except New Mexico, Puerto Rico, South Carolina, and South Dakota permit supplementation by Ford-General Motors type plans without affecting UI payments.

In 48 states permitting supplementation, an interpretive ruling was made either by the attorney general (27 states) or by the employment security agency (ten states); in Maine, supplementation is permitted as a result of a Superior Court decision and, in the remaining ten states (AK, CA, CO, GA, HI, IN, MD, NH, OH, and VA), by amendment of the UI statutes.

Some supplemental unemployment benefit plans of the Ford-General Motors type provide for alternative payments or substitute private payments in a state in which a ruling not permitting supplementation is issued. These payments may be made in amounts equal to three or four times the regular weekly private benefit after two or three weekly payments of state UI benefits without supplementation; in lump sums when the layoff ends or the state benefits are exhausted (whichever is earlier); or through alternative payment arrangements to be worked out, depending on the particular supplemental unemployment benefit plan.

Relationship with Other Statutory Provisions

Some states have no provision for any type of disqualifying income except pensions and others have only two or three types. This does not necessarily allow benefits to all individuals in receipt of the types of payments concerned. When states do not pay benefits to such individuals, they rely upon the general able-and-available provisions or the definition of unemployment. Many individuals receiving workers' compensation, other than those receiving weekly allowances for dismemberment, are not able to work in terms of the UI law. However, receipt of workers' compensation for injuries in employment does not automatically disqualify an unemployed individual for unemployment benefits. Many states consider that evidence of injury with loss of employment is relevant only as it serves notice that a condition of ineligibility may exist and that an individual may not be able to work and may not be available for work. Similarly, individuals receiving Social Security Disability Insurance (SSDI) payments may not be automatically disqualified for benefits.

SECTION 6. OVERPAYMENTS

In General

This chapter deals with state law provisions that pertain to identifying, establishing, and collecting UI benefit overpayments. All states' laws have provisions addressing these matters. A state's law generally differs in the treatment of overpayments in which the individual is not at fault or is not committing fraud, and overpayments in which the individual has committed fraud or willful misrepresentation, or concealed material facts. In addition, state laws contain provisions for fines and imprisonment for willfully or intentionally misrepresenting or concealing facts material to a determination concerning the individual's entitlement to benefits.

Nonfraud and Nonfault Provisions

Waivers

Many states provide that, if the overpayment is without fault or fraud on the individual's part, the individual is not liable to repay the amount overpaid. The following table lists some of the reasons states waive recovery of the overpayment.

Table 6-1. Waiver of nonfraud or nonfault overpayments

State	Agency Error	Employer Error	Equity or Good Conscience	Financial Hardship	Other
AL		X			
AK			X		
AZ			X		
AR			X		
CA				X	
CO			X	X	
CT	X				
DC				X	
FL		X			
GA			X	X	
HI			X		
ID	X	X			
IL			X		
IN	X	X			
IA		X			
KS	X			X	
LA			X		
ME			X		
MD	X			X	
MA			X		
MI	X		X		
MN					X
MT	X	X		X	
NE			X		
NH					X
NJ			X	X	

State	Agency Error	Employer Error	Equity or Good Conscience	Financial Hardship	Other
NC					X
ND			X		
OH	X	X			
OR			X		X
PA					X
RI			X		
SC			X		
SD			X	X	
TN		X	X		
UT				X	
VT					X
VI			X		
WA			X		
WI			X		
WY			X	X	

GENERAL NOTE: The following states do not have overpayment waiver provisions: DE, KY, MS, MO, NM, NY, OK, PR, TX, VA, and WV.

Recovery Provisions

All state laws provide for recovering benefits paid to individuals who later are found not to be entitled to them. In addition to direct repayment, states utilize several tools to recoup these funds. States may, at the discretion of the agency, recover nonfraud and fraud overpayments by deducting from future benefits payable (benefit offset); and, under specific circumstances, benefit offset is mandatory. States also recover overpayments from an individual's Federal income tax refund through the Treasury Offset Program. Similarly, states may also offset overpayments with state tax refunds due to the individual, or by the interception of lottery winnings, or they can compel repayment by pursuing civil action in state court. Finally, some states assess interest and penalties on outstanding overpayment balances. The following table provides information about how states recover nonfraud overpayments.

Table 6-2. Recovery of nonfraud overpayments

State	Benefit Offset		Offset with State Tax Refunds	Civil Action Permitted	Interest Assessed
	Offset Against Future Benefits	Number of Years Limited			
AL	100%	No	Yes	Yes	No
AK	100%	No	Yes	No	No
AZ	50% - 100%	No	Yes[1]	No	10% per year from month after overpayment established
AR	100%	4 years from date of final determination	Yes	Yes	10% annually once final overpayment has force and effect of judgment of Circuit Court
CA	25%	6 years from date overpayment notice mailed	Yes	No[2]	No
CO	25%	No	No	Yes	No
CT	50%; if WBA <$100, then 25%	No; may write off as uncollectible after 8 years	Yes	Yes	No
DE	50%	5 years from end of BY	Yes	Yes	No
DC	100%	No	Yes[1]	Yes	No
FL	100%	Commenced within 7 years from date overpayment is established	No	Yes	No, unless and until a civil judgment is entered
GA	50%	7 years from release date of the notice of determination and overpayment	Yes	Yes	No
HI	100%	2 years from date of mailing notice of redetermination or final appeal decision; after, may offset % agreed to by individual	No	Yes	No

State	Benefit Offset		Offset with State Tax Refunds	Civil Action Permitted	Interest Assessed
	Offset Against Future Benefits	Number of Years Limited			
ID	100%	5 years from date of final determination	Yes	Yes	No
IL	25%	5 years from date overpayment decision issued	Yes	Yes	No
IN	100%; if agency error, then 50%	No	Yes	Yes	No
IA	100%	10 years from date of last activity	Yes	No	No
KS	100%	No	Yes	Yes	1.5% per month if 2 years old
KY	25%	5 years from last day of BY	Yes	Yes	No
LA3	100%	No	Yes	Yes	No
ME	10% of 1st $100 WBA; 50% of rest	No	Yes	No	1% per month starting 1 year after decision is set up in system
MD	100%	No	Yes	Yes	No
MA	100%; 50% if nonfault and individual requests	No	Yes	Yes2	No
MI	Up to 20%	3 years from date of payment	Yes	Yes	Yes
MN	50%	6 years from date overpayment is determined	Yes[1]	Yes	No
MS	100%	5 years from last day of week overpaid	Yes	Yes	1% per month on principal balance after 1st full month overpayment established
MO	100%	No; may write off as uncollectible after 5 years of no activity	Yes	Yes	No

Table 6-2. (Continued)

State	Benefit Offset		Offset with State Tax Refunds	Civil Action Permitted	Interest Assessed
	Offset Against Future Benefits	Number of Years Limited			
MT	50%; higher if individual permits	5 years; must file lien against individual's real and personal property to extend to 10 years	Yes	No	Yes
NE	Any amount per week and any amount up to MBA	3 years from end of BYE in which overpaid weeks were paid	Yes	Yes	No
NV	50%	5 years from date overpayment established	No	No	No
NH	1% - 10%	10 years from date overpayment decision is final	No	Yes	1% per month on principal balance from 1st day of month after decision if not paid within 60 days
NJ	100% or 50%	No	Yes[1]	Yes	2% annually 6 months after debt established if no formal payment agreement
NM	100%; 50% or 75% if request approved	No	Yes	Yes	No
NY	50%	No	Yes	No	No
NC	50%	No	Yes	Yes[2]	No
ND	Minimum 50%	No	Yes[1]	Yes	18% starting 180 days after establishment of overpayment or 180 days from date of final appeal determination
OH	100%	3 years from date decision is final	Yes	No	No

State	Benefit Offset		Offset with State Tax Refunds	Civil Action Permitted	Interest Assessed
	Offset Against Future Benefits	Number of Years Limited			
OK	100%	No; except for administrative error, 1 year from expiration of BY current at time overpayment established	Yes; administrative error	Yes; administrative error	1% per month starting date overpayment determined
OR	100%	5 years from week decision became final for nonfault or nonfraud overpayments; no time limit for fault overpayments	Yes (if fault overpayment)[1]	Yes	If fault, 1% per month from 1st day of month following 60 days after final decision
PA	33⅓% (nonfault); 100% (fault)	4 (nonfault), 7 (fault) years from date of application for benefits	No	Yes	Computed annually based on the IRS rate
PR	50%	5 years from date overpayment established	No	No	No
RI	100%	No	Yes	Yes	No
SC	100%	No	Yes	No	No
SD	100%	No	No	Yes	12% per year upon establishment of fault overpayment or 6 months after establishment of nonfault overpayment
TN	100%	After the expiration of 6 years from overpayment determination	No	Yes	No
TX	100%	No limit for overpayment absorptions on subsequent BYs	No	Yes	1% per month from 30 days after served (when becomes judgment)
UT	50% (nonfault) or 100% (fault)	If nonfault, 3 years from date decision is final; if fault, 8 years from effective date of judgment lien	Yes (fault only)	Yes (fault only)	No, unless it goes to judgment
VT	100%	5 years from determination date	Yes[1]	Yes	No

Table 6-2. (Continued)

State	Benefit Offset		Offset with State Tax Refunds	Civil Action Permitted	Interest Assessed
	Offset Against Future Benefits	Number of Years Limited			
VA	100%; 50% if administrative error[4]	No	Yes	Yes	No
VI	Depends on amount and ability of individual to repay	2 years from date overpayment was established	Yes[1]	Yes	No
WA	50% (up to 100% depending on claimant request)	No	No	Yes	1% per month (simple interest) after ≥ 2 minimum monthly payments are delinquent
WV	100%	5 years from last day of week overpaid	Yes	No	No
WI	100%	No	Yes[1]	Yes	No
WY	100%	First 5 years from effective date of claim resulting in overpayment	Yes	Yes	No

[1] AZ, DC, MN, NJ, ND, OR, VT, VI, and WI - provision found in non-UI law (all other states' provision found in UI law).

[2] CA - summary judgment proceedings may be initiated if the claim was based solely on income received as an elected official; MA and NC - do not pursue civil action based on policy.

[3] A penalty of $20 or 25% of outstanding balance is imposed.

[4] If overpayment due to administrative error an individual is allowed to repay solely by voluntary repayment agreement, and the agency will not resort to any other methods of collection unless the individual breaches the agreement.

Fraud Provisions

Recovery Provisions, Fines, and Criminal Penalties

For fraud, including willful misrepresentation generally and concealment of facts, states utilize the same methods to recover overpayments as they do for nonfraud overpayments. However, most states can pursue criminal action in court, which can lead to fines and prison sentences. Further, states can administratively assess additional fines or penalties.

Federal law requires a mandatory penalty assessment for fraudulent claims. States are required to assess a penalty of not less than 15 percent of the amount of the erroneous payment against claimants committing fraud in connection with state and/or Federal unemployment compensation programs. The penalties are mandatory for any fraudulent payments, and the penalty assessments must be immediately deposited into the state's account in the unemployment trust fund and used for the payment of unemployment compensation.

Although UI benefit fraud typically involves an individual's attempt to obtain or increase benefits, it also includes employers who attempt to prevent or reduce benefits to eligible individuals, and employers who help an individual attempting to fraudulently claim benefits. The following table reflects state law provisions on how states treat benefit fraud. A state's policy may be different (e.g., it may not, in fact, pursue criminal prosecution) and can change.

Table 6-3. Treatment of fraud

State	Recovery of Overpayments Through Offset			Monetary Assessments			Max Prison Time Imposed When Fraud Committed By	
	Benefits		State Tax Refunds	Interest Charged	Fines or Penalties on Claimant	Fines or Penalties on Employer	Claimant	Employer
	Reduction in WBA	Number of Years Limited						
AL	100%	6 years from date overpayment is final	Yes	2% per month	4 x WBA to maximum benefit amount; 15% of overpayment	\$50 - \$500	1 to 20 years under Classes B & C felony charges1	1 year
AK	100%	No	Yes	No	50% of each fraud overpayment	X[1]	5 years	X[1]
AZ	100%	No	Yes[2]	10% per year	15% of overpayment	\$2,500	Depends on individual's record	6 months
AR	100%	No	Yes	10% per year	15% of overpayment	\$20 - \$200	60 days	60 days
CA	100%	6 years from mailing	Yes	7% until summary judgment filed; 10% until paid in full	30% of overpayment	\$20,000	1 year minimum	1 year minimum
CO	100%	No	No	No	\$25 – \$1,000 fine; 65% of overpayment penalty	\$25 - \$1,0003	6 months	6 months
CT	100%	8 years	Yes	1% per month	50% 1st offense; 100% subsequent offense	X[1]	1 year minimum	1 year minimum

State	Recovery of Overpayments Through Offset			Monetary Assessments			Max Prison Time Imposed When Fraud Committed By	
	Benefits		State Tax Refunds	Interest Charged	Fines or Penalties on Claimant	Fines or Penalties on Employer	Claimant	Employer
	Reduction in WBA	Number of Years Limited						
DE	100%	5 years from end of benefit year	Yes	18% per year	\$20 – \$50; 15% of overpayment	\$20 - \$200	60 days	60 days
DC	100%	No	Yes[2]	No	\$200; 15% of overpayment	\$1,000	60 days	6 months
FL	100%	Commenced within 7 years from date established	No	No, unless and until a civil judgment is entered	X; 15% of overpayment	\$5,000	5 years	5 years
GA	50%	7 years from release date of notice of determination and overpayment	Yes	1% per month	15% of overpayment	Up to \$1,000 for basic fraud; at least \$1,000 for multiple counts	12 months per count	X[1]
HI	100%	2 years from mailing or final appeal decision; after, if individual agrees (percentage up to individual)	No	No	X[2] 15% of overpayment	\$20 - \$200	5 years	60 days

Table 6-3. (Continued)

State	Recovery of Overpayments Through Offset			Monetary Assessments			Max Prison Time Imposed When Fraud Committed By	
	Benefits		State Tax Refunds	Interest Charged	Fines or Penalties on Claimant	Fines or Penalties on Employer	Claimant	Employer
	Reduction in WBA	Number of Years Limited						
ID	100%	8 years from final determination date	Yes[2]	Yes	25% 1st instance; 50% 2nd instance; 100% 3rd instance and subsequent[2]	\$20 - \$200 and 10 x WBA	X1	X[1]
IL	100%	No	Yes[2]	No, unless suit filed and judgment entered; then 9% per year	Up to \$500 fine; plus additional 15% of overpayment	Up to \$500	180 days	180 days
IN	100%	No	Yes	0.5% per month	25% 1st instance; 50% 2nd instance; 100% 3rd instance and subsequent; 15% of overpayment penalty	X[4]	6 - 36 months or 2 - 8 years	6 - 36 months or 2 - 8 years
IA	100%	10 years from date of last activity	Yes	No	15% of overpayment	50% of tax owed	10 years	
KS	100%	No	Yes	1.5% per month	25% of overpayment	\$20 - \$200	60 days	60 days
KY	100%	10 years from end of applicable BY	Yes	1.5% per month	\$500 -\$10,000; 15% of overpayment	\$500 - \$10,000	1 - 5 years	1 - 5 years

State	Recovery of Overpayments Through Offset			Monetary Assessments			Max Prison Time Imposed When Fraud Committed By	
	Benefits		State Tax Refunds	Interest Charged	Fines or Penalties on Claimant	Fines or Penalties on Employer	Claimant	Employer
	Reduction in WBA	Number of Years Limited						
LA	100%	No	Yes	No	Penalty is greater of $20 or 25% of overpayment balance	$50 - $1,000	10 years	30 – 90 days
ME	100%	No	Yes	1% per month	50% 1st incident, 75% 2nd incident, 100% other incidents	X[1]	X[1]	X[1]
MD	100%	No	Yes	1.5% per month	Up to $1,000; 15% of overpayment	Up to $1,000	90 days	90 days
MA	100%	No	Yes	1% per month until total interest = 50% of overpayment	Fine of $1,000 - $10,000; 15% of overpayment	$2,500 - $10,000	6 months to 5 years	1 year
MI	100%	3 years from overpayment	Yes	Yes	100% - 1st instance 150% - 2nd instance overpayment amount5	100% - 1st instance 150% - 2nd instance	1 year	1 year
MN[6]			Yes[2]	1.5% per month	40% of overpayment	X[1]	20 years	20 years
MS	100%	5 years from last week overpaid	Yes	1% per month	$100 - $500 fine; 20% of overpayment	$100 - $1,000	30 days for each fraudulent week	6 months
MO	100%	No; may write off as uncollectible after 5 years of no activity	Yes	No	25% - 100% of overpayment	25% - 100% of fraudulent amount	6 months for each violation	6 months for each violation

Table 6-3. (Continued)

State	Recovery of Overpayments Through Offset			Monetary Assessments			Max Prison Time Imposed When Fraud Committed By	
	Benefits		State Tax Refunds	Interest Charged	Fines or Penalties on Claimant	Fines or Penalties on Employer	Claimant	Employer
	Reduction in WBA	Number of Years Limited						
MT	100%	5 years; 10 years if lien filed	Yes	Yes	50% of overpayment	\$50 - \$500	Depends on recommendation of district attorney or employer	30 days for each false statement
NE	100%	3 years from end of applicable benefit year	Yes	No	Up to \$500 fine; 15% of overpayment	Up to \$500	90 days for each count	90 days
NV	100%	10 years from date overpayment established	No	Civil judgments only (6% per year)	15% of overpayment[7]	\$2,000	10 years	10 years
NH	1% – 10%	10 years from date overpayment decision is final	No	1% per month	Up to \$4,000 fine; 20% of overpayment	Up to \$100,000	15 years	15 years
NJ	100%	No	Yes[2]	5% for CY 2009	25% of total overpayment	\$100 to \$1,000 per offense	Decided by court	90 days
NM	100%	No	Yes	No	Up to \$100; 25% of overpayment	Up to \$10,000	30 days	30 days

State	Recovery of Overpayments Through Offset			Monetary Assessments			Max Prison Time Imposed When Fraud Committed By	
	Benefits		State Tax Refunds	Interest Charged	Fines or Penalties on Claimant	Fines or Penalties on Employer	Claimant	Employer
	Reduction in WBA	Number of Years Limited						
NY	100%	No	Yes2	9% per year (civil action only)	$500; the greater of $100 or 15% of overpayment	$500	1 year	1 year
NC	100%	No	Yes	No	Up to $200 fine; 15% of overpayment1	Up to $200	2 years	2 years
ND	100%	No	Yes[2]	18% per year	$10,000 fine; 15% of overpayment	$1,000	10 years	30 days
OH	100%	6 years from date overpayment is final	Yes	14% per year	Up to $1,000; 25% of overpayment	Up to $1,000	6 months	6 months
OK	100%	No	Yes	1% per month	Up to $500 fine each week after conviction; 25% of overpayment	$50 - $500	6 months	90 days
OR	100%	No	Yes2	1% per month	15 - 30% of overpayment	$100 - $500	X1	90 days
PA	100%	10 years from date applied for benefits	No	Computed annually based on IRS rate	$100 - $1,000; 15% of overpayment	$100 - $1,500 per offense	30 days per week illegally claimed	30 days per offense
PR	100%	5 years from date established	No	No	X[1] 15% of overpayment	$1,000	X1	1 year

Table 6-3. (Continued)

State	Recovery of Overpayments Through Offset			Monetary Assessments			Max Prison Time Imposed When Fraud Committed By	
	Benefits		State Tax Refunds	Interest Charged	Fines or Penalties on Claimant	Fines or Penalties on Employer	Claimant	Employer
	Reduction in WBA	Number of Years Limited						
RI	100%	No	Yes	1.5% per month	Greater of $1,000 or double value of fraud; 15% of overpayment	Greater of $1,000 or double value of fraud	1 year	1 year
SC	100%	No	Yes	No	$20 - $100; 25% of overpayment	$20 - $100	30 days for each offense or week claimed	30 days
SD	100%	No	No	12% per year	$2,000; 50% of overpayment – 1st instance and 100% overpayment subsequent	$1,000	1 or 2 years	1 or 2 years
TN	100%	No	No	1.5% per month	30% of overpayment for 1st incident; 50% for subsequent	X[1]	1 year (minimum)	1 year (minimum)

State	Recovery of Overpayments Through Offset			Monetary Assessments			Max Prison Time Imposed When Fraud Committed By	
	Benefits		State Tax Refunds	Interest Charged	Fines or Penalties on Claimant	Fines or Penalties on Employer	Claimant	Employer
	Reduction in WBA	Number of Years Limited						
TX	100%	No	No	1% per month	$4,000; 15% of overpayment	$4,000	Depends on whether prosecuted as misdemeanor or felony	X[1]
UT	100%	No	Yes[2]	No, unless it goes to judgment	The fines or penalties on individuals is 100% of overpayment (civil) and up to $10,000 (criminal)	Up to $20,000	15 years	15 years
VT	100%	5 years from determination date	Yes[2]	No	Up to $508; additional 15% of overpayment	Up to $50	30 days	30 days
VA	100%	No	Yes[2]	No	Up to $1,000; 15% of overpayment	Up to $1,000	1 year	1 year
VI	Depends on amount and ability of individual to repay	2 years from date overpayment is final	No	No	$50 - $200	$50 - $200	60 days	60 days

Table 6-3. (Continued)

State	Recovery of Overpayments Through Offset			Monetary Assessments			Max Prison Time Imposed When Fraud Committed By	
	Benefits		State Tax Refunds	Interest Charged	Fines or Penalties on Claimant	Fines or Penalties on Employer	Claimant	Employer
	Reduction in WBA	Number of Years Limited						
WA	100%	No	No	1% per month	$20 - $250; 15% of overpayment 1st offense; plus additional 25% of overpayment 2nd offense; plus additional 50% of overpayment 3rd and subsequent offenses	$20 - $250	90 days	90 days
WV	100%	10 years from last week overpaid	No	Yes	$100 - $1,000 fine; plus additional 20% of overpayment	$20 - $200	30 days	30 days
WI	100%	No	Yes[2]	No	Up to $25,000	Up to $25,000	Up to 10 years	Up to 10 years

State	Recovery of Overpayments Through Offset			Monetary Assessments			Max Prison Time Imposed When Fraud Committed By	
	Benefits		State Tax Refunds	Interest Charged	Fines or Penalties on Claimant	Fines or Penalties on Employer	Claimant	Employer
	Reduction in WBA	Number of Years Limited						
WY	100%	No	Yes	No	20% of overpayment and additional 5% of unpaid balance every 6 months thereafter until paid	$750	5 years	5 years

GENERAL NOTES: All states pursue civil action to recover fraud overpayments except AK, MA, NE, NC, PR, and SC. All states impose monetary assessments and prison time on employers who fraudulently act to prevent or reduce an individual's benefits. In addition, some states impose assessments/prison time for abetting an individual's fraudulent receipt of benefits. Where these penalties differ, the higher is shown.

[1] AL, AK, CT, GA, ID, ME, MN, NC, OR, PR, TX, and WV - penalty assessed under misdemeanor or felony statutes. Also for AL - in lieu of fines, if found guilty required to pay restitution in at least the amount of benefits fraudulently obtained.

[2] AZ, DC, HI, ID, IL, MN, NJ, NY, ND, OR, UT, VT, VA, and WI - provision found in non-UI law.

[3] Individual receives 1.5 x benefits due for weeks delayed, thus increasing employer's experience rate.

[4] The employer is assigned the rate for the year in which the violation occurred and the following 3 years. If employer is already paying the highest rate at the time of the violation, or the increase in the contribution rate described in this table is less than 2%, the employer will pay an additional 2% of the employer's taxable wages for the year in which the violation occurred and the following 3 years.

[5] Overpayment made through identity theft 4 x overpayment amount.

[6] Benefit offset not possible since individuals committing fraud are ineligible for benefits until they fully repay the amount owed.

[7] May impose additional penalties: 5% if overpayment >$25 to $1,000; 10% if overpayment >$1,000 to $2,500; 35% if overpayment >$2,500;

[8] If not prosecuted, assessed 1 penalty week for each week of fraud; however if fraud committed within the past 3 calendar years, and fraud committed again, assessed 2 penalty weeks for each week of fraud. Limited to no more than 26 penalty weeks in any BY.

Write-off of Overpayments

After exhausting its options to recover overpayments, most states will permit the UI agency to write off (that is, cancel as uncollectible) certain overpayments. The criteria for writing off overpayments vary. Usually, it depends on how long the overpayment has been outstanding. However, most states have established additional criteria. The following table provides information on states' write-off provisions.

Table 6-4. Write-off of overpayments

State	Nonfraud		Fraud	
	Age Requirement	Other Criteria	Age Requirement	Other Criteria
AL[1]	6 years from final decision	Bankruptcy or death	6 years from final decision	Death
AK[2]	2 years from last payment	Death	2 years from last payment	Death
AZ[1]	5 years from final decision			Bankruptcy or death
AR		Death		Death
CA[1, 2]	6 years and 1 month from overpayment mail date; if judgment, 10 years and 1 month from judgment	Immediately if overpayment ≤$9.99 and no payment activity for 6 months	6 years and 1 month from overpayment mail date; if judgment, 10 years and 1 month from judgment	Immediately if overpayment ≤$9.99 and no payment activity for 6 months
CO[1, 2]	5 years from determination that debt is uncollectible	Administratively impracticable to collect	7 years from determination that debt is uncollectible	Administratively impracticable to collect
DE[2]	3 years	Overpayment debt is wholly or partly uncollectible	3 years	Overpayment debt is wholly or partly uncollectible
DC[1]	3 years after BY ending date	No claim with current BY and balance, and no repayment within 180 days	3 years after BY ending date	No claim with current BY and balance, no repayment within 180 days, case referred for prosecution
FL[1]	2 years from establishment	Bankruptcy or death	5 years from establishment	Bankruptcy or death

State	Nonfraud		Fraud	
	Age Requirement	Other Criteria	Age Requirement	Other Criteria
GA[1]	3 years older than 1st day of current quarter		4 years older than 1st day of current quarter and last transaction is 1 quarter old	
ID[2]	5 years from final decision	Account activity	8 years from final decision	Account activity
IL2, 3		If uncollectible		Legally uncollectible
IN2	3 years from BYB of claim; civil judgment extends by 10 years (can extend again)		6 years from BYB of claim; civil judgment extends by 10 years (can extend again)	
IA[2, 3]	10 years from last activity		10 years from last activity	
KS[1]	5 years from last transaction		10 years from last transaction	
KY[2]	5 years from last day of benefit year		10 years from last day of BY	Not if individual has been prosecuted for offense
LA[2]	5 years from BYE of overpaid claim and from last acknowledgement of debt or penalty assessment	Bankruptcy	10 years from determination date and from last acknowledgement of debt or penalty assessment	Bankruptcy
ME[1]	6 years from establishment	<$25	6 years from establishment	<$25
MD1	5 years from establishment		5 years	
MA[1, 2]	5 years from last claim for benefits	No further contact with individual	5 years from last claim for benefits	No further contact with individual; after review and approval of Commissioner

Table 6-4. (Continued)

State	Nonfraud		Fraud	
	Age Requirement	Other Criteria	Age Requirement	Other Criteria
MI[1]	3 years from determination date unless civil action filed, individual made false statement, or determination requires restitution; 10 years if judgment		6 years from determination date unless civil action filed, individual made false statement, or determination requires restitution; 10 years if judgment	
MN[2]	6 years from date determined	Bankruptcy or death	10 years from date determined	
MS[2]	5 years from last day of week overpaid		5 years from last day of week overpaid	
MO[2]	5 years from establishment with no activity	Must be uncollectible	5 years from establishment with no activity	Must be uncollectible
MT[2]	5 years from establishment; 10 years with lien	Bankruptcy or death	5 years from establishment; 10 years with lien	
NE[1, 3]		Bankruptcy, death, incarcerated 5+ years, or can't be located and overpayment 10+ years		Bankruptcy, death, incarcerated 5+ years, or can't be located and overpayment 10+ years
NV	3 years from establishment		3 years from establishment	
NH[2, 3]		If in best interest of state		If in best interest of state
NJ[2]	6 months to 1 year from date of delinquency	Depends on date of last payment, proof and date of individual contact	6 months to 1 year from date of delinquency	Depends on date of last payment, proof and date of individual contact
NY[1]	6 years from latest action		6 years from latest action on overpayment; if judgment, 20 years from date judgment filed	

State	Nonfraud		Fraud	
	Age Requirement	Other Criteria	Age Requirement	Other Criteria
NC[2]		Death		Death
ND[1]		Bankruptcy, death, inability to locate claimant, or current status of employment		
OH[2]	3 years from final decision		6 years from final decision	
OK[2]	1 year from end of current BY when overpayment established	Administrative error only		
OR[2]	5 years from final decision; if nonfault overpayment, after 5 years	≤ state max WBA or uncollectible; also, must be no payments within last 3 months	5 years from final decision	≤ 1/2 state max WBA or uncollectible; also, must be no payments within last 3 months; not if conviction
PA[2]	If nonfault, 4 years from application for benefits date; 7 years if fault	Not written off if liened	10 years from application for benefits date	Not written off if liened
PR[2]	5 years from establishment	Bankruptcy or death	5 years from establishment	Bankruptcy or death
RI[1]	5 years from detection and no refund activity	Bankruptcy, death, or any overpayment ≤$100; system allows reactivation of overpayment if individual files a claim and/or starts to repay	5 years from detection and no refund activity	Bankruptcy, death, or any overpayment ≤ $100; system allows reactivation of overpayment if individual files a claim and/or starts to repay
SC[2]	5 years from establishment		6 years from establishment	
SD[2]		Bankruptcy or death and 10 years or more		Bankruptcy or death and 10 years or more
TN[2]	6 years from establishment		6 years from establishment	

Table 6-4. (Continued)

State	Nonfraud		Fraud	
	Age Requirement	Other Criteria	Age Requirement	Other Criteria
UT[3]	Fault overpayments subject to accounting write-off after 3 years if deemed uncollectible; mandatory write-off as to offset at 8 years	Nonfault overpayments	Accounting write-off after 3 years if deemed uncollectible; no write-off as to benefit eligibility	
VT[2]	5 years from determination date; if judgment order, 8 years from judgment date	Bankruptcy or death	5 years from determination date; if judgment order, 8 years from judgment date	Bankruptcy or death
VA[2]	7 years from determination date	Bankruptcy or death	7 years from determination date	Bankruptcy or death
VI[1]	2 years from final decision	Deceased w/o assets, incarcerated for a long time, permanently disabled or physically unable to work and w/o assets, is no longer in VI, or cannot be located		
WA		No cost-effective means of collecting		No cost-effective means of collecting
WV[2]	5 years from last day of week overpaid	Bankruptcy or death	10 years from last day of week overpaid	Bankruptcy or death
WI[1]	7 years from decision	Bankruptcy or death with no assets; no collection activity in 3 years; no assets or wages found	7 years from decision	Bankruptcy or death with no assets; no collection activity in 3 years; no assets or wages found

State	Nonfraud		Fraud	
	Age Requirement	Other Criteria	Age Requirement	Other Criteria
WY[2]	8 years from effective date of claim; can write off any time if deceased with no assets or insolvent with no assets	Cannot locate, totally unable to work, and covered wages < ½ of average state weekly wage		Cannot locate, totally unable to work, and covered wages < ½ of average state weekly wage

GENERAL NOTE: For additional information, consult state law, regulations, and policy. CT, HI, NM, and TX - are not included in this table since they do not write off overpayments.

[1] Write-off provisions found in policy.

[2] Write-off provisions found in law.

[3] Write-off provisions found in regulation.

SECTION 7. APPEALS

In General

This chapter provides information about state law provisions concerning appeals authorities and time limitations for review for first-level appeals, second-level appeals, and judicial review.

The Social Security Act requires states to offer "opportunity for a fair hearing before an impartial tribunal, for all individuals whose claims for unemployment compensation are denied." Hence, all states' laws provide for a right to appeal. Further, all but a few states' laws provide for a second-level appeal. In all states, individuals who are not satisfied with the outcome of the administrative appeal(s) may appeal their cases in the state court system, federal courts, and, as a last resort, the U.S. Supreme Court. In all states, employers who have an interest are granted the right to appeal decisions on claims as well.

As a result of *California Department of Human Resources Development v. Java*, 402 U.S. 121 (1971), once a UI claimant has been found eligible for benefits, such claimant will continue to receive benefits until a decision is issued reversing the determination allowing benefits. Thus, an employer's appeal will not affect the continuance of payment of benefits until a subsequent decision is issued denying benefits. The majority of state laws specifically provide for the payment of benefits pending an appeal of a determination or decision allowing benefits, while other states have either interpreted their laws or have been required by court order to follow this procedure. In all states, this procedure applies to any determination or decision issued allowing benefits.

Most states specify that findings of fact, conclusions of law, or final orders made by a UI hearing officer or board of review will not be binding in any separate or subsequent proceeding brought in any judicial, administrative, or arbitration proceeding in that state or of the U.S. government. The states that do not specify this are listed in the table below. Some states' laws provide that information obtained in connection with the UI law may not be used in certain civil lawsuits as well.

Table 7-1. States that do not specify that findings, conclusions, or orders of hearing officers are not binding in any other proceeding

Alabama	Delaware	Hawaii	Kentucky	Maryland
Mississippi	Puerto Rico	Rhode Island	South Carolina	Virginia
Virgin Islands	West Virginia			

First-and Second-Level Appeals

First-Level Appeals

An individual who disagrees with a determination denying benefits has the right to file an appeal of that determination. The determination becomes final unless a timely appeal is filed. In some states, a special examiner is designated to re-determine the original claim before an appeal. Also, an employer who disagrees with a determination paying benefits may file an appeal of that determination. Typically, all states' laws provide that appeals at the initial stage will be conducted by one person called a referee, examiner, or administrative law judge.

In all but a few states, the decision of the first-level appeals body is final in the absence of further appeal. In other states, the official may reconsider his/her decision within the appeal period.

Second-Level Appeals

Any interested party who disagrees with a first-level appeals decision must file a timely appeal of that decision to the second-level appeals body or the decision becomes final. Some states provide that a contested determination involving a labor dispute shall be appealed directly to the second-level appeal body. A few states have no second-level appeals body. In those states, the next appeal level is to the courts. About half of the states with second-level appeals have a board of review, board of appeals, or appeals board to hear cases appealed from the decision of the first-level appeals body. Most of these boards consist of three members. The members of the appeals boards generally represent labor, employers, and the public. Some common requirements related to the composition of an appeals body are: location of residence; political affiliation; whether the individual is an attorney or not; or whether the individual is designated as an employer or employee representative.

In the rest of the states with second-level appeals, appeals are handled by an existing commission or agency head.

Time Limits for Filing Appeals and Filing with Appellate Entities

The number of days for filing a first- or second-level appeal varies among the states, and ranges from 7-30 days after mailing, delivering, or electronically transmitting the notice of determination or decision. Many states extend the time for filing appeals for good cause. Some states specify that a "day" is defined as a calendar day. Some states that do not define "day" extend the due date for filing appeals when the last day for filing or the date of mailing falls on a Saturday, Sunday, holiday, or any other day the state agency is closed. State-specific information for filing first- or second-level appeals can be found in the following table.

Table 7-2. Time limits for filing appeals and filing with appellate entities

State	First-Level Appeals	Second-Level Appeals	
	Number Of Days For Filing	Number Of Days For Filing	Appellate Entity
AL	15# after mailing; 7# after delivery	15# after mailing date	Board of Appeals
AK	30 after mailing or personal delivery; an additional 3 days if mailed	30 after mailing or personal delivery; an additional 3 days if mailed	Commissioner
AZ	15# after mailing; 7# after delivery	30# after mailing or electronic transmission	Appeals Board
AR	20# after mailing or delivery	20# after mailing or delivery	Board of Review
CA	30# after mailing date on notice or personal service	30# after mailing date on notice or personal service	Appeals Board
CO	20# after mailing or personal delivery	20# after mailing or personal delivery	Industrial Claim Appeals Office (Panel)
CT	21# after notice mailed or provided	21# after mailing	Board of Review
DE	10# after mailing	10 after decision is final	UI Appeal Board
DC	15# after mailing or actual delivery	NO SECOND-LEVEL APPEAL	
FL	20# after mailing or delivery	20# after mailing or delivery	Reemployment Assistance Appeals Commission
GA	15 after mailing or delivery	15 after mailing or delivery	Board of Review
HI	10 after mailing or delivery	NO SECOND-LEVEL APPEAL	
ID	14 after mailing or delivery	14 after actual mailing or delivery	Industrial Commission
IL	30# after mailing or delivery	30# after mailing or delivery	Board of Review
IN	10# after mailing or delivery; an additional 3# if mailed	15# after mailing or delivery; an additional 3# if mailed	Review Board
IA	10# after date of administrative law judge's decision	15# after date of administrative law judge's decision	Employment Appeal Board
KS	16# after mailing or delivery	16# after mailing or delivery	Board of Review
KY	15 after mailing	15 after mailing	UI Commission
LA	15 after mailing date of document	15 after mailing date on Administrative Law Judge's decision	Board of Review

State	First-Level Appeals	Second-Level Appeals	
	Number Of Days For Filing	Number Of Days For Filing	Appellate Entity
ME	15# after mailing	15# after mailing	UI Commission
MD	15# after mailing or delivery	15# after mailing or delivery	Board of Appeals
MA	30 after mailing or delivery	30 after mailing	Board of Review
MI	30 after mailing, by facsimile, or other electronic method	30 after mailing, by facsimile, or other electronic method	Board of Review
MN	20# after mailing, facsimile, or electronic transmission	NO SECOND-LEVEL APPEAL	
MS	14 after notification or mailing	14 after notification or mailing	Board of Review
MO	30 after date of notification or mailing	30 after date of notification or mailing	Industrial Commission
MT	10 after mailing	10 after mailing	Unemployment Insurance Appeals Board
NE	20# after delivery or mailing	NO SECOND-LEVEL APPEAL	
NV	11 after mailing or personal service of determination or redetermination	11 after mailing or delivery	Board of Review
NH	14# after mailing	14# after mailing	Appellate Board
NJ	7# after delivery, 10# after mailing	20# after notification or mailing	Board of Review
NM	15# from the date on the notice	15# from the date on the notice	Board of Review
NY	20 after mailing or personal delivery	20 after mailing or personal delivery	Appeal Board
NC	15 after notification or mailing, whichever is earlier	10* after notification or mailing, whichever is earlier	Board of Review
ND	12 after mailing or service	12 after mailing or service	Bureau
OH	21# after mailing of determination or redetermination	21# after mailing	Unemployment Compensation Review Commission
OK	10# from mail date	10# from mail date	Board of Review
OR	20 after mailing or delivery	20 after mailing or delivery	Employment Appeals Board

Table 7-2. (Continued)

State	First-Level Appeals	Second-Level Appeals	
	Number Of Days For Filing	Number Of Days For Filing	Appellate Entity
PA	15# after mailing	15 after mailing	Unemployment Compensation Board of Review
PR	15 after mailing or delivery	15 after mailing or delivery	Secretary of Labor
RI	15# after mailing	15 after mailing	Board of Review
SC	10 after mailing	10# after mailing	Appellate Panel
SD	15 after mailing	15 after mailing or notification	Secretary of Labor and Regulation
TN	15# after mailing or delivery, whichever occurs first	15# after mailing or delivery, whichever occurs first	Commissioner's designees
TX	14# after mailing	14# after mailing	Commission
UT	15# from date of decision unless other specified on decision	30# from date of the decision	Appeals Board
VT	30 from date of the determination or decision	30 from date of the determination or decision	Employment Security Board
VI	10 after mailing or delivery	NO SECOND-LEVEL APPEAL	
VA	30# after of mailing date of the determination or delivery	30 after mailing or delivery	Office of Commission Appeals
WA	30 after mailing or notification, whichever is earlier	30 after mailing or notification, whichever is earlier	Commissioner's Review Office
WV	8# after mailing or delivery	8# after mailing or delivery	Board of Review
WI	14 after mailing or being given to such party, whichever occurs first	21 from the date of the decision	Labor and Industry Review Commission
WY	28# after mailing	28# after mailing	Employment Security Commission

# Indicates "calendar" days; * Indicates "working" days; If unmarked, type of "days" is not specified.

Judicial Review

The decision of the second-level appeals body or the first-level appeals body, in states without a second- level appeals body, becomes final unless an appeal is filed for judicial review. All states provide for appeals to the courts for judicial review. In general, the time limit for filing ranges from 10 to 30 days as shown in the table below. States that designate a specific period of time to exhaust actions before the second administrative appeals body decision becomes final provide an additional period of time in which to seek judicial review, commencing with the date the decision is final.

Table 7-3. Judicial review

State	Number of Days for Filing		Court of Initial Jurisdiction
	After Notification[1]	Other	
AL	30 from the date the Board decision becomes final		Circuit Court in county in which claimant resides; or if claimant not residing in state, claimant must file in the county in which claimant last worked or resided
AK		Within 30 days after date of entry of the decision	Superior Court
AZ	30	30 days after date of mailing or electronic transmission of the decision	Court of Appeals
AR	30#		Court of Appeals
CA		Within 6 months of date of decision, or date it is designated a precedent, whichever is later	Superior Court; by court rule, no statutory provision
CO	21#		Court of Appeals
CT	30#		Superior Court in Hartford or district where appellant resides
DE	10 + 10		Superior Court
DC		30 days after decision is final	D.C. Court of Appeals
FL		Within 30# days of date of entry of decision (prescribed by appellate rules)	District Court of Appeals in appellate district in which claimant resides or the job separation arose, or in the appellate district where the order was issued
GA	15 + 15		Superior Court in county or city in which the claimant last worked

Table 7-3. (Continued)

State	Number of Days for Filing		Court of Initial Jurisdiction
	After Notification[1]	Other	
HI		30 days after service of decision	Circuit Court in county in which claimant resides, or in county or city in which claimant last worked
ID	42		Supreme Court
IL	35		Circuit Court in county in which claimant resides or county where business is located; non-resident may file suit in Circuit Court of Cook County
IN	15; or 30[#] days from date of notice of intention to appeal filed within the 15-day period		Indiana Court of Appeals
IA	30[#] after date of notice		District Court in county in which claimant resides; non-resident may file suit in District Court of Polk County or where claimant last worked
KS	16[#]		District Court in county where claimant resides; non-resident may file suit in Shawnee County District Court or in county in which business is located
KY		20 days after date of decision	Circuit Court in county or city in which claimant last worked
LA	15 days of the mailing date		District Court where claimant resides; or if claimant not residing in state at time for filing petition, claimant may file in District Court in the parish in which claimant resides or in parish in which the Louisiana Workforce Commission is domiciled
ME	10		Superior Court in county in which plaintiff lives or does business
MD	30		Circuit Court of County of Baltimore, or one of the Circuit Courts in a county in Maryland
MA	30		District Court in county in which claimant resides, or in county or city in which claimant last worked, or in district of employers usual place of business

State	Number of Days for Filing		Court of Initial Jurisdiction
	After Notification[1]	Other	
MI	30		Circuit Court in county in which claimant resides, or last worked, or county in which business is located
MN	30[#]		Court of Appeals
MS	10 + 10		Circuit Court of the county where party resides, the county in which the action arose, or in the county of employment
MO	10 + 20		Appellate Court; appeals on interstate claims will be in Court of Appeals for the Western District
MT	30		District Court in county in which claimant resides
NE	30		District Court in county in which claimant resides or last worked
NV	11		District Court in the county where employment was performed
NH	30		Supreme Court
NJ	45 of mailing date		Superior Court, Appellate Division
NM	30		District Court in county in which claimant resides
NY	20		Supreme Court, Appellate Division, Third Department
NC	30		Superior Court in county in which claimant resides or county in which business is located
ND	30		District Court
OH	30		Court of Common Pleas in county in which claimant resides or last worked, or in county in which business is located
OK		30 days from mailing date	District Court in county in which claimant resides; non-resident may file suit in District Court of Oklahoma County
OR		30 days after order is served	Court of Appeals
PA	15 + 30		Commonwealth Court
PR	30		Superior Court in county in which employer or employing unit has its place of business
RI	30		District Court - Sixth Division, State of Rhode Island
SC	30		Administrative Law Court
SD		30 days of the date of decision	Circuit Court

Table 7-3. (Continued)

State	Number of Days for Filing		Court of Initial Jurisdiction
	After Notification[1]	Other	
TN		30 days after decision of commissioner has become final	Chancery Court in county in which claimant resides; non-resident may file suit in Chancery Court of the county in which employer is located
TX	28[2]		County Court in county in which claimant resides; non-resident may file suit in Travis County Court or in county in which claimant last or principle place of business is located
UT		30 days after date of decision	Utah Court of Appeals
VT		30 days after date of decision	Supreme Court
VA	30		Circuit Court where claimant last worked
VI	30		District Court of the Virgin Islands
WA	30		Superior Court; appeals on intrastate claims filed in petitioner's choice of Thurston County or county of residence or business; appeals on interstate claims in Thurston County
WV	30		Circuit Court of Kanawha County
WI	30		Circuit court of the county where plaintiff resides, except if the plaintiff is a state agency, the proceedings must be in the state where the defendant resides; if the plaintiff is a non-resident of Wisconsin, the proceedings must be in the Circuit Court of Dane County; cases can be brought in any other county circuit court if the parties and the court agree
WY	30		District Court of Natrona County, or in county in which claimant resides, or in county in which business is located

[#] Indicates "calendar" days

[1] Where two figures are shown, the first figure is the number of days after which the decision is final and is the time claimant has to exhaust actions before administrative appeals bodies; the second figure is additional time allowed to seek judicial review. Notification may include postal or electronic mailing, in-person delivery, or other methods of notice.

[2] Claimant may request a rehearing within 14 days of the date that the second-level appeals decision is mailed; starting on the 15th day, the individual may file for judicial review with the civil court.

Section 8. Temporary Disability Insurance

In General

Temporary Disability Insurance (TDI) programs are designed to provide wage replacement for nonwork-connected sickness or injury. The TDI program complements the UI program by providing benefits to individuals who do not meet the UI program's "able" to work requirement. Although Federal law does not provide for a federal-state TDI system, the SSA and FUTA both authorize the withdrawal of employee contributions from a state's unemployment fund for payment of TDI.

Six states operate TDI programs. In California, New Jersey, Puerto Rico, and Rhode Island the TDI programs are administered by the state employment security agency. The Hawaii law is administered by the Temporary Disability Income Division of the Department of Labor and Industrial Relations. The New York law is administered by the state's workers' compensation board.

> *Historical Note:* Rhode Island passed the first TDI law in 1942; California followed in 1946, New Jersey in 1948, New York in 1949, Puerto Rico in 1968, and Hawaii in 1969.

Definition of Disability

The scope of the program depends in part on the type of disabilities compensable. The intent of the laws is to compensate for nonwork-connected sickness or injury. This purpose is achieved through the definition of disability or through other eligibility conditions.

In general, the laws define disability in terms of the inability of an individual to perform the regular or customary work because of the individual's physical or mental condition. California also specifically includes individuals suspected of being infected with a communicable disease, acute alcoholics, and drug addicts undergoing treatment. Hawaii's definition of disability includes organ donation. The Puerto Rico law and two of the special programs for the unemployed who are disabled in New Jersey and New York contain more strict requirements with respect to disability during unemployment. The New Jersey law provides that individuals must be continuously and totally unable to perform the duties of their job. The New York and Puerto Rico laws provide that individuals must be unable to perform any work for which they are reasonably qualified by training and experience.

Exclusion from Disability Payments

Hawaii, New Jersey, New York, and Puerto Rico have provisions for excluding payments for disability caused by willful, intentional, or self-inflicted injuries. A disability acquired in the perpetration of an illegal act is excluded in California, Hawaii, New Jersey, New York, and Puerto Rico. California also prohibits payment due to incarceration. New York also excludes disabilities resulting from an act of war after June 30, 1950. California and Puerto Rico prohibit payments for any period of confinement in an institution as a drug addict, dipsomaniac, or sexual psychopath. In Puerto Rico, benefits are not payable for disability in cases caused by, or in relation to, abortion performed for medical reasons or in cases where complications have arisen due to abortion.

Uninterrupted Period of Disability

All states except Rhode Island have defined consecutive periods of disability resulting from the same or related cause or condition.

Table 8-1. Consecutive periods of disability

CA	Consecutive disability periods due to same or related cause and separated by not more than 14 days
HI	Consecutive periods of disability due to same or related cause and not separated by an interval of more than 2 weeks
NJ	Consecutive periods of disability due to same or related cause and separated by not more than 14 days if individual earned wages from his last employer during the 14-day period

NY	Consecutive disability periods caused by same or related injury or sickness if separated by less than 3 months
PR	Consecutive disability periods caused by same or related illness or injury if separated by less than 90 days

Coverage

Coverage for the purpose of TDI varies among the six states; therefore, no state TDI coverage provision is the same. Services are covered for TDI if an employer meets the definitions shown in the table below. In all states with TDI laws, under specified conditions, states may allow certain exemptions from coverage and certain elections of coverage.

Table 8-2. Coverage provisions

CA	Employers of one or more workers and $100 in quarterly payroll, agricultural employees, certain domestic workers who are paid $1,000 or more, and employees of nonprofit hospitals
HI	Employers of one or more workers
NJ	Employers who paid $1,000 in any year
NY	Employers of one or more workers on each of at least 30 days and domestic workers who work a minimum of 40 hours and are employed on each of at least 30 days; individuals can elect out on grounds that they are entitled to Old Age and Survivor's Insurance benefits
PR	Employers of one or more workers on any day of current or preceding calendar year
RI	Employers of one or more workers at any time, except that individual workers can elect out on religious grounds

Financing

In California and Rhode Island, the benefits and administration of the programs originally were financed wholly or mainly by employee contributions that formerly went to UI. In New Jersey, employers have always contributed substantially (up to 50 percent, historically) for TDI. In addition to providing that current employee contributions are deposited in the disability fund, the legislatures in these states provided for transfer to the disability fund of some or all of the employee contributions collected under the UI law.

Type of Fund

In Rhode Island, all contributions are paid into a pooled state fund and all benefits are paid from that fund. In California, New Jersey, and Puerto Rico, coverage under a private plan (usually with an insurance company) may be substituted for coverage under the state fund if the private plan is approved by the agency as meeting certain requirements of the law. Contributions are then paid into the private plan and benefits are paid by it, generally one plan for disabilities beginning during employment and one plan for disabilities beginning shortly thereafter. In Puerto Rico, benefits under a private plan are paid to individuals for periods of disability that begin during unemployment or while employed in noninsured work.

The Hawaii and New York laws are similar to an employer liability law in that they require employers to take positive action to provide disability insurance for their workers, with employees contributing to the cost. In New York, the employer may provide the protection through self-insurance, or through buying an insurance contract from either a private insurance company or the state insurance fund, which is a state-operated competitive carrier originally organized for workers' compensation. In New York, employers may purchase Enriched Disability Benefits Insurance coverage to provide benefit levels for employees above the statutory requirements. Also, there is a special fund for disability benefits, operated by the state, for benefits to the unemployed. In Hawaii, employers may provide protection through private plans with an authorized insurance carrier or through approved self-financing. In addition, there is a special state fund for unemployed workers and employees of bankrupt or non-complying employers.

Amount of Contributions

The TDI contribution rates for both employees and employers vary among the states. All six states require employees to pay contributions to finance TDI. Only four states require employers to pay TDI contributions.

The following table shows the amount of TDI contributions required for both employers and employees.

Table 8-3. Amount of contributions

State	Employer Contributions	Employee Contributions	Taxable Wage Base
CA	None; optional; may elect to pay all or part of employee amount	0.1 – 1.5% of TWB[1]	$118,371
HI	At least ½ plan costs, plus additional costs, plus additional costs not charged to employee	Up to ½ plan costs, but not more than 0.5% of avg. weekly wages	$1,088.08 weekly
NJ	0.1% - 0.75% of TWB[2]	0.19% of TWB	$34,400
NY	Balance after employee contributions	0.5% of wages paid (up to 60¢ weekly)	None
PR	0.6% of TWB which is shared by employer and employee[3]		$9,000
RI	None	1.1% of TWB	$69,300

[1] Rate may not decrease from the previous year's rate by more than 1.2%; the 2019 rate is 1.0%.

[2] Percent of TWB of each employee based on experience rating; rate may decrease to 0.1% or increase to 1.1% on basis of employer's reserve ratio, how long a covered employer, and the status of the state UI fund as a whole.

[3] Contributions may or may not be equally shared.

Financing Benefits for Disability during Unemployment

In Rhode Island, all benefits are paid from the state fund with no distinction between disabilities beginning during employment and those beginning during unemployment. In California, where contracting out is permitted, there is no distinction between the amount of benefits payable to the employed and the unemployed, but the latter are charged to a special account in the state fund depending on whether the workers were covered by the state plan or a private plan when employed. Each voluntary plan pays 14 percent of the amount due annually for contributions into the state fund to finance benefits to persons who are either unemployed or in noncovered work at the time their period of disability commences. In Puerto Rico, private plans must finance some or all of the disability benefits payable to workers for periods of disability that begin during unemployment or employment in uninsured work.

The separate New Jersey program for disability during unemployment is financed principally by interest on employee contributions withdrawn from the unemployment trust fund. Additional costs of such benefits may be assessed against all employers up to 0.1 percent of taxable wages.

Hawaii levied a temporary contribution rate of 0.2 percent on the taxable wages of subject employers from July to December 1969 to establish the Special Disability Fund from which benefits are paid during unemployment. Additional amounts are assessed against insurance carriers and self-insured employers as needed.

In New York, a temporary contribution from January 1 to July 1, 1950, of 0.1 percent on the first $60 in weekly wages by both employers and employees (i.e., not more than 60 cents a week each) established the fund from which benefits were first paid for disability during unemployment. This fund has been maintained at $12 million (by statute) by interest earned by the fund, by certain fines and penalties, and, when necessary, by an assessment against all carriers including the state fund.

Administrative Costs

Administrative costs under five programs are paid from the contributions; in Hawaii, such costs are paid from general revenue. Under the terms of the SSA and FUTA, employee contributions withdrawn from the unemployment trust fund are not available for payment of costs of administration. In New Jersey, 0.01 percent of taxable wages is credited to the administration account. In California and Puerto Rico, necessary administrative expenses, as determined by the State Director of Finance (California) or the Secretary of Labor (Puerto Rico), are withdrawn from the disability fund and each private plan is assessed a share of the total amount expended for added administrative work arising out of the voluntary plans.

New Jersey employers covered by the state fund pay an extra assessment for the costs of maintaining separate accounts for experience-rating purposes. In New Jersey, employers with private plans are assessed the additional administrative costs attributable to private plans in proportion to covered wages, with a maximum annual assessment of 0.5 percent of wages. Included in this assessment is a prorated share of the administrative costs of the system for the unemployed.

In New York, the state insurance fund is limited to 25 percent of contributions for administrative expenses. The administrative costs to the state of the programs for both employed and unemployed workers, not including the expenses of the state fund as a carrier, are assessed against all carriers, including the state fund, in proportion to covered wages, with no limit.

Benefit Provisions

Table 8-4. Benefit year and base period

State	Benefit Formula	Benefit Year	Base Period
CA	Differs from UI	No BY; rights determined with respect to continuous disability period established by valid claim	First 4 of last 5 CQs preceding disability
HI	Differs from UI	1-year period beginning with 1st week of disability for which valid claim is filed	None; see tables in TDI statute for period used for qualifying employment and WBA
NJ	Differs from UI	No BY but statutory minimum and maximum benefits in any 12-month period	52 calendar weeks immediately preceding calendar week in which disability period began
NY	Differs from UI	No BY; maximum benefits limited in terms of any 52 consecutive weeks	No BP as used in UI; see tables in TDI statute for period used for qualifying employment and WBA
PR	Same as UI for agricultural and nonagricultural workers up to $64 WBA	No BY; maximum benefit limited in terms of any 52 consecutive weeks	First 4 of last 5 completed CQs immediately preceding 1st day of disability
RI	Similar to UI	Begins Sunday of calendar week in which individual first became unemployed due to illness and has filed a valid claim for TDI (52 consecutive weeks; 53 if overlaps with any quarter of BP of prior claim)	First 4 of last 5 completed CQs immediately preceding BY or last 4 completed quarters if individual fails to meet qualifying wage requirement

Table 8-5. Qualifying wages or employment

State	Additional Information
CA	Flat $300 in base period
HI	14 weeks of employment with at least 20 hours in each week and wages of $400 during the 4 completed CQs immediately preceding 1st day of disability
NJ	20 weeks of employment at 20 times the minimum wage during the base year or 1,000 times the minimum wage during the base year; or $8,500 in earnings for individuals who have not established 20 base weeks; $172 base week
NY	Employ one or more persons on each of 30 days in a calendar year
PR	Flat $150 in base period
RI	(1) 200 x minimum hourly wage in 1 quarter and BPW of 1½ x HQ, and BPW must be at least 400 x minimum hourly wage, or (2) paid total BPW of at least 3 x total minimum amount required in (1) above

Table 8-6. Weekly benefit amount and duration of benefits

State	Weekly Benefit Amount	Duration
CA	$50 - $1,252	Up to 52 weeks
HI	$1 - $632	Up to 26 weeks in BY
NJ	$10 - $650	Up to 26 weeks or period necessary for benefits to equal ⅓ of total wages in base year
NY	$20 - $1701	Uniform potential 26 weeks in any 52 consecutive weeks or for any single period of disability
PR	Non-agricultural workers: $12 - $113 Agricultural workers: $12 - $64	Uniform potential 26 weeks in any 52 consecutive weeks
RI	$98 - $852 plus dependents' allowance (equal to the greater of $10 or 7% of the individual's benefit rate for each dependent, up to 5 dependents)	1 - 30 weeks

The TDI benefit provisions are shown in the tables provided. In all states, eligibility for benefits depends on proof of disability and continuation of such disability. Some states also have special provisions for individuals with specific circumstances (e.g., military service, trade affected, unemployed, etc.).

Table 8-7. Waiting period

State	Additional Information
CA	7 consecutive days of disability at the beginning of each period of disability
HI	7 consecutive days of disability at the beginning of each period of disability
NJ	7 consecutive days of disability commencing with the Sunday of the week in which the claim is filed; becomes compensable after benefits have been paid for all or some part of each of the 3 weeks immediately following the waiting week
NY	7 consecutive days of disability at the beginning of each period of disability
PR	7 consecutive days of disability at the beginning of each period of disability; no waiting period for agricultural workers who become disabled during continuous period of unemployment; no waiting period required for regular benefits for hospitalized individual or for individual unemployed and disabled for more than 14 days
RI	Waiting week eliminated 7/1/2012; as a condition of eligibility, an individual must have been unemployed due to nonjob-related injury or sickness for at least 7 consecutive days

Partial Weeks of Disability

In the temporary disability programs, benefits are paid for partial weeks on a different basis from partial unemployment (except in the New Jersey program) for compensating disability during employment.

Table 8-8. Partial weeks of disability

State	Additional Information
CA	Benefits payable for less than 1 week will be paid in increments of 1/7 WBA
HI	Benefits payable for less than 1 week will be paid in increments of 1/5 WBA
NJ	Benefits payable for less than 1 week will be paid in increments of 1/7 WBA; payment for part week rounded to next higher dollar
NY	Benefits payable for less than 1 week will be paid in increments of the WBA divided by the number of the employee's normal workdays per week (daily benefits computed on basis of normal number of workdays per week)
PR	Benefits payable for less than 1 week will be paid in increments of 1/7 WBA rounded to higher dollar
RI	For each day of qualifying unemployment, worker receives benefits at the rate of 1/5 WBA for each workday up to 4/5 WBA rounded to next higher dollar

Benefits under Private Plans

The California law requires that private plans provide benefit rights greater than those under the state plan in all respects. In Hawaii, New Jersey, and Puerto Rico, private plan benefits must be at least as favorable to workers as those under the state plans. Hawaii permits deviations from statutory benefits if the benefits provided under the private plan are actuarially equal or better. In New York, adherence to a statutory formula is not required whether workers are insured with the state fund or with a private carrier. Benefits must be actuarially equivalent to the statutory formula. Cash benefits in the formula in Table 8-4 may be reduced if the plan of insurance includes a shorter waiting period or other benefits, such as hospitalization benefits; weekly benefits may be less than 50 percent of wages if maximum duration is more than 26 weeks. Employees may be required to contribute more than 0.5 percent of wages paid if additional benefits warrant the extra cost.

Survivors' Benefits

In California and New Jersey, if a claim for disability benefits was not filed by an otherwise eligible individual prior to his death, a claim may be filed by a person who legally would be entitled to such benefits. Puerto Rico provides a lump sum death benefit of $4,000 to dependents of workers. Death benefits are payable upon the sudden death of an insured worker from injuries or an accident compensable under the law, or death resulting within 52 weeks of an onset of a disability because of sickness or injury. However, benefits may not be paid for death or injury caused by an automobile accident that is covered under the Automobile Accident Social Protection Act.

Disqualification and Nonmonetary Eligibility Provisions

Eligibility Requirements in Addition to Wages

Under all the programs, for TDI eligibility, individuals must be in a nonwork status because of disability, and they may be declared ineligible if they withdrew from the labor force for reasons other than disability. A California claimant who has been disqualified from UI is presumed to be disqualified from disability benefits for such weeks unless the claimant establishes that he/she is suffering a bona fide illness or injury, and the agency finds that there is good cause for paying such benefits. However, a claimant who is otherwise eligible for disability benefits is not disqualified from receiving those benefits because of a labor dispute disqualification for UI.

A disability claimant in Hawaii must be in current employment; i.e., an individual who was performing regular service prior to the onset of the disability and who would have continued in employment but for the disability. In addition, a disability claimant is ineligible for benefits during any period in which the claimant would be disqualified for UI because of a labor dispute or during any period in which the claimant performed work for remuneration, was unemployed because of an intentional self-inflicted injury, or attempted to obtain benefits through fraud, or failure to file a claim for disability benefits within 90 days after the commencement of the period of disability or as soon as was reasonably possible.

In New Jersey, a covered governmental employee must exhaust all sick leave before becoming eligible for disability benefits. New Jersey claimants for disability benefits beginning during employment also are ineligible if they would be disqualified for UI benefits because of a labor dispute, unless the disability began before the disqualification. New Jersey claimants must be under the medical care of a legally licensed physician or other qualifying medical personnel.

In Hawaii and New Jersey, claimants for disability during unemployment must meet all the requirements for UI except ability to work; they are not eligible for disability benefits for any week of disability more than 26 weeks after the last week of covered employment. Although the benefit formula in New York is not related to the benefit formula for UI, individuals who are or would be disqualified from UI benefits are disqualified from disability insurance benefits.

Relationship to Workers' Compensation

None of the TDI laws is intended to replace workers' compensation, although the relationship between the two programs differs among states.

In California, a claimant who is receiving or is entitled to receive workers' compensation for the same temporary disability is not eligible for disability benefits unless the disability benefit is higher than the weekly workers' compensation payment; in that case, the claimant is entitled to the difference from the disability fund. If the claimant's eligibility for workers' compensation has not been determined, he/she may receive disability benefits subject to reimbursement from any workers' compensation benefits subsequently awarded for that week. Full benefits are payable irrespective of cash payments under a workers' compensation law for permanent disability.

Hawaii does not permit duplication of benefits unless a claimant is receiving workers' compensation payments for permanent partial or total disability previously incurred. However, if a claimant's right to benefits under workers' compensation is disputed, the individual may receive disability benefits until his disability becomes compensable under workers' compensation. If a claimant subsequently receives workers' compensation payments, these payments are proportionately allocated among employers or insurers according to the amount of disability benefits paid by them.

In New Jersey, both the definition of disability and the eligibility conditions exclude disability benefits for any week for which workers' compensation, other than for permanent total or partial disability, is payable. However, if a claim for workers' compensation is contested, temporary disability benefits may be paid to an otherwise eligible claimant until his/her disability becomes compensable under the workers' compensation law.

The New York law defines disability to exclude illnesses or accidents arising out of or in the course of employment, whether or not worker's compensation is payable. It further provides that no benefits are payable for any period with respect to which workers' compensation, other than permanent partial benefits for a prior disability is paid. In Puerto Rico and Rhode Island, a claimant may receive disability benefits if there is doubt as to his eligibility for workers' compensation. If the claimant later receives such benefits, he/she is liable for repayment of the disability benefits. Puerto Rico limits the maximum weekly benefit amount payable while a claim for workers' compensation is under dispute to $65. However, if the claimant is later found eligible for disability benefits, the claim will be recomputed. In addition, in Puerto Rico, no disqualification is applicable if the worker's compensation payment was made on account of partial permanent disability occurring prior to the disability for which disability benefits are claimed.

Effect of Other Types of Income on Eligibility

Other types of income that affect eligibility include wages, employer pensions, old-age benefits, and survivors' insurance benefits.

In Rhode Island, claimants collecting TDI who return to work on a partial basis lose their TDI benefits. A claimant who earns less than the weekly benefit rate would be entitled to a partial UI payment. The partial payment allows a person to earn and keep the first 20 percent of the weekly benefit amount without any penalty. After earning more than 20 percent of the weekly benefit amount, the benefits are reduced dollar for dollar. All earnings are taken into consideration in offsetting the partial benefits. New Jersey and Puerto Rico take such wages into account and limit the total of wages and benefits to the claimant's weekly wages immediately prior to the disability. In Puerto Rico, a pregnant worker may not be paid during any period in which she is receiving benefits under the Act to Protect Working Mothers unless such benefits are less than her weekly disability benefit amount, in which case she may receive the difference. California provides that the daily combination of such wages and disability benefits shall not exceed one-seventh of the claimant's weekly wage, excluding overtime pay, immediately prior to the disability. Also in California, individuals are entitled to receive, for any day, if otherwise eligible, disability benefits reduced by the amount of a permanent disability indemnity if the permanent disability indemnity is less than the amount the individual would otherwise receive as disability benefits under the law.

New York deducts from the benefits any payment from the employer or from a fund to which the employer contributes, except supplementary benefits paid pursuant to a collective bargaining agreement. New Jersey applies the UI formula for partial benefits to claimants receiving disability benefits during unemployment. Also, a claimant's disability benefit is reduced by the amount of any pension plan to which his most recent employer has contributed. In Puerto Rico, any claimant receiving any pension payments or retirement income is denied benefits unless, subsequent to receipt of the pension or retirement payment, he/she has performed services in insured work for at least 15 weeks immediately preceding the disability.

Administration

The systems of disability insurance coordinated with UI use the same wage record procedures for both programs. Claims procedures, however, necessarily differ for UI claimants and for claimants who are not able to work. Disability claims are filed by mail. The first claim or notice of disability is normally filed after the end of the first week of disability. All claims are sent to the central office in both New Jersey and Rhode Island. In California, both the initial and continued claims are sent directly to one of the field offices. In New York, employed workers file claims with their employers, and unemployed workers with the workers' compensation board.

Under all the laws, medical certification of disability in connection with claims is required from the claimant's attending doctor, with minor differences in the types of medical personnel permitted to certify. California, Hawaii, and New York accept certifications from an authorized religious practitioner with respect to the illness of a member of his/her group. All state laws give the agency authority to require that claimants, without cost to themselves, submit to examination by a designated licensed physician.

Individuals who are dissatisfied with determinations on their disability claims have the right to appeal under all state laws. In states with disability and UI coordinated, the appeal is to the UI appeal bodies; in New York, to the workers' compensation board; and in Hawaii, to the referee for temporary disability benefits. In the states with private plans, a private-plan claimant may also appeal to the state's unemployment appeal tribunal.

Appendix I. Acronyms Used in This Document

AAW	average annual wage
ABP	alternative base period
AW	annual wage
AWW	average weekly wage
BP	base period
BPW	base period wages
BY	benefit year
CQ	calendar quarter
CY	calendar year
DA	dependents' allowance
EB	extended benefits
EBP	extended base period
FUTA	Federal Unemployment Tax Act
HQ	high quarter
HQW	high quarter wages
IUR	insured unemployment rate
MQ	multi-quarter
OP	overpayment
SEA	self employment assistance
STC	short time compensation
SSA	Social Security Act
SUTA	state unemployment tax act
TDI	temporary disability insurance
TUR	total unemployment rate
UC	unemployment compensation
UI	unemployment insurance
UTF	unemployment trust fund
WBA	weekly benefit amount
WW	weekly wage

State Abbreviations

The term "state" includes the Distict of Columbia, the Commonwealth of Puerto Rico, and the Virgin Islands.

AL	Alabama
AK	Alaska
AZ	Arizona
AR	Arkansas
CA	California
CO	Colorado
CT	Connecticut
DE	Delaware
DC	District of Columbia
FL	Florida
GA	Georgia
HI	Hawaii
ID	Idaho
IL	Illinois
IN	Indiana
IA	Iowa
KS	Kansas
KY	Kentucky
LA	Louisiana
ME	Maine
MD	Maryland
MA	Massachusetts
MI	Michigan
MN	Minnesota
MS	Mississippi
MO	Missouri
MT	Montana
NE	Nebraska
NV	Nevada

NH	New Hampshire
NJ	New Jersey
NM	New Mexico
NY	New York
NC	North Carolina
ND	North Dakota
OH	Ohio
OK	Oklahoma
OR	Oregon
PA	Pennsylvania
PR	Puerto Rico
RI	Rhode Island
SC	South Carolina
SD	South Dakota
TN	Tennessee
TX	Texas
UT	Utah
VT	Vermont
VA	Virginia
VI	Virgin Islands
WA	Washington
WV	West Virginia
WI	Wisconsin
WY	Wyoming

Appendix II. UI Information Online

(https://oui.doleta.gov/unemploy/)

Federal

On the left column of the page, click on "UI Legislation" and scroll down to the categories below:

- Under "Overview," click on "Unemployment Compensation: Federal-State Partnership" Brief explanation of the UI program; updated annually
- Under "Overview," click on "Chronology of Federal Unemployment Compensation Laws" Digests of UI law since the program was established in 1935
- Under "Federal Guidance," click on "UIPLs and other Advisories" Directives and Advisories interpreting federal law, sorted by type of directive/advisory and federal fiscal year; new documents issued periodically

State

On the left column of the page, click on "UI Legislation," scroll down and click on "State Law Information" for the links below:

- Click on "Most Recent Comparison of State UI Laws" Detailed information on state UI law; updated annually
- Click on "Most Recent Significant Provisions of State UI Laws publication" Key elements of state UI programs; updated semiannually

UI Data

On the left column of the page, click on "UI Data" and select the links below:

- Click on "Weekly Claims Report"
  UI claims data at the national and state levels; issued weekly
- Click on "Benefits and Claims," then click on "Quarterly Data Summary"

Overview of the status of the UI program at the national and state levels; updated quarterly

- Click on "Program Projections" then click on "UI Outlook" Projections of revenues and outlays; updated semiannually
- Under the heading "Direct Data Access" click on "Chartbook" Assorted UI-related charts illustrating national and state-by-state data series; updated periodically

Information concerning the creation of the Unemployment Insurance program in the 1930s is available at https://www.ssa.gov/history.

APPENDIX III. FEDERAL UNEMPLOYMENT TRUST FUND

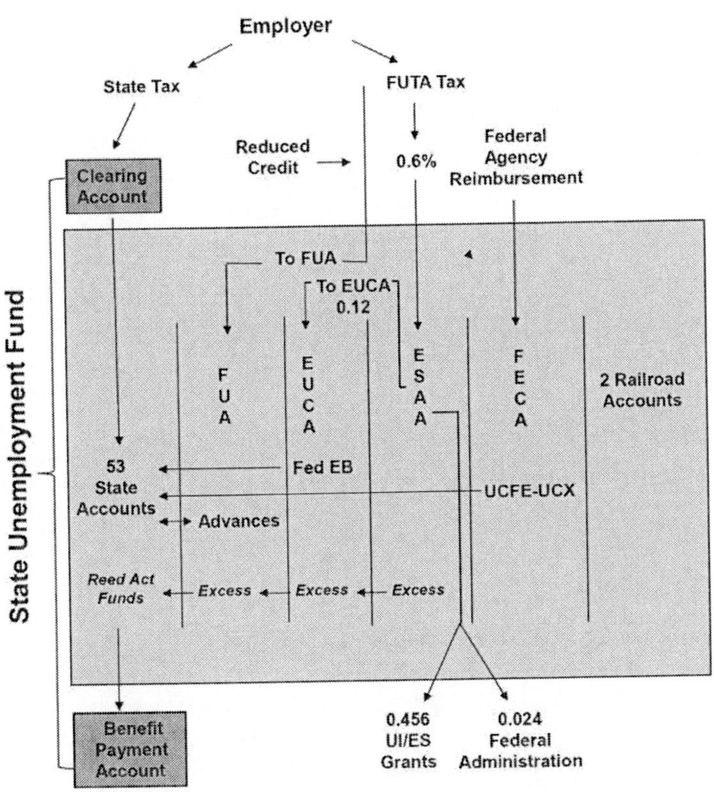

INDEX

D

E